THE VIRGINIA HOUSE OF BURGESSES

1750–1774

THE VIRGINIA HOUSE
OF BURGESSES

1750-1774

by

LUCILLE GRIFFITH

Revised Edition

THE UNIVERSITY OF ALABAMA PRESS

University, Alabama

For
Lorraine Pierson

ACKNOWLEDGMENTS

No student works in a vacuum; he is constantly dependent on libraries, books, and people who make research and writing possible. I certainly am no exception and I gladly acknowledge my great debt to a number of people without whose help this study of the House of Burgesses could never have been done.

Probably my greatest debt is to the late Dr. Hallie Farmer, former head of the Social Science Division, Alabama College, who got me off to graduate school and who, by her unflagging interest in the Burgesses, made it possible for me to do research after I returned to Alabama College at a faster rate than I had dared hope. Her successor, Dr. John Bennett Walters, was equally generous with office help.

A second debt is to Professor Edmund S. Morgan, under whose supervision this study was begun. He kept me out of many pitfalls that I would have fallen into if left to my own devices, and pointed out larger meanings that I would have missed. While many changes have been made in the text, the outline is the one that he approved.

The personnel of the several libraries where I have worked have been more than kind: the Alderman Library, University of Virginia; The Birmingham Public Library; Virginia State Library; the libraries of the College of William and Mary, Colonial Williamsburg, the Virginia Historical Society, and Alabama College.

Three of my colleagues, Dr. Eva Golson, Dr. Anne Eastman, and the late Dr. Ethel Marshall, have read the whole work or parts of it. Their wise suggestions kept me from making some grievous blunders.

I am very grateful to the officials of the Southern Fellowship Fund and Colonial Williamsburg for the summer grants-in-aid which helped the financial pinch while I was doing the research. Colonial Williamsburg also provided a second grant in the summer of 1969 for the revisions of the present edition.

L.B.G.

Montevallo, Alabama
Fall, 1969

TABLE OF CONTENTS

PROLOGUE

History, Thomas Carlyle once said, is but the essence of innumerable biographies. Working on that premise, the doughty Scotsman wrote at length on many historical subjects. His *History of the French Revolution,* for example, is fundamentally a series of thumbnail sketches and longer biographies held together by the central theme of the revolution. History to him was no aimless meandering of impersonal fate but the substance of the lives of the men who lived and moved within the matrix of world events.

That people rather than abstractions have made history has long been recognized by historians. For all his belief in divine determinism and his concern with oracles and prophecies, the Father of History himself gave much attention to the role men played in the affairs of the world. Herodotus even says in the very first lines of *The Persian Wars* that, in publishing his researches, he hopes to preserve "from decay the remembrance of what men have done. . . ."[1] For Thucydides, causes exist inside the human sphere and it is the historian's business to find them and relate them to events. The pages of his account of the war between his native Athens and Sparta are sprinkled with the exploits of men like Themistocles, Cleon, Demosthenes, and hosts of others. He makes his history even more personal by interjecting numerous orations into the narrative. In our century, Charles A. Beard gave historical scholarship an impetus when he published *An Economic Interpretation of the Constitution.*[2] Although many of Professor Beard's conclusions have since been challenged, his method of examining the personnel of a body like the constitutional convention has been accepted as valid. In more recent years, two British historians, Sir Lewis B. Namier and Professor J. E. Neale, have used the biographical approach with great success in studying the English Parliament. As a result, we have new insights into the structure of politics and the composition of society in the Elizabethan and Georgian periods. We know who the members of Parliament were, to what classes of society they belonged, and the means by which they rose to places of eminence.[3]

The present study of the House of Burgesses is an attempt to apply a similar method to a colonial legislature. We are seeking answers to some of the same questions Namier and Neale asked of England. Under what kind of laws, for example, did Virginians vote? How did election laws operate in actual practice? Who voted? What kind of men were elected burgesses?

What were their interests other than lawmaking? In answering these questions, I shall follow a fourfold plan. First, I shall describe the structure of Virginia's government in the period from 1750 to 1774. In the second place, I shall give some attention to a series of controversies that affected the operation of government during the period. Next, I propose to study the system under which burgesses were elected and to see how the system worked in a few representative counties. Last, I want to find out what manner of men Virginia freeholders chose for their lawmakers. In finding the answers to these questions, I hope to shed some light on a larger question, that of why an aristocratic Virginia was in the vanguard of the movement for independence.

The House of Burgesses was only one body in the governmental structure of Virginia. It worked in conjunction with the governor, the council, and the General Court. Most of the burgesses were members of their local county courts and their church vestries. Thus they were part of both the colonial and local governments. Therefore, in any study of the House of Burgesses, it becomes necessary to examine the whole governmental structure, the functioning of each unit, and the relationship of the General Assembly to the other parts. For out of this relationship between the governors and the burgesses (and the rivalry between the House of Burgesses and Parliament), a series of controversies arose after 1750 that helps to explain how the House of Burgesses emerged by 1774 as a much strengthened body.

THE VIRGINIA HOUSE OF BURGESSES
1750-1774

1

THE OLD DOMINION
AT MID-EIGHTEENTH CENTURY

A POLITICAL PORTRAIT

Promptly at eleven o'clock on Thursday morning, February 27, 1752, Robert Dinwiddie, lieutenant governor of Virginia, opened the first session of the new General Assembly. The meeting of the General Assembly was always an important and exciting event to Virginians, who were both gregarious and politically minded. This meeting was especially so because Governor Dinwiddie, who had arrived in Williamsburg the previous November, was holding his first session. Robert Dinwiddie was no stranger to many of the men present. He had formerly lived in the colony as a customs official, and his former associates watched with particular interest his performance as chief executive. Virginia had been without a resident governor since the summer of 1749, when Governor William Gooch left for England; and no meeting of the assembly was held in the interval. Consequently, much business had accumulated that demanded the attention of the legislators.[1]

It was, therefore, with considerable zest that eighty-four burgesses (out of a possible ninety-four) from forty-five counties and four boroughs were on hand to greet the governor and open the meeting. Following a time-honored procedure, these elected representatives of the people had met already that morning with the Council in the improvised Council chamber at the College of William and Mary and had taken the oaths of supremacy and allegiance—the same ones that their English cousins took on entering Parliament. Solemnly they had promised to be "faithful and bear true allegiance" to His Majesty, George II, and had sworn that with all their hearts they did "abhor, detest, and abjure as impious and heretical that damnable doctrine" of Catholicism that "a foreign prince," the Pope, had any preeminence or authority within the realm of England. Furthermore, like all other office holders under the British government, they had taken the Test

Oath that within the last three months they had taken Holy Communion according to the rites of the English Church, "in some public church upon some Lord's day."[2] Having attended to these formalities, the burgesses had returned to their temporary quarters and waited for a summons from the governor.

Nathaniel Walthoe, secretary to the governor, appeared with the expected message: "Gentlemen of the House of Burgesses," he began, "the governor commands your immediate attendance in the Council Chamber." When the burgesses stood before the governor, he told them to return to their chamber and proceed to the choice of a Speaker. This they did. Carter Burwell, burgess from James City County, nominated John Robinson, who had been Speaker since 1738; the body elected him without opposition. Burwell and Charles Carter, of King George County, went as a committee to inform the governor of their action and to ask that they might present the Speaker. Still following prescribed ritual, Dinwiddie informed the two men that he would signify his readiness to receive them by his own messenger. Almost immediately, however, he sent Mr. Walthoe to inform the burgesses that he awaited them in the Council chamber. When the burgesses again stood in the governor's presence, the Speaker, in behalf of the House, petitioned the governor that "they might enjoy their ancient rights and privileges, such as freedom of speech and debate, exemption from arrests and protection for their estates. . . ." After replying that he "would take care to defend them in all their rights and privileges," he began his prepared speech. After expressing gratitude to the king for his appointment, Dinwiddie announced the purpose of the meeting of the General Assembly; it was to consider what they might do jointly to promote "His Majesty's interest and the prosperity" of the colony. As a good politician, he paid tribute to the popular Governor Gooch, his predecessor; he promised to support the Church of England; and in pious terms, he spoke in favor of vague generalities such as "zeal for good," "instruments of happiness," and "spirit of benevolence." For the legislative agenda, he recommended two measures: some way to speed up the procedure in the civil courts and "good correspondence" with the Indians so that white settlers on the frontier might be better protected. After the burgesses had listened politely to the speech, they returned to their quarters and appointed a six-man committee to consider the governor's speech and draw up an appropriate reply. Having chosen the Reverend William Dawson of the College as chaplain, the legislators ended the activities of the first day. The next day, which also began at eleven o'clock, the Speaker appointed the standing committees and all was ready for the business of the session.

Thus began the meeting of the General Assembly in the largest and most populous colony in America. Virginia legislators followed very closely what they thought was the English practice in most matters. When a procedure in the House of Burgesses was questioned, it was settled by conforming to the practice of the House of Commons. Consciously and legally they followed the political and religious organization and the educational pattern of the mother country. Landon Carter, for example, serving his first term in the 1752 session, was told several times that the House followed a certain procedure because it was "a standing order in the House of Commons."[3] Yet in spite of what her leaders thought they were doing, Virginia was no mere carbon copy of England. Its essentially English institutions had been adapted to New World environment and were more individual than most Virginians apparently realized. In the face of these statements, it seems advisable to examine the political structure with some care in order to see how the colony was actually governed.

The County

Virginia was an agricultural, rural colony. Assemblies had tried to promote urban centers but, with all their grandiose plans for expansion, towns were never more than country villages.[4] During "public times" when the assembly or the General Court was sitting, the population of Williamsburg swelled to three or four thousand people, but the permanent residents probably numbered less than a thousand. Williamsburg, Norfolk, Winchester, and Fredericksburg had charters that gave them town governments with mayors and aldermen, but apparently no more than four or five thousand people lived in municipalities. In Virginia, as in England, the county government was the important political unit. The central colonial government with all its power had little contact with the individual, and it remained for the county court and the county officials to implement the laws, collect the taxes, and apprehend the criminals.

The county court, made up of the justices of the peace—"gentlemen justices"—had jurisdiction over "all causes whatsoever" at the common law or in chancery within their respective counties except criminal cases involving the loss of life or limb and "except the prosecution of causes to outlawry against any person or persons." Such cases went to the General Court. Cases involving trivial sums of less than twenty-five shillings current money or two hundred pounds of tobacco could be heard by a single justice.[5] The law set the number of justices at eight, but much latitude was exercised in the matter. In fact, no county seems to have limited itself to this number. Hanover County, for example, in 1764 had twenty-four; Nansemond, at the same date, sixteen; Prince George, seventeen; Stafford in 1767, nineteen.[6] Almost every man of eminence had his first political experience on the county court; and many of them, especially the burgesses,

5

remained justices throughout their lifetime. Being a gentleman justice may have been an honor, but some appointees considered it such a thankless chore that they refused to qualify by taking the required oaths. In 1748, therefore, the assembly devised an elaborate oath for the justices and placed a fine of three hundred pounds on an appointee refusing to take it.[7]

The sheriff, who was also one of the justices, wielded large powers, but this office, too, was judged a great bother, and gentlemen frequently found reasons for refusing it. Each sheriff served only two years, but the sub- or under-sheriffs, who in many instances seem to have done most of the work, remained in office for long periods. The sheriff, or his deputy, had to execute writs and processes, keep the peace, make election returns, report quitrents, and enumerate the tithables in his county. There was much complaint about malpractices of the sheriffs and their assistants; almost every session of the Assembly during the colonial period produced a law that tried by fines, admonitions, and supervision to beg, force, or shame the sheriff into better performance of his duty.[8] Sheriffs were prohibited by law from sitting in the General Assembly.

The county clerk in some respects was comparable to the sheriff in power. In fact, when he and the sheriff worked in close harmony, they had great influence in the county because, in the intervals between sessions of the county court, the two of them had the management of affairs at the court house. In the early days and probably throughout the whole colonial period, in the absence of educated lawyers, the clerks acted as legal advisers to the people in general. Like all other county officers, they were appointed; but unlike the justices, who were nominated by the court itself, the clerks were named by the Secretary of the colony. There was no time limit to their terms and many of them stayed in office until they died. Their sons often became their successors. Many clerks sat in the House of Burgesses, a fact that Dunmore thought gave them too much power. There was little criticism of the clerks until shortly before the break with England, and then it came from two very different sources: from the county courts, which believed they ought to have the right to nominate them; and from Governor Dunmore, who thought that if he had the power of appointment he might acquire "an interest among people," which he sorely needed.[9]

Two minor county officers should be mentioned here. The constable, "as the officer of the court of a single justice," did the same duty as the sheriff and was paid the same fees. The coroner—often one of the justices—held inquests and, in the absence of the sheriff, could perform his duties.

All these were officers of the civil government. There was also a military organization. Each of the counties had a county lieutenant, a colonel, a lieutenant colonel, and a major. The militia (which included men twenty-one to sixty years of age) was divided into companies, each with a captain, a lieutenant, and an ensign. The militia was the mainstay of defense and found its chief function in repelling Indian incursions on the frontier; it saw much action against the combined forces of the French and Indians after 1754. Governor Dinwiddie reported twenty-seven thousand men enrolled out of a total estimated population of two hundred and thirty thousand.[10]

The English hundred was never transplanted successfully to the American continent, and the only subdivision of the county in Virginia was the parish. In new counties, the county and parish were coterminous; but, as the population increased, the counties were subdivided into two, three, or even four parishes. Each had a parish church, and many had two or three chapels in remote sections for the convenience of worshipers. The business of the parish was handled by a vestry of some eight, ten, or twelve prominent men, who were elected by the parish members when the parish was organized. Once elected, however, the vestry was self-perpetuating. The only way a new election could be held (this happened often) was for the Assembly to dissolve the old vestry and pass an act authorizing the parish members to elect a new one.[11] The primary functions of the vestry were to look after the affairs of the local church and to fill the pulpit when a vacancy occurred. This presentment of the minister, as it was called, was of course an American invention. In England, clerical appointments were made by the bishops. No bishop ever came to America; and his representative in Virginia, the Commissary, did not perform this function. Because the church was official and the pulpit semipublic, the governors saw no reasons why they should not assign the clergymen, and many a heated argument between the governors and the members of the vestry resulted. It worked out that the vestries inducted their ministers; but, if a pulpit was vacant for longer than a year, the governor could fill it. The vestry had more than ecclesiastical duties. As the lowest unit in the civil government it laid and collected the parish levy, cared for the poor, punished cases of immorality, bound out orphans, determined property boundaries, took the census, and built roads.[12]

The Colony

Important as the counties were in the political structure, it was the central government in Williamsburg that made the laws and interpreted them, granted land patents, levied the taxes, raised the troops, and looked after the colony in general. Here the authority of the Crown and the will of the people met. The king was represented in the person of the governor, who held office by royal commission and administered the colony by a set of instructions issued to him on his departure for America. The people of Virginia were represented in the House of Burgesses. Between the governor and the burgesses was the Council of twelve men, residents of the colony who were appointed by the king on the recommendation of the governor. In early days there was much overlapping of duties; but, by 1750, the role of each part of the government—the governor, the Council, and the House of Burgesses—had become fairly well defined and reasonably stable.[13]

The Governor

The head of the colonial government was, of course, the governor. Since the dissolution of the Virginia Company in 1624, he had been appointed by the king. The governor general, however, often chose not to leave the comforts of England for the wilds of America. It remained for the lieutenant governor, also royally appointed, to become the resident administrator and to assume the duties and titles of his superior. William Gooch, Robert Dinwiddie, and Francis Fauquier were all lieutenant governors; Lord Botetourt in 1768 was the first titular governor to come to Virginia for more than sixty years. It is uncertain how far the wishes of the governor general shaped policy or administration, but the extent seems to have varied with the man. Lord Albemarle, governor general in 1752, seems to have given the colony little concern; and, as recorded in the Dinwiddie *Papers,* his lieutenant wrote him only five letters. Lord Loudoun, on the other hand, took a very active part in affairs of the colony; it was believed he even planned to reside in Williamsburg. Dinwiddie wrote at least twenty letters to him. Of all the governors, however, Lord Jeffery Amherst was the most active, exchanging many letters with Francis Fauquier on the Indians, defense, currency, acts of the legislature, and other matters that concerned Virginia, and offering advice (and at times criticism) freely. He spent some three years in America (1758–1761) with the British forces, fighting the French and the Indians, and apparently intended to visit the colony. However, he decided to leave for England at the end of hostilities, and Fauquier journeyed to New York in order to talk over some matters of importance to the security of the colony.[14]

The British government usually bypassed the governor general in the administration of the colony. When the resident governor left England for Virginia, he was given two important documents to guide his conduct: his commission, which he read publicly on arrival in Williamsburg; and a set of instructions, for his own private enlightenment, which elaborated and explained the general powers laid down in the commission. Additional instructions were issued as need arose. The government, for example, instructed Governor Robert Dinwiddie to collect a fee for signing land patents; it advised Governor Francis Fauquier about forts on the frontier and many other matters after his arrival in America. Although drawn up in the name of the king, instructions were normally prepared by the Board of Trade, often after extensive consultation with other government officials, merchants engaged in Virginia trade, and leading colonists who happened to be in London at the time. A draft of the instructions was submitted to the Privy Council for approval before it was put in its final form. Most instructions related to government; but some applied to religion, morals, Indian trade, land, commerce, and other current issues. These instructions to the governor, which in the main he followed to the best of his ability, formed the closest tie between the colony and England.[15]

The resident governor was commander in chief of the military forces and vice-admiral. He appointed all the militia officers except those of lowest rank, but he could not declare war. He issued writs for elections, and convened, prorogued, and dissolved the General Assembly. He had extensive appointive power, which was enlarged through recommendations he made to the king. He could veto a law or insist that a suspending clause be inserted in an act to delay operation of the law until the king's pleasure was known. He could suspend sentences and pardon all crimes except treason and murder. With the Council, he issued patents to public lands. He and the Council formed the upper house of the assembly and the General Court. Furthermore, the governor of the province enjoyed an independence that many of his fellow governors in other colonies did not, in that his salary came from an export duty on tobacco. He was hence independent of the whims of the assembly for his living.

The salary, however, was not so fixed as it might seem. When Major General Amherst was made governor in 1759, Fauquier wrote him the usual congratulatory letter, indicating that the people of all ranks would "find satisfaction" in his appointment. He hoped that he could induce his new chief to travel southward during the winter months so that he might have the opportunity of showing him the part he took in "this instance of his Majesty's justice and favor." Apparently believing Amherst did not know the money value of his new office, he pointed out that according to the royal instructions the salary of three thousand pounds was to be divided between the two, each getting one-half of the living in semi-annual payments.

However, it seems to have been customary to bargain for the division. Governor Dinwiddie, Fauquier's immediate predecessor, paid to the account of the governor sixteen hundred and sixty-five pounds. Governor Gooch, on the other hand, previously paid to Lord Orkney only thirteen hundred pounds. When Gooch was relieved of his post because of poor health in 1749, Thomas Lee, president of the Council, became the resident governor; he agreed to pay Orkney twenty shillings per day "as long as he could keep the Government or during their joint lives if he could procure the Government for him."[16] This seems to have been in addition to the thirteen hundred pounds because, when Robert Dinwiddie was named lieutenant governor,

Orkney demanded three hundred and sixty-five pounds be added to the base salary, making it sixteen hundred and sixty-five pounds because, as he said, "Mr. Lee who did the business found he could afford to pay so much." If Dinwiddie would not agree to the office on such terms, Mr. Lee would. Dinwiddie, of course, took the appointment on Orkney's terms but "much to his own wrong." After Amherst had consulted Dinwiddie, then in England, he found the former governor of the opinion that even with sixteen hundred and sixty-five pounds going to Amherst "something handsome" would be left to Fauquier. Nevertheless, Amherst was willing to accept fifteen hundred pounds, provided there would be no deductions and the sum was paid in London in semiannual payments.[17]

The "something handsome" came from certain emoluments that increased the total income of the governor: an allowance from a contingent fee for the expenses of government; a "sort of" quitrent paid by some tenants living on lands formerly set aside for the governor's service, which in the 1750's was paid in corn. These were "trifles" but did add to the gross income of the chief executive. What Fauquier apparently did not mention was an occasional gift of money from the colony, a sum always questioned by certain members of the House of Burgesses. When in 1752 the House was considering a gift of five hundred pounds to Dinwiddie as a "grateful acknowledgment for his regard to the interest and welfare of the colony," Landon Carter and Edmund Pendleton objected to the "regularity of it."[18]

While the list of powers in the hands of the governor looks imposing, each chief executive complained that his power was more apparent than real. Every officer in the colony except the burgesses was appointed, yet almost none of them by the governor and council alone. The county courts named the justices, the sheriffs, the coroners, and the constables, and the governor and Council merely confirmed them. As we have seen, the secretary chose the county clerks. It seems that only the tobacco inspectors were appointed by the governor; and yet, here again, his powers were restricted because of the limitations placed on the political activities of the inspectors. True, there were certain officers for whose appointment by the king the recommendation of the chief executive was generally essential—the naval officers on the navigable rivers, the deputy receiver-general, the attorney general, and apparently the receivers of customs. These appointments were not made regularly but at the king's pleasure (which came at the death of the incumbent), and changes seldom occurred; however, they were frequent enough to keep the governor from being a mere figurehead. Nevertheless, every governor complained that his appointive power was very limited. Dunmore considered it very strange that so much power should reside in the hands of the secretary, power which gave him more authority than the governor had. At an earlier date Dinwiddie had frankly admitted that what little influence he had with the assembly resulted from persuasion alone. Fauquier, whose "constant endeavour" was to preserve harmony between the various branches of the government, depended heavily on his influence with the leaders of the assembly. Getting the House of Burgesses to authorize and finance a regiment of a thousand men at the end of the French and Indian War was an arduous task, which Amherst urged Fauquier to back with the "utmost of his influence," confident that it would have "due weight" and be productive of an "immediate acquiescence." Fauquier followed his superior's instruction, "stretched [his] influence to the utmost pitch," and was successful. But he frankly hoped he would not have to try so hard again because he could not promise equal success. Fauquier would have agreed that governors had more prestige (and therefore influence) than real power. These Virginians, Lord Anson told Fauquier at his departure for his colony, are "a good natured people whom you may lead but whom you cannot drive."[19]

After 1750, four Englishmen represented the king as governors in the colony. Robert Dinwiddie, the first governor after 1750, was an energetic Scotsman, a former merchant, who according to his standards served the crown well in the more than six years (1751–1758) he was governor. But he suffered from ill health, aggravated by a "paralitic disorder" that left him with a "quiveration" in his handwriting. He finally persuaded the English authorities to allow him to return home, and he sailed on January 12, 1758, aboard the *Baltimore*.[20] Dinwiddie had not always been on easy terms with his fellow Virginians. Some measures that he considered essential for the welfare of the country seemed to the burgesses contrary to their interests. His vigorous prosecution of the French and Indian War required money and men that the assembly was reluctant to give. His demand for a fee on land patents, which may have been sound from an imperial view-point, created an opposition that never died down completely.

When John Campbell, fourth Earl of Loudoun, was appointed titular governor of the colony on March 17, 1756, Dinwiddie tried in vain to learn the wishes of his superior. For a time, he erroneously believed that Loudoun intended to come to Virginia to assume the active governorship himself. Loudoun, in fact, seems to have wanted to replace Dinwiddie and, as an excuse to remove him, accused him of breaking the embargo against the French.[21] Since Dinwiddie had repeatedly expressed his desire to return home, everyone was pleased when he was permitted to go. In spite of "unjust clamour and complaints" against him and the discord over specific measures, Dinwiddie departed with the good wishes of the assembly and city of Williamsburg; and he retained an interest in America as long as he lived.[22]

John Blair, as president of the Council, was acting governor until Francis

Fauquier, the new lieutenant governor, arrived June 7, 1758.[23] "A very good natured gentleman," and "a most punctually diligent man," Fauquier was destined to live through some crises that would try his patience. The Parsons' Cause and the Stamp Act crisis are only the two best publicized of them. Essentially on the side of the Americans in the quarrel with the parsons, he nevertheless bitterly denounced the burgesses in their stand on the Stamp Act and promptly dissolved the assembly after their famed resolves. Endowed with an amiable disposition and an inquiring—even skeptical—mind, he delighted in good conversation such as he found in the company of Dr. William Small at the college and the youthful Jefferson. His scholarly and scientific interests made him a member of the Royal Society. He died after a long and tedious illness, which he bore "with the greatest patience and fortitude," on March 3, 1768, after having presided over the colony for nearly ten years "much to his own honour and the care and satisfaction of the inhabitants." His body was buried in the north aisle of Bruton Parish Church attended by President Blair and the principal gentlemen of Williamsburg and the neighborhood. The militia was there to pay the honors due to his memory. Editor Rind of the *Virginia Gazette* concluded a lengthy tribute to him who "in public life was equaled by few and in his private character excelled by none" with these lines:

If ever virtue lost a friend sincere
If ever sorrow claimed Virginia's tear
If ever death a noble conquest made
Twas when Fauquier the debt of nature paid.[24]

In less poetic but more succinct words, Robert Carter of Nomini Hall, a member of the Council, said of him, "He was vigilent in government, moderate in power and merciful where the vigor of justice could be dispensed with."[25]

Again President Blair became acting governor to remain in that office until late October, 1768.[26] On October 26, Norborne Berkeley, Lord Botetourt, arrived to take over the reigns of government. He was the first governor general to reside in the colony since Francis Nicholson, approximately sixty years before. No other governor after 1750 got so favorable an advance billing as Botetourt. He was not only the full-fledged governor; he was a peer of the realm with a very ancient title and a gentleman of His Majesty's Bedchamber. He was known as a "man of a very amicable character" in England, "remarkable for his great attention to business as he was said never to have been absent from the House of Commons during twenty years he was a member of it, at reading of prayers or when the House was adjourned and he has been as remarkable since he came to the House of Peers for his close attendance there." He had never married, but as a bachelor he had "ever been commended for his hospitality." He had "one of the prettiest seats in England," and it was thought he had a "very independent fortune."[27] We know now that this last was not true, because the basic motive in appointing him to the post in Virginia was to help him out of financial difficulties.[28] But this consideration did not mean that the ministry was insensible of his personal characteristics, which would certainly placate the touchy Virginians, or that he was an unwise choice.

He arrived with due fanfare aboard His Majesty's man of war, the *Rippon*, which had been detailed for the voyage. From the beginning, he was pleased with everyone and everything, and Virginians generally were happy with him. The palace he found in admirable order; he especially liked the garden behind it. The leading citizens were filled with the "highest expectations of happiness" and sincerely believed "his Lordship's conduct fully justified the very high encomiums given him by his friends." "We are very happy in our governor, Lord Botetourt," wrote Thomas Everard to John Norton, London merchant and former burgess from Norfolk, "his affability and great attention to the due administration of every part of his duty has gained him the affection" of everyone. Very soon he was beloved by all ranks of people.[29]

There was no mistaking his affability, his genteel manners, and his popularity; but the colonists expected more from the first governor general in their memory. "Thy rank and station in life placed thee in a more conspicuous point of view than most of thy predecessors," the Quakers in Virginia told him, "consequently more will be expected of thee."[30] However, there were those who reserved judgment on his politics until he met with the assembly, which he did on May 8, 1769.[31] Colonial affairs were already in a critical stage, and less than ten days had passed when the burgesses adopted a set of resolves which the governor considered "very offensive to the Parliament of Great Britain." Hastily he consulted the Council and informed its members of his intention to dissolve the assembly at once. He then sent for the House of Burgesses, who went up to attend him in the Council chamber. When they arrived, he stated bluntly: "Mr. Speaker and Gentlemen of the House of Burgesses, I have heard of your resolves and augur ill of their effect; you have made it my duty to dissolve you; and you are dissolved accordingly."[32]

Following this speech the burgesses met immediately at Anthony Hay's tavern and formed an association to prohibit trade with England, but they held no ill will toward the governor.[33] "Lord Botetourt is the most amiable man in the world to Virginians," wrote William Nelson to Francis Fauquier, son of the late governor, "tho he was obliged to dissolve the Assembly. They consider him as acting under instructions, yet they admire and revere him for his good qualities and love their governor."[34] Many prominent

13

citizens had great faith that he would become "the instrument of dawning happiness" and the means of greater harmony with England. But whatever hopes the Virginians had pinned on him were blasted by his untimely death on October 15, 1770, slightly less than two years after he took office.[35] Virginians honored Botetourt's memory by ordering a statue of him which eventually was placed in the college library.[36] "Lord Botetourt," wrote Robert Beverley to Landon Carter, "was confessedly not a man of ability and yet I believe it would puzzle the greatest analyst to put out anyone who had more universally or more deservedly recommended himself to the esteem of mankind."[37]

John Blair by seniority should have become governor again, but because of his great age he stepped aside in favor of William Nelson, who served as governor until Dunmore arrived.

John Murray, Lord Dunmore, was the last royal governor for the province. Virginians were rapidly becoming wary of the power of the British government, but they accepted Dunmore with hope and optimism and accorded him the usual courtesies of an incoming governor. He arrived on September 26, 1771. William Reynolds, late of John Norton's countinghouse in London, was among those who went across the bay to escort him to York. "He appears quite affable and is complacent enough to say he likes Virginia," young Reynolds wrote Mrs. Norton. William Nelson, who handed over the government to Dunmore, considered that from "appearance". the people would be very happy with him; he thought he discovered "many good qualities in him."[38] Richard Bland was less sanguine, but his opinion was based on a report of a madcap prank in which Dunmore and "his drunken companions sallied forth about midnight from his palace" in New York and attacked the coach and horses of the chief justice of that colony. The coach was destroyed and "the poor horses lost their tails,"[39] Whether true or false, the story made Bland reserve his judgment until Dunmore had arrived in Virginia and had an opportunity to prove his executive abilities. On his part, Dunmore wrote to Hillsborough that he hoped that by following the admirable conduct of his predecessor (Botetourt) during his own administration he would be able to carry on the business of the colony in such a manner as to give satisfaction to the king and his ministers.[40]

Dunmore, like Dinwiddie, was a Scot; like Botetourt, he was a peer with a very ancient title. Like most of his fellow governors, he had solid political experience before coming to America. Appointed governor of New York by Hillsborough in 1770, he had served about eleven months in America before being promoted to Virginia. As indicated above, he began his term in the Old Dominion under rather favorable circumstances and with very little opposition. He opposed the action of the House, however, in creating a Committee of Correspondence (1773); and, from that time on, friction increased until he and his family fled Williamsburg and took refuge aboard the *Fowey,* His Majesty's man-of-war.[41] Dunmore was hardly the boor, the "mercenary, ministerial tool" that some burgesses were wont to call him before he left the country. He seems now rather the victim, not entirely blameless to be sure, of a strength that had developed in the colony over a long period of time.

As has been seen here, the governor occupied an important place in the colony. In addition to being the chief executive with what appeared to be extensive appointive power, and chief justice of the General Court, he was the center of a court society made up of the leading Tidewater families. Virginians did not always agree with their governors, but they liked and respected them, and generally the governors merited their approval. In fact, the limits of the governor's power and the amount of his success depended more upon his personality and ability to work in harmony with the people and the General Assembly than upon legal powers. As Robert Beverley put it in a letter to Landon Carter, "I do not think it absolutely necessary that every governor of a province should be excessively learned or profoundly wise. The road is chalked out so plainly that a common capacity may manage tolerable enough when assisted by a good heart; otherwise the American governments would long since have been wrecked indeed."[42] The road "chalked out" was one of accord with the landed gentry as each successful governor from Spotswood's time had learned to follow. The "flower" of Virginia gentry was represented on the Council, which almost without exception worked in close harmony with the governor.

The Council

The Council had twelve members appointed for life by the king. A councilor received an "Esquire" after his name and "Honorable" before it, titles reserved for the most eminent men. In the absence of the governor, the president of the Council became acting governor. The Council performed a threefold purpose: as an advisory body it performed executive duties and met regularly to advise the governor on matters of policy and execution; as the upper house of the legislature, it met when General Assembly met, approving or disapproving acts of the House of Burgesses, but there is no indication that it initiated legislation during the period from 1750 to 1774;[43] and with the governor it formed the General Court, which met twice each year in April and October and exercised appellate jurisdiction over cases involving life and limb and chancery cases "of great value."[44]

The duties of a councilor required a great deal of time and attendance in the capital and for these services each member was paid one hundred pounds annual salary. "The power and duty of a Councilor of Virginia,"

15

wrote Fauquier to the Board of Trade, "is very great and extensive and . . . it requires gentlemen of the greatest abilities and most important understandings that can be found in the colony to execute it with honor to His Majesty's government and the board of which he is a part, and with advantage to the colony in general."[45] When Dinwiddie took office in 1751, the Council was composed of Lewis Burwell from Gloucester County; William Nelson and his brother Thomas, who was also Secretary of the Colony, merchants from Yorktown; William Fairfax, cousin of Lord Fairfax and actual manager of his estates in the Northern Neck, who lived at Belvoir on the Potomac not far from Mount Vernon; John Blair, nephew of the Reverend James Blair, the founder of the College of William and Mary, and a resident of Williamsburg; Dr. William Dawson, president of the College; John Lewis, who was from Warner Hall, Gloucester County; Philip Ludwell of Green Springs, James City County, who was the father-in-law of President Thomas Lee of Stratford; Philip Grymes, whose residence was Brandon, Middlesex County; Peter Randolph, from Henrico; Richard Corbin, of King and Queen County (he would shortly become Receiver-General of His Majesty's Customs); and William Beverley, who was the son of the historian Robert Beverley and lived in Essex County. It will be observed that all these gentlemen with the exception of Fairfax lived within short distances of Williamsburg, and all bore names illustrious in the colony. In fact, it would be difficult to find a group more representative of Virginia aristrocracy than these.[46] Generally conservative, the majority of the councilors could be counted on to support the governor. But in contrast to South Carolina and some of the other southern colonies, the Council in Virginia differed less with the lower house over issues and in composition than might be expected.[47]

Other Royal Appointees

There were other officers in the colony, all of them appointed by the king but most of them on recommendation of the governor. The Secretary for the Colony was "the very next in dignity to the governor." The office conferred much power and influence on the occupant. He had the right to appoint all county clerks; and as these were men of political and social influence in their respective communities, it was charged that the Secretary exercised power not justified by his office. He was keeper of the colonial seal; and all patents, writs of election, and other papers from the chief executive were issued from his office. He was custodian of the executive and the General Court records. He had an important duty to keep the English government constantly informed of affairs in the colony and send "home" copies of all public papers. Thomas Nelson, who had been ap-

16

pointed to the office in 1743, was the incumbent when Dinwiddie came to the colony and served until the end of the colonial period. Son of "Scotch Tom," an immigrant who had made a comfortable fortune as a merchant, and brother to William Nelson, who like himself was a member of the Council, he was a leading merchant and took a lively interest in the business affairs of the country. At times he kept the Secretary's office at his home in Yorktown.[48] The Auditor General, who was John Blair from 1732 until 1771, had the responsibility of examining and auditing all accounts of collectors and receivers of revenue in the colony. The Receiver General was the custodian of the revenues of the colony, among them the quitrents. However, there were certain revenues, raised under acts of the Assembly, which were not controlled by this officer but by the Speaker Treasurer, who was elected by the Assembly. Philip Grymes was Receiver General when Dinwiddie began his term of office; at his death Richard Corbin was appointed and served until the Revolution, which abolished the office.[49]

The Attorney General represented the Crown in cases at court; there was a deputy king's attorney in each county who served the same purpose on the local level. Peyton Randolph was "Mr. Attorney" from 1748 until he became Speaker at the death of Speaker Treasurer John Robinson in 1766. He was succeeded by his brother, John Randolph. Peyton Randolph, throughout his time as Attorney and Speaker, was burgess from the College (1752–1758) and Williamsburg (1758–1776). It is noteworthy that the Secretary of the Colony, the Auditor General, and the Receiver General were all members of the Council and that the Attorney General was a leading member of the House of Burgesses. Offices seldom came singly in colonial Virginia.

The House of Burgesses

The political institution that was rapidly taking the place of first importance was neither the governorship nor the Council, but the House of Burgesses. From a simple beginning in 1619 and in spite of various setbacks, the House had grown in power and prestige so that by the middle of the eighteenth century it was a force to be reckoned with. "It was not mere flattery," wrote an analyst of procedure in the House, "that prompted a justice of the peace, prisoner at the bar in 1740, to plead that the displeasure of the House, expressed in its reprimand, would cause him lasting disgrace in the colony."[50] Just how long the House had enjoyed this much prestige is uncertain, but by the 1750's it was considering itself the American counterpart of the House of Commons. It elected its speaker; it initiated not only all revenue bills but all legislation; it drew up resolutions; it sent petitions to the king; and by 1765 it even dared defy the English government.

When the first assembly after Dinwiddie's arrival sat in February, 1752, the House of Burgesses had a membership of 94, two from each of the 45 counties and one from each of the four boroughs—Jamestown, Williamsburg, Norfolk, and the College. As population increased and people moved west, the old counties were subdivided and new ones created until in 1774 there were 61, which, with the four boroughs, gave the House a total membership of 126.

Burgesses received for their service travel expenses and ten shillings for each day's attendance at the General Assembly. This was the direct pay but it was only a minor part of their reward. It was usual procedure for the Speaker at the first meeting of each new assembly to present himself to the governor and ask that the members of the House "might enjoy their ancient rights and privileges."[51] This request was made regularly, but it was considered far more than mere routine. Burgesses were asking for rights which as Englishmen they thought they were entitled to, rights which they shared with members of Parliament. These privileges (which the General Assembly had defined by law) the burgesses guarded with a jealous eye. Each burgess ten days before, during, and ten days after each session of the assembly was free in his person, servants, and estates (both real and personal) from all arrests, attachments, and "all other processes whatsoever," save for treason, felony, or breach of the peace. If a process was already pending, it could be suspended until a session was over.[52] Furthermore, sheriffs were prevented from serving any kind of writs at the courthouse on election day. Business men often found it difficult to collect debts from burgesses because of the long period of legal immunity. In 1761 for example, William Allason wrote his brother in Scotland that he had been unable to collect any part of a bill owed their store by Richard Lee, "a man of great fortune and naval officer for the South Potomac."[53] Since he happened to be a burgess, there was little time in which to bring action. Allason proposed to bring suit in "the borough court" of Williamsburg where the case could be brought to trial within a few months, for he had experienced no success either in the county in which Lee lived or at the capital.[54] In other words, burgesses were guilty of extending their privileges beyond their legal time limit and to phases of life not originally intended. To restrict these abuses, George III instructed Amherst (and indirectly Fauquier) not to "allow any protection to any member of Assembly, further than in their persons and that only during the sessions of the Assembly."[55]

These privileges admittedly had their practical value to assemblymen, but the greatest compensation was honorary. Burgesses, both during time of privilege and under ordinary circumstances, enjoyed an immunity from

18

criticism that ordinary citizens had to endure. Members of the House cared little about the social status of their critics; a violation of privilege was a violation of privilege regardless of who was guilty. Take the case of John Blair, nephew of the founder of the College. During the agitation to remove the capital from Williamsburg in 1748, Blair, one of the Council, in a conversation with a member, said, pointing to Speaker Robinson, who was passing, "There goes the man who is at the bottom of this hellish scheme and has told several lies and advanced many things that he knew to be false." He added that he had no confidence in such a man and that, although he pretended to be interested in the public good, his real motive was his private welfare. The House judged that these statements were "most scandalous and malicious reproaches" and "false expressions highly reflecting on the honor of the Speaker and the House of Burgesses." Blair apologized, and the House seems to have been satisfied.[56]

Most instances in which privilege was invoked involved, like the Blair case, "abusive and scandalous" language. In September 1758, during the heat created by the Two-Penny Act, there occurred another case of this kind. The Reverend Jacob Rowe, professor of philosophy at the College of William and Mary, in a company which he thought was private, asked how many of the burgesses would be hanged for their vote to pay parsons' salaries in money. He added he thought such men were scoundrels and vowed that, if any of them wanted to receive the sacrament from him, he would refuse it. Ordered before the House, he explained that he did not know a member of the House was present. He confessed that he had been too easily and indiscreetly provoked by some rude expression used by some of the company against "that sacred order" to which he belonged. Convinced that his offense did not arise from a lack of "due deference," the House discharged him after he paid the customary fees.[57] The burgess was William Kennon of Charles City County, whom Thomas Knox, apparently also of the company, criticized as being "a damned scoundrel for betraying private conversation" and for deviating from the truth in presenting Rowe's behavior to the House. Knox was likewise reprimanded and required to pay fees.[58]

Not all cases were this simple, nor were the allegations always false. In Surry County in 1757, an altercation took place between John Ruffin, an elderly gentleman, and William Clinch, a burgess, which illustrates the complexity of cases in which privilege might be invoked. Trouble started over a judgment of £1,209.15.5–3/4 against Clinch obtained by Ruffin and his son in Surry County Court in December 1754. Clinch seems to have had no intention of paying the sum and was using all kinds of questionable means to avoid it. On March 31, 1757, Ruffin was taken into custody by

19

the sergeant-at-arms of the House for having spoken "scandalous words" against Clinch. The Speaker read the charge against him:

John Ruffin, the House has been informed that you, on Monday last publicly declared before many members of the House, that Mr. Clinch (a member of this House) being indebted to you in a large sum of money, decoyed you into his house, shut the door upon you, and cocked and presented a loaded pistol at you (his for that purpose) and with dreadful oaths and imprecation threatened your life and compelled you to sign discharges for the whole debt, and that you were ready to prove the same when required. The House have therefore commanded me to require of you an answer to this charge.[59]

Ruffin did not apologize; on the contrary, he affirmed the truth of the statement and proved his charges. Clinch attempted still another trick by informing the Committee of Privileges and Elections, which was handling the affair, that three material witnesses were unavailable: one had gone to Georgia, another was living in Carolina, and a third had broken his collar bone. But in the end the House expelled Clinch and voted him "incapable forever of sitting or voting in the House."[60]

Another case in point involved James Pride, naval officer for York River. Pride ordered a writ served on Edward Ambler, from Jamestown, during a session of the House, "within the time of privilege." Benjamin Waller, clerk of the General Court, and William Michell, undersheriff of York County (who should have warned the recently appointed Pride of his error) were absolved from any guilt in the matter. Pride was charged guilty not only of Ambler's arrest but of a "scandalous insult," which he had written to be inserted in the *Virginia Gazette*. He was sentenced and remained closely confined in the Williamsburg jail from March 1767 to March 1768.[61] It was not a weak House, indifferent to its rights and privileges, that would jail a royal officer for abuse of privileges.

Privileges might be invoked by burgesses against one another. Leonard Claiborne of Dinwiddie was declared guilty of violating the rights and privileges of the House because he had called members of a certain vestry "not only rogues, but damned rogues." Richard Bland and John Jones, both burgesses, were members of that vestry. Claiborne vowed that after the "rising" of the assembly he would "take Richard Bland by the nose"; he called Jones a liar and threatened to bring suit against him as soon as the session was over for sums the representative owed the parish, sums which were gained, Claiborne implied, by questionable means.[62] This same Claiborne, who seems to have been often in political hot water, was once charged with planning to flee the colony while under privilege, so that he would not have to surrender some slaves the General Court had ordered him to give up.[63]

20

This use of privilege to protect its members was but one evidence of the developing strength of the House. During the long administration (1727–1749) of the amiable Governor Gooch, the burgesses had been allowed free rein in many affairs and were little prepared for having their wishes crossed. After 1750, there was a series of crises in which the colonial legislature came out the victor or else developed a line of reasoning that was useful at a future date: The Pistole Fee, the Two-Penny Act, the resulting Parsons' Cause, the Stamp Act, and the Townshend Acts. All these measures aroused legislative ire and brought forth legal opinions, petitions, pamphlets, and resolutions which employed the same techniques—and often the same arguments—that Virginians and other colonials used later at the time of Independence.

It was in these controversies that the House of Burgesses revealed its real strength—a strength that enabled it in 1776 to shake off the last remnants of royal control. This study is concerned primarily with the men who exercised that strength rather than with the uses to which they put it. Nevertheless, in order to know the men, we must examine briefly the principal controversies in which they pitted themselves against their governors and flexed their political muscles.

2

CRISES IN THE ASSEMBLY,
1750–1774

Power in the House of Burgesses began to develop rapidly during the Dinwiddie years. The exigencies of the French and Indian wars necessitated frequent meetings, and out of these sessions came not only laws but also precedents and ideas. Jack P. Greene, a close student of colonial legislative bodies, speaks of the "rather prosaic manner the lower houses went about the task of extending and consolidating their authority, with the infrequency of dramatic conflict."[1] Quietly and simply passing laws and establishing practices, "the implication of which escaped both colonial executives and imperial authorities" and even at times the colonials themselves, they were establishing precedents which, as Professor Greene points out, would soon become "fixed principles," "undoubted rights," and "inherent powers." This is doubtless true; but slow steady growth, however fundamental and lasting it is, never has the emotional impact of a dramatic crisis. For publicizing and clarifying issues, there is nothing more effective than conflict between public authorities such as Virginia experienced beginning with the Pistole Fee controversy

The Pistole Fee

On Dinwiddie's arrival in Virginia in 1751, the colony had been without a resident governor for more than two years. During that time, the acting governors (Robinson, Lee, and Burwell) and the Council had continued to make land grants in large amounts. These grants apparently needed the signature of the governor; hundreds of them had accumulated in the Secretary's office. Additionally, the land office business increased because Dinwiddie himself was an active member of the Ohio Company, the leading land company operating beyond the mountains. After Dinwiddie's arrival, when several persons applied for their patents, the clerk in the secretary's office took a number of applications to the governor for his signature. This he refused to give and commanded that no more should be brought to him until further notice, so that for some time the office was completely closed. The governor reportedly said that he could not sign any until after the General Assembly adjourned. The governor was still in high favor, especially since in both private conversations and public utterances he had given the "strongest assurances that he would make the true interest in Virginia . . . the great rule of his administration." Consequently, no one took the trouble to inquire why the patents were stopped; on the contrary, "the whole country entertained the most grateful sense of, and placed the highest confidence in, his declaration. . . ."[2]

Dinwiddie had taken this action only after seeking advice from the Council about taking a fee for affixing the seal of the colony on land patents. He was of the opinion that he was "justly entitled to and might reasonably insist upon it" since it was agreeable to the practice of all other governments in America. At a meeting of the Council on April 22, 1752, the ten members present—William Fairfax, John Blair, William Nelson, William Dawson, John Lewis, Thomas Nelson, Phillip Grymes, Peter Randolph, Richard Corbin, and Philip Ludwell[3]—agreed with the governor and advised him to begin collecting a fee of one pistole for affixing the seal to the land patents. The governor seems to have waited until he had approval also from the Board of Trade before he began collecting the fee. He received the permissive letter and read it to the Council a year after he had first brought up the matter. "We find that the Governors of other His Majesty's provinces do take a fee on the like occasion, and as a pistole appears to us to be a reasonable charge, we have no objection to your taking that fee according to the advice of your Council," read the communique from the Lords of Trade.[4]

By the middle of November, the ruling had been in force long enough for protests to come in from counties in the central part of the colony: Henrico, Chesterfield, Cumberland, Albemarle, and Amelia Counties, and—a week later—Dinwiddie County. The petitions from the freeholders and other inhabitants complained of the hardships they labored under being obliged to pay this new fee over and above the fees that were customarily charged and asked that the House give them relief.[5] The burgesses followed the usual procedure of turning over the petitions to a committee. Charles Carter of King George County was chairman, and other members were: Richard Bland of Prince George County, William Randolph of Henrico County, Beverley Whiting of Gloucester, Christopher Robinson of Middlesex, Benjamin Harrison of Charles City, Edmund Pendleton of Caroline, James Power of New Kent, John Martin of King William County, Joshua

23

Fry of Albemarle, Augustine Claiborne of Surry, and Philip Johnson of King and Queen County. Only two members came from the petitioning counties, Fry and Randolph; the others were all from the Tidewater area.[6] In the beginning, the burgesses seem to have doubted that Dinwiddie had ordered the fee and merely inquired if the sum was collected at the governor's direction, or if it had originated with the clerks in the Secretary's office. Charles Carter for the committee reported on November 27 that they had prepared an address to the governor on the matter. In this address they asked him if the action was by his direction and, if so, by whose authority he demanded it.[7]

The next day the governor, having received the message from the lower House, summoned it to the Council chamber and read his reply. "The welfare and happiness of Virginia I have very much at heart . . . ," Dinwiddie began. "I have been influenced by no other motive and my conduct upon all extraordinary occasions has been requested by the advice of the Council. I shall always show a just regard for the House of Burgesses in everything that properly lies before them, and they may remain assured that I shall not demand, or take, any fee without proper authority. The pistole fee . . . which is the subject of your address, is by my direction. Agreeable to my instructions, I advised with the Council at this point, who unanimously agreed and advised me to take the above fee which, together with the powers I have received from home, will sufficiently justify my proceedings herein." He ended by expressing the hope that they would not think that he was acting in an arbitrary manner but recognize that he was "properly invested with regular power and authority" in demanding this small fee.[8]

In all probability Dinwiddie, armed with ample reasons, considered the matter closed. The burgesses, however, were far from satisfied and were frankly annoyed at the governor's insinuations that the affair was none of their business. They believed that "it is the undoubted right of the Burgesses to inquire into the grievances of the people, of which we take the above demand to be one." There were certain "terms and conditions upon which His Majsty and his royal predecessors had been pleased to grant" the colony which his Honor could not alter or infringe, even with the advice of the Council. This was the main theme in a "humble address" in which the burgesses replied to the governor. Dinwiddie himself was getting annoyed and snapped, "I am not unacquainted with the just privileges of the House of Burgesses." His duty to his king and his regard for liberty would always influence his conduct, he said. He would gladly hear the complaints of the people if they "were well grounded, and the grievances really felt." The fee related solely to the disposal of the king's land, "a matter of favor from the crown and not a matter relative to the administration of government. . . ." It was his care and concern "for the improvement of His

24

Majesty's revenue of quitrent" that prompted him to be "more earnest" in adhering to his former opinion and insisting on the fee which was confirmed to him by "unquestionable authority."[9] "I have had an unhappy difference with our House of Burgesses," the governor wrote the Bishop of London shortly thereafter, a difference he believed to be caused primarily by the Reverend William Stith, president of the College of William and Mary, who argued that this measure was "an attempt to lay taxes upon people *without* law" which made it certainly *"against* law and an evident invasion of property." Stith was the author of a toast used widely in opposition to the act—"Liberty and Property and no Pistoles."[10]

Up to this point the House believed that they had behaved in a "most dutiful and justifiable manner," while the governor's replies had been unsatisfactory and "a means to create fears and uneasiness in the minds of His Majesty's faithful subjects." It was time for stronger action on the part of these faithful subjects. The House therefore passed some resolutions, *nemine contradicente.* The strongest of these stated the legal and moral reasons the burgesses had for objecting to the fee: "Resolved, That the said demand is illegal and arbitrary, contrary to the characters of this colony, to His Majesty's, and his royal predecessors' instructions to the several governors and the express order of His Majesty King William . . . in his Privy Council, and manifestly tends to the subverting the laws and constitution of this government."[11] The last resolve agreed to the sending of a "dutiful and loyal address" to His Majesty, which stated that the demand of the fee was "a great grievance, a discouragement to the settling of the frontiers . . . and a prejudice to His Majesty's quitrents"; it begged for "his royal and paternal interposition" that the colonists might be relieved of this "illegal demand." The committee to draw up the address to the crown was the same that had handled the matter from the beginning.

Affairs in Virginia obviously had reached an impasse; and both sides, the governor and the burgesses, made identical moves in appealing to England; Dinwiddie through the resident agent, James Abercromby, and the burgesses through the Attorney General for the colony, Peyton Randolph, for whose trip they appropriated twenty-five hundred pounds public money. The Council entered the fray, too, by sending an address which defended the governor.[12] These communications reached the Privy Council on January 31, and the hearing was set for the early summer.[13] William Murray, Attorney General for the Crown in the Newcastle government and therefore counsel for Dinwiddie, opened the case at the Cockpit on Tuesday, June 18, 1754.[14] The pistole fee was small, he stated, in comparison to the value of the land. The land was quitrent free,[15] and the patentees desired more to keep settlers out than to cultivate it. The fee was a reasonable amount; it was collected with the consent of the Council and was customary in all the other colonies.

It was not the fee, he said, that had been the source of all the disturbance, for the governor had been willing to let all the patents in the office before April 17, 1752, pass in the usual manner. If the colonists had been willing to accept this concession, all would have been well. But the legality of the fee—the right of it at all—had become the question. It was the position of the attorney that the king had absolute property in all the lands in the colony. If, he concluded, the fee was too large, it could be reduced.

Mr. Forrester replied for the assembly.[16] He began by reviewing the historical facts in the case. Both the practice of collecting the fee and the hardships caused by it had come to the attention of the House when the six counties complained to the Assembly in November, 1753. The House had thereupon proceeded in a parliamentary mannner: it had appointed a committee to inquire into the matter; it had addressed the governor to ask by whose authority he demanded the fee; it had sent a second address in which it cited the case of Lord Howard, whose similar action had been declared illegal; and it had voted the fee illegal. It was the opinion of the burgesses that the governor had power to regulate fees, but not to create new ones. And as for the consent of the Council, "Virginia councilors were too good courtiers to their governor to say anything was unjust that was pleasing, anything unreasonable that was profitable. . . ." It was poor reasoning that Virginia should follow the policy of allowing such a fee simply because the other colonies did so; besides, no other colony provided so amply for their governor in salary and residence. One thing Virginians wanted clear was that they were not objecting to their sovereign, but protesting "against the usurpation of a viceroy."

At this point in the proceedings the king's counsel spoke. "The question is not whether the fee complained of is reasonable or not, or whether the Assembly have behaved properly or not, but whether His Majesty can demand any fee at all upon granting out his lands." The king, he stated flatly, had absolute right to all the lands in the colony and had the right to dispose of them as he pleased "without the consent of any power whatever." Then he lapsed into scorn for "This *little* Assembly who because they now enjoy the happiness of a mild government have presumed to demand that as a matter of right which was here before indulged them. . . ." The counsel for the Virginians had been careful to point out the parliamentary manner they had followed, but he objected to it. "The Assembly have authorized the Attorney General to appoint an agent and to allow him two hundred pounds per annum in order to be perpetually trying to your lordships. This little Assembly—this puny House of Burgesses—have boldly dared to do what the House of Commons in England never presumed to attempt." He, like the attorney before him, reasserted that the king had the right to demand and collect any fee he chose. The sum may have been trivial, he said, but the proceedings of the assembly had made the matter most important, and their conduct had been "so unwarrantable that they have put it out of your lordships' power to show them the least countenance or indulgence."

This outburst seems to have had the desired effect on the representatives of the colony. Their reply was confined to a restatement of the facts in the case, protestations of loyalty as evidenced in their liberality in "provision for the exigencies of the government." But, they concluded, "they cannot, they ought not, tamely to submit to the oppression of their governor." Except for this show of spirit, the statement of the attorney for the colony sounds quite chastened.

For all his bias, Murray, who had opened the case, came near the truth as both sides saw it when he said that the whole thing boiled down to two questions: first, how much right the king had and whether the Assembly could curtail the king in his right; and second, whether the governor was within his limits in the mode in which he collected the fee. The governor's position was that the lower house was a subordinate lawmaking body and, where the king's decisions were concerned, counted for nothing. On the other hand, the counsel for the burgesses was saying that even authorities in London could not abridge or modify established practice and usage in Virginia.

Three days after the hearing, the Privy Council recommended to the king that the address of the House of Burgesses be rejected. There was so much confusion about the matter, however, that the Council felt it advisable for His Majesty "to order the Lords Commissioners for Trade and Plantations to prepare a letter to the Governor of Virginia to regulate his conduct with regard to his taking the fee of a pistole and to make other regulations relative to the grants of land as may be most conducive to the welfare of the province of Virginia and the benefit of your Majesty's revenue and service."[17] Thus, so far as official England was concerned, the matter ended. It remained only for the Board to communicate the decision to the Council in Virginia.

Meanwhile, opponents to the fee were elaborating on their early resolutions. The crisis—for such it was—had given several Virginians the opportunity to engage in writing political pamphlets; how many we do not know, but at least Landon Carter and Richard Bland from the assembly. Landon Carter's *A Letter from a Gentleman in Virginia to the Merchants of Great Britain, Trading in that Colony* was printed in London. The author reviewed the case, analyzed the conduct of both the governor and the burgesses, and concluded with a strong defense of the House.[18] The product of Bland's pen, *A Modest and True State of the Case* (published later as *A Fragment on the Pistole Fee*), had wide circulation. Bland could not see that the demand was either legal or reasonable. "The rights of the subjects

27

are so secured by law," he wrote "that they cannot be deprived of the least part of their property without their own consent. Upon this principal of the law, the liberty and property of every person who has the felicity to live under a British government is founded." The question was not, and should not be, the smallness of this demand, but the lawfulness of it; if it was the law, the same power that imposed one pistole could impose a hundred. Liberty and property were precious vessels whose soundness was destroyed by the least flaw, their usefulness lost by the smallest hole. "Impositions destroy their beauty, nor are they to be soldered by patchwork which will always discover and frequently widen the original flaw." The demand for a pistole fee was an attempt to break through the legal forms and must be opposed in every possible way.[19]

When the General Assembly met in October, 1754, Landon Carter referred to it as the "Harmonious Session." The affair of the pistole fee had been settled at home "and both parties having got something, both seemed to hug themselves with a victory." The governor had the right to charge a fee on all patents that he signed over one hundred acres (but only on lands east of the mountains), and he had the satisfaction that the king's attorney (Peyton Randolph) had been "turned out for presuming to go home as an agent." The "country" gained a victory in getting the fee restricted to those patents of land made after 1752. Patents issued before that date, lands beyond the mountains, and tracts of less than one hundred acres were exempt. And furthermore, Virginia had the "assurance that, if the attorney asked for his place, he was to have it again," and the governor would sign the act appropriating twenty-five hundred pounds to pay for his expenses.[20] Dinwiddie was sure he was the winner in the contest over the "silly fee" and felt that the people were sensible to "unjust clamor and complaints" against him. He forgave them and he felt they were on "perfectly easy" terms again. This settlement must go down in history as an example of the perfect political compromise since it seemed to give to each side a satisfied feeling of complete victory. Nevertheless, Dinwiddie was uncertain as to the procedure in collecting the fee and even the lands to which it applied. The Board of Trade seems to have been in some doubt too, for the governor had to write to it several times before getting a satisfactory answer. The governor finally was ordered to sign all the patents issued before 1752, and "any demand of arrears of quitrent" without fee; he could collect the fee on new patents. Dinwiddie may not have liked the order to sign gratis the old patents, but he believed that the land thus alienated would soon be put on the rent roll and would thereby increase the revenue of the colony.

Here in 1753 and 1754, the burgesses developed a pattern of protest that they used often thereafter. They began with respectful and dutiful addresses to the governor; and, if these failed to accomplish their goals, they

28

sent humble petitions to the king. They even used the same reasons, arguing that the fee was taxation without their consent and therefore a violation of their charter rights and an infringement of their laws. The Pistole Fee controversy, in fact, may be called the opening battle of the Revolutionary War.

The Two-Penny Act

The furor caused by the pistole fee, important as it was, was mild in comparison with that stirred up by the Two-Penny Act.[21] There were actually two of these acts, but the first one in 1755 aroused comparatively little protest; it was the second one in 1758 that caused the trouble, although in content they were much alike. The year 1755 was very dry, and many inhabitants in the colony made no tobacco at all with which to pay their public dues. To relieve the distress of the taxpayer, the assembly passed an act at the October, 1755, session to enable the inhabitants to discharge their tobacco debts in money at the rate of 16s. 8d. per hundredweight. It was to be in force for ten months and no longer. Because it was a temporary measure for immediate relief, it did not have a suspending clause.[22] Three years later a similar measure was necessary. By September, it was certain that the "unseasonableness" of the weather would cause a "prodigious diminution" of the staple crop in 1758. To relieve the distress that normally attended such scarcity, the assembly passed another act which would allow, as did the one in 1755, the sheriffs to collect money instead of tobacco and to pay persons entitled to sums out of the public levies in money. It, like the earlier measure, had neither suspending nor retroactive clause and was to be in effect for only one year.[23]

This act did not single out any particular group, but applied to all officers alike. It was the clergy alone who protested. Ministers of the Established Church, of whom there were more than sixty in Virginia, were paid in tobacco like all other public officials.[24] Since 1696 each minister had been entitled to sixteen thousand pounds, plus casks, annually. Their real wages had fluctuated as the market price of the staple rose and fell.[25] Clergymen with large families may have been underpaid, but most of them were able to manage very well with this salary and the income from the parish glebes. When they protested against the 1758 act, it was not against being paid in money but against the rate of exchange, which they considered far too low. Because of the acute shortage of the commodity, tobacco would have brought a high price on the market, an advantage which the clergymen would have welcomed.

These Two-Penny Acts, like all other legislation, had to go to England for final approval by the Crown. Since they were in harmony with the

29

long established practice of passing temporary legislation to relieve acute distress in the colony, no one seems to have foreseen the possibility of the king's vetoing them. But this he did. On August 10, 1759, the Privy Council declared both acts null and void *ab initio* because they, in effect, repealed an act of 1748 which reaffirmed the earlier act making the sixteen thousand pounds of tobacco the legal salary. The act of 1748 had received the royal sanction and could not be repealed by a piece of local legislation.

The king in council did not reach this decision unaided. The 1755 act, which had passed by one vote only, had caused a great deal of uneasiness among the clergymen, and they had sent letters and memorials to England, asking for redress. But the law was of short duration and the following seasons good; the salaries were about up to normal again so that no action was taken. Leading clergymen and even some of the burgesses and councillors believed that the 1758 measure was at best of doubtful legality, but "the obnoxious law" passed in spite of their protests, even if by a very narrow margin; Landon Carter says, by one vote only. Francis Fauquier, then governor, took part with the assembly, according to Meade, caring little for its justice or legality but much for his standing with the people.[26] It was high time, the clergy thought, that they should take steps to defend their rights. Consequently, the leading ministers of the Williamsburg area met and made an address to the Crown pleading their grievances. The Reverend John Camm, pastor of the York-Hampton parish, leader in the movement, was sent by the clergy to present their cause in England. It was largely due to his pleading that the Two-Penny Acts were vetoed.

During his stay of some eighteen months in England, Camm, "whose delight . . . [was] to raise a Flame and live in it," was able to get a decision from the Privy Council that the courts in America could be used to regain the back pay—that which was lost by the low evaluation of tobacco due the clergymen. Camm lost no time in having his attorney institute proceedings against the collectors in his parish to recover his salary in tobacco. The laws had been disallowed on August 10; on November 14, William Nelson reported that a suit had been commenced. A Committee of Correspondence composed of the two Nelsons and Philip Grymes from the Council; John Robinson, Charles Carter, Richard Bland, Landon Carter, George Wythe, and Robert Carter Nicholas from the House took the report under advisement and concluded that York-Hampton parish's cause was the whole colony's cause. Seeing in it a test case, the Committee recommended that it be taken to the House for consideration, partly because the expense of defending it would be too costly for a single parish.[27] Both sides seem to have anticipated appeal to the General Court and to England. Camm lost in the Virginia court with councillors Byrd, Tayloe, Thornton, Burwell, and Blair voting against him and the Nelson brothers abstaining because they were vestrymen in the parish. When Camm took his case before the Privy Council, it was finally thrown out (1767) because of a technicality. It was common belief at the time that this was a mere pretext and that the English government was unwilling to give the colonists any new cause for irritation so soon after the repeal of the Stamp Act.[28]

Other ministers brought similar suits in other counties: the Reverend Mr. Warrington in Elizabeth City, the Reverend Alexander White in King William, and the most celebrated of all, the Reverend James Maury in Hanover. It was in this last case that the youthful Patrick Henry made his maiden appearance before a jury—and won.

The House and Council had been divided on the Pistole Fee but were united in the new contest facing the colony. Together the two bodies drew up a petition to the king in October, 1760. "Melancholy and dreadful prospect of a general famine," it said, had faced the people in 1758, and they had petitioned the General Assembly to alleviate their distress in some manner. The royal government was too far away to be consulted before many of the faithful subjects perished, and the Two-Penny Act was the way the assembly handled the problem; it was an act based on the principle of humanity and "intended to preserve the people from rapine and destruction." In no way did the assemblymen intend "to lessen the influence and prerogatives of the crown." For a hundred years, the assembly had repealed, altered, or amended such general laws as had proved burdensome or inconvenient, and which had not received the royal approval. The petitioners hoped that what former assemblies had been allowed would be continued with the present one.[29] The legislators here were arguing their case on necessity and ancient custom; others would defend their stand on the same question on less conservative grounds.

The petition was couched in mild and polite terms, but the verbal attacks of Richard Bland, Landon Carter, and Patrick Henry were violent. Bland, having successfully tried his talents at pamphleteering in the Pistole Fee case, entered into the affray with a zest that warmed the hearts of the other champions of Virginia. He was joined by Carter, also an experienced pamphleteer, who loved a good fight at any time, and together they waged a paper war with the Reverend Mr. Camm.[30]

Of these pamphlets, those written by Richard Bland were the most closely argued. Bland was burgess from Prince George from 1742 until the end of the colonial period, one of the longest careers in the history of the Assembly. He was one of the most learned of Virginians in history and constitutional law. He was a "wary old experienced veteran . . . staunch and tough as whitleather" with "the look of musty old Parchment," whom his fellow colonials, half in criticism, half in affection, called "Old Spectacles," "Spectacle Dick," and the "Old Antiquary."[31] America, he argued, was not

31

conquered territory, but English colonies. Under English government all men were born free and were subject only to laws made with their consent. Englishmen need not be told these facts for they already knew them and valued them as a vital part of their constitution, which placed them "without the reach of the highest executive power in the state." Colonists were born free with all rights and liberties of English subjects; they had a right to representation in the legislature which made laws for their internal government "and without any such representation . . . no law can be made."[32] External matters, Bland admitted, belonged to the British Parliament, but the internal to the local government. The legislature of the colony had a right to enact any law that should be necessary for this internal government; it possessed the power to "make, ordain and constitute laws, statutes, and ordinances for the public peace, welfare, and good government of the colony."[33] Again, as he had in the Pistole Fee case, Bland cited Calvin's case in which Lord Coke said, "where the King by Charter or Letter Patent grants to a country the laws of England or a power to make laws for themselves, [neither] he nor his successors can alter or abrogate. . . ." If this be true, Bland said, the colony which held such rights and liberties by charter from the Crown, and had enjoyed them uninterruptedly for nearly one hundred fifty years, could not be deprived of them.[34]

The Two-Penny Act had received the assent of Governor Fauquier; and, so far as Bland could see, this was all that was necessary to make it legal. The king could not give his assent to every piece of colonial legislation in person, and his royally appointed governors acted for him. The General Assembly had a right to present any act "relative to the internal government" to the governor, and the governor had the right to give or refuse his assent; but once he had given it, only the king could undo the act, and even his action was restricted by rights which he had granted to others. He was, in short, a constitutional, limited monarch, and "submission, even to the supreme magistrate, is not the whole duty of a citizen."[35]

These arguments were not far different from the ones used in the Pistole Fee case, but there was one new note. The people, Bland said, had "an original right to a legal government" which "had been confirmed [not granted] to them by charter."[36] This more nearly approached the natural rights theory than anything hitherto suggested. It was not long, however, before natural rights became the favorite argument of protesting Americans.

If it was the role of Richard Bland to provide the constitutional arguments in the case, it was the role of Patrick Henry to furnish the oratory and emotional appeal. Henry had established himself as a lawyer by 1763 but certainly had won no fame until the Reverend James Maury entered a suit, similar to John Camm's in York, for the recovery of his back salary.[37] The trial was to become one of the most famous in Virginia colonial history. Maury, although he can in no way be judged an unbiased observer, left the only contemporary account of the proceedings. From the beginning, Mr. Maury could see that the cards were stacked against him and other clergymen of the Establishment. The dissenting population in Hanover, where the trial was brought, was large, and three of the popular new sect, "The New Lights," were included on the jury over the protest of the plaintiff. As the trial proceeded, Henry rose and "harangued" the jury for an hour, mostly on points "much out of his depth." The law of 1758, he said, was a good law, a law of general utility and could not be annulled without breaking "the original compact between king and the people." The king, therefore, in disallowing the act, "from being the father of his people had degenerated into a tyrant, and had forfeited all rights to his subjects' obedience." To the complete exasperation of the clergymen, he told the jury that the only purpose of the Established Church and clergy in society was to "enforce obedience to civil sanctions . . ." and when a clergy ceased to serve that purpose, the community had no further need for them; instead of useful members of the state, they deteriorated into enemies of the community. Unless the jury were disposed "to rivet chains of bondage" on their own necks, he hoped they would use the opportunity to rebuke those who had the temerity "to dispute the validity of such laws authenticated by the only authority which could give force to laws for the colony, the authority of legal, representative government and of a "kind and benevolent and patriot governor." This was strong talk, and "the more sober part" of the audience was horrified. According to Maury, Peter Lyons, one of the lawyers for the plaintiff, called out to the Bench that the gentleman had "spoken treason." Whatever the merits of the Parson's cause, the jury, under the spell of Henry's oratory, was out only five minutes. It returned with its decision: one penny's damages. The law had been disallowed; so the jury had no alternative but to bring in a verdict of damages, and it brought in the least possible amount. It was an unmistakable victory for the colony.[38]

Henry had dared attack the integrity of his sovereign; and, although he later apologized for his hasty words, he nevertheless had suggested that the king could become a tyrant. Although this theme did not have any great popularity until Tom Paine gave it wide currency in his pamphlet, *Common Sense,* Virginians were becoming familiar with ideas that might prove useful at a later date. In the controversies over the Pistole Fee and Two-Penny acts, most of the arguments used for independence in 1775–1776 were tried —and found equal to the emergency.

No one in Virginia liked the Stamp Act, not even the staunchest supporters of royal prerogative. The House was divided over the Pistole Fee; a large part of the clergy had been arrayed against a majority (but by no means all) of the burgesses about the Two-Penny Act; but Virginians were of one accord in opposing the Stamp Act. This does not mean, of course, that they agreed on reasons for opposing it or on the manner in which opposition should be expressed, but the Stamp Act did evoke an extraordinarily unanimous hostility, and from that hostility grew the clearest and fullest statement that Virginians had yet made. It was, moreover, a statement in which Virginians were joined by other colonists. The Pistole Fee and Two-Penny Acts had been only local in scope; in 1764–1765, Virginians for the first time faced a crisis along with other Americans.

The Stamp Act grew out of the financial difficulties of the British Empire following the French and Indian War. When peace was restored in 1763, after nearly nine years of fighting, England found herself saddled with a staggering debt that had been incurred largely in America. The new empire in America would require troops to anglicize and patrol it; so even more of the imperial expenditures would be used there. The House of Commons was faced with the unpleasant task of finding a new source of revenue. The Sugar Act was expected to bring in some, but not all, of the needed monies; there remained a substantial deficit which George Grenville, head of the Ministry, proposed to make up with a duty on legal papers in America. A year of grace was given the colonists in which they could debate the proposition and suggest any other method of raising the sum, the exact amount of which was never given.

News of the proposed stamp duty reached Virginia sometime before mid-June, 1764. Grenville had followed a mysterious course in the whole matter. He had announced in a speech on March 9 the possible alternative the colonies might have, but at no time did he send this proposal to the governors of the colonies.[39] The next day after the speech, March 10, Edward Montague wrote of it to the Committee of Correspondence of the Burgesses. His letter arrived in Virginia sometime before June 15, when the Committee replied to him that it was "much alarmed at the attempt in Parliament to lay a duty on the several commodities . . . and the proposal for a Stamp Duty." He was requested to oppose this with all his influence and, as far as he dared, insist on the injustice to the colonists and "particularly taxing the internal trade of the colony without their consent."[40] If the colonists hoped for better news, they hoped in vain because each new dispatch brought only "truly alarming" news that gave them "fresh apprehension of the fatal consequences that may arise to posterity for such a precedent."[41]

Already Virginians were looking askance at the power that Parliament was exercising. The members of the Committee desperately wished that their "just liberties and privileges as free born British subjects were once properly defined"; then much misunderstanding would be prevented, and the people of Virginia would never "entertain the most distant inclination to transgress their just limits." But this had never been done. There were, they said, some limits beyond which even the king could not go; one of the most important of these was that subjects could not be made subservient to laws which they had no part in making. Parliament out of the "plenitude of its power" had regulated the trade between the mother country and the colonies, and even placed export duties, "but to fix a tax upon such parts of our trade and concerns as are merely internal" seemed to the Americans an act of impertinence. It could not be denied that Parliament had power if it chose to use it, but no one in his right mind would conceive that any "man or body of men, however vested with power" had a right to do anything that was contrary to reason and justice or that tended to the "destruction of the Constitution." Furthermore, in order to prevent a precedent of being taxed in this unconstitutional manner, the Committee "supposed that this country would rather agree to lay on themselves any reasonable apportionment of the sum intended to be raised in the colonies." Nothing could be done, they said, until the sentiments of the General Assembly were known; and, since it did not meet until October 30, the agent was urged to use all his influence in getting the matter postponed until after that date.[42]

The assembly had been sitting two weeks when on November 14 Peyton Randolph, the Attorney General, brought in a report from the committee that had under its consideration the state of the colony. He submitted some resolutions which stated the colonial objections to the proposed bill,[43] and recommended an address to the king and memorials to both houses of Parliament. The address to George III implored his protection and begged that they might continue to enjoy "all their natural rights and civil rights as men and descendants of Britons," rights which would be violated "if laws respecting the internal government and taxation of themselves" were imposed by any power other than that derived from their own consent. In spite of this strong statement, the address emphasized the fact that Virginians were a loyal people, willing to contribute their just proportion of the expenses needed for the defense and security of America—provided they were left free to raise it by "modes least grievous."[44] The memorial to the House of Lords entreated "those hereditary guardians and protectors of British liberty and property" not to let the people of the colony "be enslaved or oppressed by laws respecting their internal polity, and taxes imposed on them" in a manner that was unconstitutional. The tax would be especially objectionable at that particular time because the people were already burdened by the expenses of the recent war.[45] The memorial to the House of Commons stressed the already heavy tax burden of the country and pointed out that not only would an increase in taxation be a burden, it would "violate the most sacred and valuable principle of the Constitution."

These were only resolutions recommended by the committee. But the House adopted them with minor amendments, and a select committee set to work to embody the wishes of the Assembly in formal addresses and memorials which were ready and adopted a month later, on December 18. In the petition to the king the burgesses reminded him that "their internal polity and taxation . . . are derived from their own consent" and that it was "essential to British liberty that laws imposing taxes on the people ought not to be made without the consent of representatives chosen by themselves. . . ." To the British Parliament they said that even if it were proper for that body "to impose taxes on the colonies at all" which "the remonstrants take leave to think would be inconsistent with the fundamental principles of the constitution," the year 1764 was an ill-chosen time to do it.[46] Fauquier had not seen the memorials when he reported to the Board of Trade in December, but he understood "the subject matter of them is praying to be permitted to tax themselves."[47]

In spite of protests, official and personal, American and English, the Stamp Act was passed on March 22, 1765, to become effective the following November 1. For some Virginians like Speaker John Robinson, Attorney General Peyton Randolph, and lawyer George Wythe the passage of the bill ended whatever right of protest the colonists had. The measure had become a law of the realm, and Virginians, like all other Americans, had no choice but to obey it. Charles Carter expressed a common feeling when he wrote his tobacco merchant in London, "For God's sake, what will become of America and particularly the poor colony of Virginia" which was already so "heavily laden" with taxes; all were "ruined and undone."[48]

There were, however, some "hot and giddy" members in the House who refused to admit that all hope was lost. At some time early in the May session of the Assembly, the text of the act arrived; on the 4th, the House resolved itself into a committee of the whole to consider what steps could be taken as a result of the action of Parliament.[49] In spite of threats, no overt action had been taken against the act, and, as the meeting drew to a close, Governor Fauquier probably began to relax. But on May 29 things began to happen thick and fast. Fauquier's official report to the Board of Trade is the best contemporary account of these events.[50]

On Wednesday the 29th of May, just at the end of the session when most of the members had left town, there being but 39 present out of 116 . . . a motion was made to take into consideration the Stamp Act, a copy of which had crept into the House; and, in a Committee of the whole House, five resolutions were proposed and agreed to—all by very small majorities. On Thursday the 30th they were reported and agreed to by the House, the numbers being as before in the Committee, the greatest majority being 22 to 17, for the 5th resolution 20 to 19 only. On Friday the 31st, there having happened a small altercation in the House, there was an attempt to strike all the resolutions off the journals.[51] The 5th, which was thought the most offensive, was accordingly struck off, but it did not succeed as to the other four. I am informed the gentlemen had two more resolutions in their pocket, but finding the difficulty they had in carrying the 5th which was by a single vote . . . they did not produce them. The most strenuous opposers of this rash heat were the late Speaker, the king's attorney, and Mr. Wythe, but they were overpowered by the young hot and giddy members. In the course of the debates I have heard that very indecent language was used by a Mr. Henry, a young lawyer who had not been a month a member of the House, who carried all the young members with him. . . .[52]

If more members "had done their duty by attending to the end of the session," the governor thought, Patrick Henry and his crowd would have been outvoted. His report convinced the authorities in England that the "ill-advised resolutions owed their birth to the violence of some individuals who, taking advantage of a thin assembly, so far prevailed as to publish their own unformed opinions to the world as the sentiments of the colony."[53]

Fauquier was of course not present in the House. There is, in fact, only one eyewitness account, that of an unidentified Frenchman who was travelling in Virginia and arrived in Williamsburg from York at noon on the 30th.[54] It is from him that we learn the details of the "indecent language." When he reached the capital, he went immediately to the assembly, where he was "entertained with very strong debates" about the duties that Parliament wanted to lay on the American colonies. Shortly after he had entered the room, "one of the members stood up and said that he had read that in former times Tarquin and Julius had their Brutus, Charles had his Cromwell, and he did not doubt but some good American would stand up in favor of his country, but (says he) in a more moderate manner, and was going to continue when the Speaker of the House rose and said he, the last that stood up had spoken treason and was sorry to see that not one of the members of the House was loyal enough to stop him before he had gone so far, upon which the same member stood up again (his name is Henry) and said that if he had affronted the Speaker or the House" he was sorry but that from his interest in his "country's dying liberty" he had spoken with too much heat. He begged the pardon of the Speaker and the House,

37

and there the affair was dropped. The "hot debate" on the duty itself continued the next day.[55]

For all the furor they caused, these famous resolves adopted by a rump House contained nothing that had not been said before. As printed in the *Journals of the House of Burgesses,* the Virginians were again pleading for the rights of Englishmen, rights from early charters, the right of a people to impose their own taxation and long uninterrupted enjoyment of "the inestimable right of being governed by such laws respecting their internal polity and taxation as are derived from their own consent. . . ."[56] These arguments had become as familiar as an old friend who could be called upon in time of need. This time, however, the influence of the well-worn phrases went beyond the local colony. In slightly different forms, the resolves were published first in the *Newport Mercury* and later in the *Maryland Gazette* and other papers.[57] Although no Virginians attended the Stamp Act Congress held in New York in October, the declarations that that body drew up, and the petitions which it sent to the king and both houses of Parliament contained all the principles which Virginians had been debating for years.

It is a well-known fact that, through the combined efforts of the colonists, the merchants in the American trade, and other friends in England, the Stamp Act was repealed on March 18, 1766.[58] The Resolves were the official act of the burgesses, but there was other opposition to it, probably less orthodox but admittedly effective. If there were no stamps available, some Virginians argued, none could be bought and consequently the act could not be enforced. George Mercer, son of John Mercer of Marlborough in Stafford County, had been appointed stamp distributor and was due to arrive with the stamps for his own colony and for Maryland well before the November 1 date for the act to go into effect. But even before his arrival there was opposition. Colonel Mercer, Governor Fauquier reported to the Lords of Trade, had been "ill-treated in effigy at some places farther up the country."[59] Williamsburg was quiet; and, if he could get all the jurors and witnesses at the capital for the General Court to go home before Mercer arrived, he was hopeful that they could "weather the storm which seems ready to burst over the northern colonies."

But the court dragged on and was still in session when Mercer arrived on October 30. Fearing trouble, Governor Fauquier thought it proper to go to the coffee house.

> My particular reason for going there was that I might be an eyewitness of what did really pass and not receive it by relation from others. The mercantile people were all assembeled as usual. The first word I heard was 'one and all' upon which, as at a word agreed on before between themselves, they all quitted the place to find Colonel Mercer at his father's lodgings where it was known he

was. This concourse of people I should call a mob did I not know that it was chiefly if not altogether composed of gentlemen of property in the colony, some of them at the head of their respective counties and the merchants of the country, whether English, Scotch, or Virginians, for few absented themselves. They met Colonel Mercer on the way just at the Capitol.[60]

There they stopped him and demanded to know if he intended to resign or to continue in his office as distributor of stamps. Only twenty-two years old, impressed with the importance of his office but totally unprepared for any opposition from his fellow countrymen, Mercer was at a loss for what to say. Pushed for an answer, he finally agreed to give one by five o'clock the following afternoon. Fearing for Mercer's physical safety, the governor appeared at his side at the coffeehouse where they all had converged and took him home to the palace for the night. Even after long and earnest discussions, Fauquier was not sure what the young man planned to do the next day.

At the appointed hour young Mercer appeared at the Capitol and read a statement before a crowd that was much increased over the previous day "by messengers having been sent into the neighborhood for that purpose." In the statement he tried to explain why he had accepted the position and assured his listeners that he meant only good for his fellow Virginians. And then he resigned. "This declaration," stated the *Gazette,* "gave such general satisfaction that he was immediately born[e] out of the Capitol gate amidst the repeated acclamations of all present." Then he was conducted to a public house where they held "an elegant entertainment," which already had been ordered, apparently in anticipation of the event. He was greeted with redoubled acclamations, drums, French horns, and other noise makers. "As soon as night set in, the whole town was illuminated, the bells set a ringing and every mark of joy shown at the Gentleman's declining in such a genteel manner to act in an office so odious to his country." Never, the editor stated, had there been so much general rejoicing on such short notice.[61]

On Friday, November 1, the day the Stamp Act was to go into effect, the judges of the General Court met at the usual hour; but the king's attorney, Peyton Randolph, was the only lawyer present. After twice proclaiming the opening of the Court, when no one appeared, Governor Fauquier called Colonel Mercer and in open court asked him whether he could supply it with proper stamps so that it might continue its business. Mercer replied that he could not. The clerk of the court, on being asked, said that it would be illegal to operate without stamps. Therefore, after consulting with his "brother judges on the Bench," Fauquier adjourned the court until the following April 10.[62]

The winter of 1765–1766 was a trying time. The courts were closed so that the people had no recourse to justice; the county governments were suspended for want of stamped paper; the General Assembly, which was scheduled to meet in March, was delayed by the governor until May and eventually to September; no lands were patented. Some shipping continued because of a technicality. Mercer had brought no stamps for the custom-houses; so, since none were available, officials passed ships with a statement to that effect, but the number of ships reported was very small. Alexander Purdie, insisting he could not publish a taxed newspaper, suspended publication of the *Virginia Gazette*. However, tired of an "involuntary recess of four months and believing in the advantages of a newspaper to a community," he began publishing it again on March 7.[63]

But the colony was far from quiet, and Governor Fauquier felt that he was sitting on the proverbial powder keg. "Never in the course of my whole life," he wrote the Lords of Trade, "[have I] been in a situation which required so much circumspection." He was often at a loss to know how to proceed and then often dissatisfied with his "determinations."[64] Once he had hoped that action of a full House of Burgesses would "quash" the violent resolves of the "very thin house." But after the events attending Mercer's arrival, he had changed his mind and believed practically all leading Virginians hated the Stamp Act and were working actively for its repeal. He could see only "much heat, violence, and resolution" and no way through this "gloomy prospect."

Word of the repeal did not reach Virginia until news of it appeared in the *Gazette* on May 2. However, there had been rumors earlier. On March 1, Secretary Conway wrote Fauquier that repeal was being debated and shortly thereafter the *Gazette* reported that an article in an unidentified English paper outlined a proposal by which the colonies could raise their tax money as they pleased and thus eliminate the Stamp Act. On March 31 Secretary Conway sent a circular letter to the colonial governors announcing the repeal of the Stamp Act; on June 9, Fauquier publicly proclaimed it.[65]

Great was the rejoicing at the news. The governor reported that "loyalty and gratitude shone forth" at his proclamation. There were church services, balls, illuminations, public dinners, and much drinking of toasts throughout the colony.[66] By mid-July, nearly every institution was functioning normally; commerce was brisk, courts were open, and business went on in the usual channels. The Governor reported that all was very quiet, "tho there seems to be too general an inclination not to submit to laws."[67]

The Townshend Acts

The "interval of happiness" following the repeal of the "late oppressive Stamp Act" was very short. Virginians had hardly ceased rejoicing over its repeal when news reached America in the summer of 1767 that a new batch of colonial laws had been passed, called collectively the Townshend Acts. Virginians were alarmed immediately at this new evidence of ministerial tyranny, but it was not until the following April that they began to make official protests. "Sundry Freeholders" from several counties—Westmoreland, Chesterfield, Henrico, Amelia, and Prince William—sent petitions to the House "as the only true and constitutional representative people of Virginia" that it would take under its consideration the "fatal tendency" of Great Britain to make laws that were destroying their ancient rights and privileges as freemen.[68] In the preceding years, the colonists had learned a great deal about the use of petitions and the weight of concerted protest. Their petitions of April, 1768, took on the tone less of a suppliant than of a child grateful for past favors and confident that new injustices would be removed. The burgesses who drew up these papers were Richard Bland, chairman, Robert Carter Nicholas, Edmund Pendleton, John Woodbridge, Archibald Cary, John Blair, Dudley Digges, John Page, Jr., Severn Eyre, Benjamin Harrison, and John Anderson. The burden of the argument was the same, but there were a few new touches. For the first time in an official petition, the memorialists faced squarely the problem of virtual representation. They frankly admitted that American representation in Parliament was impossible, but this was just another way of pressing home the point that "respecting their internal polity or taxation" they were bound only by laws of their own making. Governor Botetourt was impressed with the sincerity of their opinions. "I must not venture to flatter you with hopes that they will ever willingly submit to the being taxed by the Mother Country," he reminded the Earl of Hillsborough in February, 1769; "the reverse is their creed; they universally avow a most ardent desire to assist upon every occasion but pray to be allowed to do it as formerly," by requisition.[69]

To the House of Lords they said they were claiming nothing other than their "natural rights" and were far from wishing "an independency of their parent kingdom"; instead, they rejoiced at "their reciprocal connections" which were essential to the happiness of both.[70]

Public discontent simmered for a year, and it was only at the next assembly that it reached the boiling point. The new assembly had been sitting only eight days when, on May 16, Bland offered some resolutions to the House of Burgesses which contained little of the filial devotion of the year before, but a blunt statement of rights. The resolutions spoke of "the sole right of imposing taxes" on the inhabitants of that colony as being vested then and always in the House of Burgesses; and of the "undoubted privilege" of the inhabitants to petition their king for redress of grievances.[71] It was not to be expected that Governor Botetourt could or would let these resolutions, "very offensive to the Parliament of Great Britain," go un-

41

noticed. The next day, having advised the Council of his intentions, he summoned the House before him and dissolved it.[72]

The Stamp Act resolves may have been adopted because the larger part of the burgesses had already started home from the capital, leaving only the "young and giddy" among the thirty-nine to act on them. This could not be said of the 1769 resolves, which were passed by the "fullest house that was ever known."[73] The people seem to have expected events to turn out as they did, and were ready. The governor dissolved the assembly at noon; immediately, the "late representatives of the people," with the "greatest order and decorum," went up the street to Anthony Hay's Raleigh Tavern, elected Speaker Peyton Randolph the moderator, and proceeded to adopt some nonimportation resolutions and eventually to organize the "Association" by which the signers made a nonimportation-nonexportation agreement to last until the Townshend Duty Act was repealed. Eighty-eight burgesses signed it.[74] "We surely must have been thought the most short-sighted, weak, pusillanimous creatures upon the earth," Treasurer Robert Carter Nicholas, one of the signers, wrote Arthur Lee a few days later, "if it was imagined that we would be silent and patient under the greatest injuries." Of what significance was it for Americans to protest "a paltry" Stamp or Revenue Act, he asked, if they would tamely submit to measures fraught with mischiefs a thousand times more alarming and destructive?[75]

Whatever peace the colonies had with Great Britain after this date was merely an uneasy truce. Planters were suspicious, merchants cautious, and lawyers resentful. Some, like John Page, Jr., and Robert Carter Nicholas, were hopeful the Association would be the means of forcing England to repeal the "disagreeable" acts, since it was easily within the power of Parliament "by a single act . . . to restore things to their former happy channel. . . ." Nicholas, who at his most extreme was a moderate at heart, pledged "religiously to adhere to" the Association and was persuaded that it would in time perfect the good work.[76] Others, both Americans and their friends in England, were less sanguine. Landon Carter, who was repelled by the act of independence in 1776, was nevertheless one of the progressive group in 1769. "Fine language this," he exploded in his diary, "as if there could be any half-way between slavery and freedom; certainly one link of the former preserved must be the hold to which the rest of the chain might at any time be joined when the forging smiths thought proper to add it."[77] John Norton, a former burgess but in 1769 a leading merchant in London, would have preferred to see "performances" rather than "the strong promises" that Lord Hillsborough was making.[78] To Arthur Lee, the whole affair appeared hopeless because Lord Hillsborough himself had said that reconciliation was impossible unless the whole authority of England was given up, and of course the "dull arbitrary lord" would not accept that.[79]

There were many little incidents and great uneasiness that indicated widening breach between the colonies and the mother country. The House, led by Jefferson, Richard Henry, Francis Lightfoot Lee, Dabney Carr, and Patrick Henry, created a standing Committee of Correspondence in 1773 which kept it in touch with other parts of British America.[80] The stage was being set for a showdown. One more explosion of major proportions took place before the final rupture. On Tuesday, May 24, 1774, Robert Carter Nicholas, who was one of the most devout men (clergy included) in all Virginia, was persuaded by Thomas Jefferson and his fellows (Henry, the two Lee brothers, and "three or four more") to introduce a resolution they had "cooked up," calling for a day of fasting, humiliation, and prayer in sympathy for Boston, which was threatened with the destruction of her civil rights and the evils of civil war. The resolution, appearing as a broadside, came to the hands of Governor Dunmore, who thought it "reflected highly" on His Majesty and Parliament. He promptly dissolved the assembly. There was another election and one short meeting of the new assembly, but for all practical purposes, the House of Burgesses was ended.

Richard Henry Lee, who in spite of his devotion to the cause of liberty never lost his love of, nor admiration for, England, once lamented that for all "the excellent pattern furnished by the mother country," Virginia's government was "exceptionally contrived."[81] The "happily poised" English constitution and government was a fine blend of monarchy, aristocracy, and democracy. In Virginia, so Lee thought, there was entirely too much power in the hands of the Crown, a fact which led to the diminution of the third element in the system, democracy. Lee and most of his fellow Americans failed to recognize that, after the Glorious Revolution, Parliament quietly but none the less surely was becoming the real government for Britain. And, in spite of his complaints, the House of Burgesses was just as surely becoming the body of real strength in Virginia. Virginians needed only one more crisis to reach the ultimate in their stand against the power in the British government. As shown in the foregoing pages, the lawmakers for this colony had used most of their constitutional arguments in the 1750's over the Pistole Fee and the Two-Penny Act. In succeeding events the petitioners had ample opportunity to restate and refine their arguments so that by 1774 they had reached a mature constitutional position. Even if they had not had full faith in their arguments in the beginning, they convinced themselves by frequent repetitions of them. Virginians were divided when independence finally came, with the Attorney General, most of the councilors, and a few burgesses remaining loyal to the Crown; but, generally speaking, the leaders of the Revolution had been the leaders in the House of Burgesses. In addition to working out a legal and constitutional position, they had devised methods of circumventing the governor and operating in the absence of an assembly. The Committee of Correspondence and the Associations were instruments of their own making by which Virginians kept in touch with the other colonies and worked in unison for a common cause.

This place of preeminence was no accident. It was the handiwork of a group of men who were using their rights as Englishmen. The House of Burgesses was no abstract concept, but a body of men—399 of them between 1750 and 1774—who besides serving their country, made a living, belonged to the Church, and were elected by their constituents. It is the main purpose of this study to secure greater knowledge about these men, how they were elected, what they did besides serve their country, how they made a living, and who they were in private life.

3

"THE FLAME OF BURGESSING"

Elections, Election Laws, and Electioneering

Virginia followed the English practice of holding elections only at irregular intervals. Her elections were of two kinds: general elections and by-elections. General elections, at which every seat in the House of Burgesses had to be chosen, followed a dissolution of the assembly for any one of a variety of reasons. By-elections were held in individual counties to fill vacancies resulting from death or resignation during the term of the assembly; these were numerous because no vacancies were filled by appointment. There were eight general eelctions between 1750 and 1774.

General Elections

When Governor Dinwiddie arrived in the colony, he dissolved by proclamation the old assembly which had been elected in 1748.[1] The new assembly met February 27, 1752, at the college because of repairs being made on the Capitol. It lasted through eight sessions until November 8, 1755. The occasion for its dissolution was an act "for advancing and securing the public credit," which contained a plan for a loan office and an emission of two hundred thousand pounds in paper money which Dinwiddie believed would have had insufficient security.[2] Thinking it would be to "His Majesty's service and the good of this dominion," he took a chance on a new election. No new assembly, he thought, could be "so bad as the last." It had indeed made a burning issue of his policy in regard to land patents, had hired Peyton Randolph as its own agent, and had sent him to England on twenty-five hundred pounds Virginia money appropriated in a rider to a defense bill.

New elections were held in December, 1755.[3] Dinwiddie must have been convinced very early that little good would come of the new assembly.

45

Although 41 new members were elected out of a total of 104, the leadership was much the same. Speaker John Robinson, Benjamin Harrison of Charles City County, Edmund Pendleton, and Peyton Randolph, all of whom had formed the leadership of the earlier House, were returned by their constituents. Furthermore, at the very first session of the new assembly, the House, annoyed that it was unable to get a quorum for a vote on several important measures, sent the sergeant-at-arms with the mace into the General Court room where the Governor and the council were sitting to compel some errant burgesses to attend to their duty.[4] Dinwiddie considered the act an affront to the dignity of the governor and court.

He returned to England within two years after this election and left President John Blair to preside over the affairs of the colony until a new lieutenant governor could be appointed.[5] With the arrival of Francis Fauquier, this assembly was ended and a new election called.

Burgesses who were elected in July 1758 had, in all, seven meetings. The last one, from October 6, 1760 to April 10, 1761, was one of the longest in the history of the House.[6] George II died on October 21, 1760; and, on February 12, Fauquier proclaimed George III king. A new sovereign necessitated the dissolution of the old assembly and the election of a new one. As early as February 17, Fauquier had announced to the Board of Trade that he would dissolve it as soon as it finished its business.[7] In his closing message to the House, the governor praised the burgesses "for the readiness and alacrity with which they had engaged in the measures recommended" to them for the assistance of the armed forces in America. He called them his friends and expressed sadness at parting with them and said he could "never expect, or even desire, to meet an assembly composed of gentlemen more acceptable" to him than these "who happily found the means of joining" their duty to His Majesty with their interest in their colony, "which can never be separated but to the disadvantage of both." He hoped that their constituents would see their conduct, approve the "whole tenor of it," and show their approbation by returning the same gentlemen at the next election.[8]

The second election under Fauquier (May 1761) returned a larger percentage of the old members than some earlier elections, but the results in getting docile burgesses were no better than in earlier elections. Fauquier dissolved the assembly on June 1, 1765, when he heard of the Stamp Act Resolves.[9]

Hoping to replace the "hot and giddy" young members who had supported Patrick Henry in his resolves, Fauquier called a third election. If we knew the names of the burgesses who voted with Henry, we would be in a better position to interpret the changes in personnel resulting from the election. From the 41 new men returned, it is difficult to see that the

46

governor was any better off after the election.[10] Polls for burgesses were held in July, 1765, but the new assembly was prorogued until November 6, 1766, some fifteen months later. The last of the three sessions ended on April 16, 1768, and the assembly was terminated by Lord Botetourt, who had replaced the deceased Fauquier the preceding fall.[11]

Botetourt, the first resident titular governor since Francis Nicholson in 1705, dissolved the assembly on October 27, 1768, and ordered elections to be held in November. This assembly had the shortest life in the period. Meeting for the first time on May 8, 1769, it was dissolved on May 17 because of its opposition to the Townshend Acts.[12] As indicated earlier, however, Virginians seem to have nursed little resentment toward the governor for this action.

The assembly that was elected in September 1769 and met for the first time on November 7 was to continue until after the death of Botetourt; Lord Dunmore dissolved it on October 12, 1771. It gave a great deal of attention to enforcing the nonimportation association formed in 1769 and to drafting a new election law. The last of the three sessions was convened by President John Blair, who was again the acting governor.

The election of November 1771 was the last to be held under anything like normal circumstances. Convened on the following February 10, the assembly met on three different occasions. On May 26, 1774, at the end of the third session which had begun with the governor urging "prudence and moderation" and the burgesses promising only "coolness and delibera-tion," the House voted June 1 a day of fasting and prayer for Boston. When Dunmore heard of the action, he summoned the burgesses before him and sent them home. "I have in my hand," he said, "a paper published by order of your House, conceived in such terms as to reflect highly upon His Majesty and the Parliament of Great Britain, which makes it necessary for me to dissolve you, and you are dissolved accordingly."[13] There was to be one more election, and the assembly continued at least in name until Independence, but the House of Burgesses ceased to be a lawmaking body after May, 1774, and became instead a revolutionary organ.

From this account it may be seen that elections in Virginia in the years between 1750 and 1774 resulted from two causes. One was the arrival of a new governor who dissolved the old assembly and issued writs for electing a new one as a matter of course. Four times during the period—at Din-widdie's arrival in 1752, Fauquier's in 1758, Botetourt's in 1768, and Dunmore's in 1771—such an occasion arose. The other cause was action which the governor deemed a violation of the prerogatives of the Crown or Parliament. On four occasions, four different governors, believing that the House had gone beyond the limits of a colonial legislature, ordered new elections. Dinwiddie objected to the legality and economics of a loan office and the emission of paper money; Fauquier knew that the Stamp Act Resolves denied certain basic principles in the relation between colony and mother country; Botetourt in 1769 recognized in the resolves against the Townshend Acts a further denial of the right to tax; and Dunmore saw in setting a day of prayer for rebellious Boston an open sympathy for an act of defiance. The death of the ruling monarch brought the election of 1761. Although there was no regular time to hold elections, circumstances were such that, in a twenty-four-year period, freeholders went to the polls eight times or, on the average, once in three years. One might conclude that, in the absence of laws for holding them regularly, death and taxes combined to give the colony fairly frequent elections.

Election Laws

The law under which elections were held had been in effect since 1705, the fourth year of Queen Anne's reign. Only once had it been amended—in 1736 under King George II. Two major revisions were attempted in the 1760's; but these acts, although passed by the assembly and signed by the governor, were disallowed by the home government. So, except for minor amendment, the law remained unchanged after 1736.

The law of Queen Anne's time was entitled "An act for regulating the election of Burgesses, for settling their privileges and ascertaining their allowances."[14] Under it, freeholders had the "privilege and liberty" of electing "two of the most fit and able men" from each county to represent them in the House of Burgesses. The law gave in great detail the process of holding an election and the qualifications for voting.

At least forty days before the governor proposed to have a meeting of an assembly, he signed election writs which the secretary of the colony within ten days sent to the sheriff in each county. Within three days after that officer received them, he was to send copies to each minister in the county or, if the parish had no resident clergyman, to the reader. These gentlemen were to read them immediately after divine worship on every Sunday until the election. The copy bore the place of the election, and the date, which had to be at least twenty days after the sheriff received the writ. In order to be sure that the information was properly publicized, the law required that the minister or reader send his copy back with "a certificate of publication."[15]

The right to vote extended to all freeholders except men under twenty-one years of age, women, Negroes, and recusant convicts. The law did not specify the size of the freehold. A freeholder who failed to vote was subject to a fine of 200 pounds of tobacco; and any nonfreeholder who tried to vote, 500 pounds. Elections were held at the court house by the sheriff,

48

who was subject to severe fines in tobacco for failure to carry out any part of his responsibility. When the polling was over, the sheriff was to announce the winners and send a copy of the returns to the secretary in Williamsburg.

In order to assure honest elections, fairly taken, and to keep electioneering within the bounds of reason, legal restrictions were placed on campaign practices. As soon as election writs were out, the law said, no candidate, nor anyone on his behalf, was to "give, present, or allow, to any persons or person having voice or votes in such election, any money, meat, entertainment, or provision, or make any present, gift, or reward, or shall at any time hereafter make any promise, agreement, obligation, or engagement to or for" any person who had a vote. The penalty for violating any part of this act was simple, but severe: any candidate so doing was incapacitated from sitting in the House.[16]

Two amendments were made in the 1705 law before 1750. The law of 1736 raised the voting requirement from a freehold of unspecified size to one hundred acres of unimproved land or twenty-five acres with a house and plantation.[17] Later legislation made sheriffs and tobacco inspectors ineligible for seats in the House of Burgesses.[18]

These election laws, however elaborate and detailed, proved so unsatisfactory that twice the assembly attempted a complete revision of them. The Act of 1762, "An act for directing and better regulating the elections of burgesses, for setting their privileges and for ascertaining their allowances," would have required an election every seventh year and a meeting of the assembly once every three years.[19] The amount of land that composed a freehold was reduced from one hundred acres of unimproved land to fifty acres, but the twenty-five acres with house and improvements remained the same. It restated that certain people were ineligible to election: sheriffs, tobacco inspectors, and anyone who held a "place of profit" under the British government. Instead of the county being responsible for the burgesses' salaries, money for this purpose could be taken from the treasury of the colony if there was a sufficient balance. The act had a suspending clause, which meant that it would not become law until the home government approved it.

The home government vetoed it, however, just as the governor predicted it would, although he had signed the bill. He foresaw that it would be deemed an encroachment on the royal prerogatives, which he was duty-bound to support.[20] In an opinion handed down by Matthew Lamb, counsel to the Board of Trade, it was stated that: "The province of Virginia is in the same situation as the rest of His Majesty's American provinces in respect to choosing, continuance, and dissolution of their assemblies. The governors who act under His Majesty's commission have authority to exercise what belongs to his royal prerogatives in that respect, and presumably have usually done so. Therefore, it seems unnecessary and improper that any law should be passed wherein that power should be restrained, fixed, or altered. And I am of opinion that this act which limits the continuance of the assembly and fixes the times for holding the same is an infringement of His Majesty's prerogative in the manner it has usually been exercised and that notwithstanding the suspending clause therein that the lieutenant governor should not have given his assent thereto. And I submit . . . that this act should not be confirmed."[21] This opinion was not dated, but it must have been later than 1766, for on December 20 of that year Richard Henry Lee was complaining to his brother Arthur that, although four years had passed since the enactment of the law, it had not had the royal approbation. A thorough reform in the "faulty parts" of the constitution, Lee believed, was urgently needed. How, he queried, with so good a pattern as the English constitution, could Virginia's government be "so exceptionally contrived"?[22]

Undismayed at the fate of this bill, the House undertook a new revision in 1769, with no better results. Debate and action on the measure was the center of attention for two meetings of the assembly, November 7–21, 1769, and May 21–June 28, 1770. On November 20, 1769, leave was granted to bring in a "bill to explain and amend an act of Assembly made in the fourth year of the reign of Queen Anne. . . ." Richard Bland of Prince George and Archibald Cary of Chesterfield composed the committee to prepare and bring in the bill.[23] Eight days later Bland presented his report. Final action on the bill, however, was not taken until the beginning of the June 1770 session.[24]

The new bill omitted the section on septennial elections and triennial assemblies, but contained many other features of its predecessor.[25] The fifty acres or twenty-five acres with house and improvements remained the same, but the size of the house—at least twelve feet square—was now specified. The length of ownership previous to voting was reduced from one year to six months. The actual voting process was the same as in the earliest bills, but failure to execute any portion of it carried a fine in money instead of tobacco. Voting could be continued a second day when more freeholders appeared than could be polled before sunset. A voter was required to swear that he had the necessary freehold only if someone, presumably an election clerk or one of the candidates, questioned his ownership. The Quakers had become strong enough to receive recognition of their conviction against oath-taking; they were only required to make a declaration of their land. The procedure after election day was more detailed here than in earlier acts. Reflecting the popular distrust of sheriffs, the act names several frauds for which the sheriff could be fined one hundred pounds in current money. The act closed, as did the one of 1762, with a suspending clause. It is uncertain what happened to this act in England. We do know that twice the Board of Trade considered it but ordered it to "lye by" until the members could get more information. In all probability the outbreak of hostilities came before the matter was resolved.[26] We also know that the law never went into effect. The colony, therefore, as far as election laws went, was still where it was in 1736. Elections in Virginia in the quarter century before independence were regulated by the acts of 1705 and 1736 and by certain customary practices, which the governors thought consistent with British practice.

Election Procedure

Elections were always held at the courthouse "where the county court is accustomed to be held"; there were no other polling places. If a man voted, he rode to the county seat to do it, regardless of how far away he lived. The hours for keeping the polls open were not designated in the law and, judging from cases of disputed elections, varied from place to place. The law said only that the sheriff should go to the door of the courthouse and announce the opening of the polls; at the end of the balloting he proclaimed the closing. Voting might, and often did, continue until after dark if the freeholders there had not voted earlier and even on a second day if necessary. The evidence suggests, however, that voting normally required only one day.

On election day the sheriff was in charge. He opened the polls and conducted the voting. If there were only two candidates or only token opposition, and the results could be seen clearly "upon the view" (voting being oral), all that remained for the sheriff to do was to close the polls and make a certified copy of the results, which he was to send the secretary within twenty days. If it could not be decided "from the view" who was elected, the process became more complicated and the sheriff more important. The sheriff, or in his absence an undersheriff, with the consent of the freeholders, appointed as many election clerks as to him seemed "fit." He administered to these men an oath by which they promised a "true and impartial taking of the poll." He then provided them with the necessary books in which to keep records of the voting. The name of each candidate was written at the head of a column or the top of a page, and the names of the freeholders casting their votes for him listed below.

When a freeholder voted, he stepped up, took an oath that he was a freeholder in that county and that he had not been polled before in that election, and stated his choices, which were duly set down. Each freeholder had two votes and both had to be cast at the same time; he could not save one until later in the day. All this was done under the watchful

51

eyes of the candidates, or persons representing them, who were present to see the "poll fairly taken." When the sheriff thought everyone had voted, he closed the polls by making proclamation three times at the courthouse door. He then proceeded to count votes, probably with the assistance of the clerks and under the observation of the candidates, although the law was not specific here. If the vote was tied, the sheriff, or the undersheriff, as a freeholder, had the right to cast his ballot for the man of his choice. He then "returned the burgesses," which may have included both the announcement to the waiting crowd and the written form to the secretary in Williamsburg. The law was specific about the form to be used. It read: "By virtue of this writ to me directed, in my full county, held at the courthouse of my said county, upon the _____ day of _____ in the _____ year of the reign of _____ by the grace of God, of England, Scotland, France, and Ireland, Queen, defender of the faith, and by the assent of my said county, I have caused to be chosen (two burgesses) of my said county, to wit, A. B. and C. D. to act and do as in the said writ is directed and required." The process was the same in a by-election. From the time the writs reached the county until the returns were sent to the secretary, the sheriff had complete charge of the election. Virginians often complained that this concentration of power led to abuses; and, after every election, the burgesses found it necessary to subpoena sheriffs to correct their returns.

There were many alleged violations of the corrupt practices code. When a defeated candidate believed that campaign tactics had gone beyond legal limits, he had the right to petition the House of Burgesses to investigate the "undue election and return" of the incumbent. Such contested elections were handled according to a set procedure. After the petition had been heard at the bar of the House, the case was sent to the Committee of Privileges and Elections. The petitioner had to give the list of the voters he objected to and otherwise state his complaints to the committee, which was empowered to send for persons, papers, and records needed in making a thorough investigation. After it had examined witnesses and collected pertinent information, the committee reported its findings to the House, which had the final vote on the matter.

Many contested elections resulted from illegal campaign practices. The testimony in two cases taken by the Committee on Privileges and Elections will serve to illustrate. In Lunenburg at a by-election in 1757 when Thomas Nash was returned, the barkeeper Bacon supplied free liquor to all who applied in the name of Mr. Nash, but told others bluntly there was "no liquor for Marrable," another candidate. This treating seems to have been against Nash's advice and without his knowledge, and his election was upheld when the question was taken to the House for settlement.[27] Not long afterwards, when this same Matthew Marrable and Clement Read were elected, Henry Blagrave complained of Marrable's treating;[28] and in 1772, the same charge was made against Blagrave.[29]

Holding elections only at the courthouse made it necessary for freeholders living at great distances to make at least a part of the journey a day early. Taking care of potential voters could, and often did, lead to trouble for the victor. Such a situation developed for Stephen Dewey of Prince George County at the election of 1752. On the day before elections, reported Edwin Conway for the Committee of Privileges and Elections,

> a great number of the freeholders . . . supposed to be near eighty, who all, except a few, lived remote, some thirty, and others more, miles from the court house, went to the dwelling house of the sitting member, the earth being then covered with snow, and the weather excessive cold, where they continued till the next day, and during that time were kindly and hospitably entertained by the sitting member who gave them sufficient meat and drink, lodged as many of them as he could, and gave them some drams of rum in the morning . . . the sitting member or any person for him did not invite them to come there, nor then, nor at any other time, solicit any of them to vote for him . . . that the greater part of them did vote for him, and intended to do, before they went there. . . .

A few were drunk the next morning, but they had not been sober when they arrived. On election day, Dewey's wife got help to prepare a hogshead of punch, which Drury Thweat, who had done the mixing, set up about a hundred yards from the courthouse door. When the polling began, Thweat went inside to see how things were going. In his absence, one of the Dewey Negroes announced that all who had voted or would vote for his master might drink as much as they pleased. This invitation was endorsed by Mrs. Dewey's young brother, William Hall, who urged several people to drink. All this was taking place while Dewey was attending the poll. He testified later that he knew nothing of it and that

> on the day of election before the freeholders began to poll when a person asked whether he might not have some punch, declared that none ought to be drank before the poll was concluded. And that the friends of the sitting member, when they were informed that some persons were drinking his punch, immediately went to the hogshead, and having pulled out the cock, stopped it up.[30]

The House, convinced of the truth of his testimony, voted fifty-three to seven that Dewey was duly elected.

Who could vote in colonial Virginia? The act of 1705 stated simply that all freeholders could vote, provided that no "feme-sole, feme-covert, infant under age or recusant convict" should exercise the right. A freeholder was defined as "every person who hath an estate real for his own life or the life of another or any estate of any greater dignity." No minimal limits to the value or size of the freehold were set. Very small amounts of land must have been used in early times to qualify a freeholder because this is one part of the act that was amended by the law of 1736. "Whereas divers frauds have of late been practiced to create and multiply votes in elections . . . ," began the later act, "by making leases of small and inconsiderable parcels of land upon feigned considerations and by subdividing lots of ground in town in prejudice of the rights of the true freeholders and contrary to the true intent and meaning of the laws in that behalf."[31] It would appear from this that the requisite property was very small and that almost anyone could vote before 1736. Evidently some persons had found it worthwhile to acquire small parcels of land simply in order to qualify as voters. In the revision of 1736, as has been noted, voting was restricted to the owners of one hundred acre freeholds that had no improvements, or twenty-five acres with a house and plantation which the freeholder had owned for at least a year, unless he had acquired it by "descent, marriage, marriage-settlement, or devise." It should be observed that residence in a county was not a prerequisite. From the wording of the law it would appear that a man could vote in as many counties as he had freeholds. Whether he did or not, is not certain, but elections were held on different days and it would have been physically possible to do so. Residents of Williamsburg and Norfolk had somewhat more lenient suffrage requirements—any person was entitled to vote who owned a lot and house in the town or had visible property to the value of fifty pounds, or who had served as an apprentice five years in the city and had become a householder. In the revision of the Williamsburg charter in 1742, the potential voter with the fifty pounds visible property had to have been a resident for twelve months before he could exercise this privilege.[32]

Judging from testimony taken in contested elections, the requirement of land was rigidly adhered to. Under such laws how many people—what proportion—had the right to vote and how many actually exercised the right? In the eighteenth century there was no more relationship between the number who could vote and those who did than there is in the twentieth; therefore the questions must be taken up separately. Neither question is easily answered since the student is hampered by incomplete, inadequate, and fragmentary information.

Thomas Jefferson seems to be largely responsible for the commonly accepted belief that only a small portion of the white male inhabitants of Virginia could vote. Writing to the Frenchman, Francois Marbois, in 1781, he expressed the view that the majority of the men in the state could not vote, that the roll of freeholders generally did not include half of those on the rolls of the militia or of the tax gatherers.[33] Recently Jefferson's statement has been given support by Jackson T. Main in an article in the *Mississippi Valley Historical Review*. Mr. Main has examined the tax rolls of the 1780's and has concluded that a very large portion of white males, between one-half and three-fourths, were landless and therefore without the suffrage.[34] Both Jefferson and Main are writing of a postwar period, but the qualifications for voting were the same under the Constitution of 1776 as they were in the colonial period after 1736. Therefore, the percentage of people having a voice in the affairs of the government should be essentially the same. It remains to be seen if it was.

There are no tax lists for the colonial period such as Mr. Main uses, so the student must turn to other sources. There are a few documents which are of great help in solving the problem. Early in 1756, Governor Robert Dinwiddie reported to the Board of Trade a list of tithables which was made up of all white males sixteen years and over, and all blacks both male and female above the same age. Dinwiddie's list is broken down into whites and blacks.[35] There is a similar list for 1773, which is not broken down, but which gives the total number of tithables for each county.[36] The first federal census taken in 1790 is of use in determining what the population trend had been over a period of years. All three lists give numbers only; the first two include tithables, and the federal census tabulates people in the same age groups. Dinwiddie advised the home government that the total white population could be determined by multiplying the white tithables by four; and, in general, the 1790 census bears out the truth of his statement.[37] According to colonial law only white males above twenty-one years of age could vote, but the lists of tithables and the census divide the population at the age of sixteen rather than twenty-one. Jefferson's estimate that a fourth of the white male population over sixteen was between sixteen and twenty-one is the only clue that has been found thus far of any value in determining the number of tithables old enough to vote. Jefferson arrived at that number from an examination of the militia rolls.[38] Whether he was correct or not, his number is the only one we have.

Help in determining the number of property owners comes from a source only recently discovered. John Blair, Auditor General for Virginia, reported to the Board of Trade the number of freeholders in 1763. His figures were based on the colonists who paid quitrent to His Majesty's government. Blair admitted that the report contained some information based

55

on guesswork but said it was as accurate as he could make it.[39] The greatest shortcoming of the paper is that it contains no statistics for the counties in the Northern Neck. As tenants of the Fairfaxes, the inhabitants of that area paid rent to the proprietors rather than to the king. Even with the Fairfax lands missing, the report includes figures for forty-one, or two-thirds, of the total number of counties. There are no population figures for any time within eight years of 1763. To fill in the breach, a comparison of the statistics for 1755, for 1773, and for 1790 becomes valuable. There are admitted inaccuracies and even more probable errors, but the figures give as accurate knowledge as is possible to attain; any other figures are only guesswork.

Ten counties for which Blair lists the freeholders had an increase of less than 200 white males above 16 for the thirty-five years from 1755 to 1790.[40] Some counties actually reported losses at the first federal census. It seems safe to assume that at no time during the years after 1755 did the population of these counties vary materially. Charles City, for example, had 537 white tithables in 1755 and only 532 in 1790. Such figures suggest that in 1763 the number must have been near the same. In that year Blair reported 231 freeholders, or 43 percent of the total white male population above 16. York County had 562 in 1755 and 630 in 1790. Blair said there were 200 freeholders, which made up only 35.6 percent of the white males above 16. In the other counties, the freeholders made up fifty or more percent of the white males above 16. Cumberland, in the center of the colony, had 704 white tithables in 1755 and, in spite of the rapid development of the area, only 885 in 1790. There were 586 freeholders in 1763, which is 83.24 percent of the 1755 number or 66.21 percent of the 1790 number. Elizabeth City, like Charles City, was a small county whose white tithables increased very little—from 316 in 1755 to 390 thirty-five years later. The totals for 1773 indicate there were only 82 more persons in the county than were there eighteen years earlier in 1755. The population therefore can be counted as stable. One hundred seventy people, or 53.8 percent of the 1755 white tithables, paid quitrents in 1763. The white men over 16 in Essex County increased only 19 in thirty-five years (from 889 to 908), and 69.7 percent of the 1755 number could vote in 1763. In James City, the total white tithables increased just one, and of the 394 in 1755, two hundred—50.8 percent—could vote in 1763. Mr. Main found 56.5 percent of the Middlesex County men landless in the 1780's, but in 1763 the figures show an entirely different situation. There were 371 white tithables in the county in 1755 and 280 freeholders in 1763, or 75.5 percent of the total tithable men. The white males over 16 had increased from 371 to 407 in 1790 and, even considering the later figure, 68.8 percent were still landowners and potential voters. Four hundred of King William's 702 were freeholders—nearly 57 percent. In Surry 63 percent could vote

56

and in Warwick 69 percent. For the ten counties whose population can be predicted with a fair degree of accuracy, 60.7 percent of the white males were freeholders and therefore potential voters. This percentage is again based on white tithables and aged 16 and above; if figured on the 25 percent less that Jefferson said were below voting age, the percentage of men who could vote would be even greater.

The statistics for the above counties, because of static population, can be considered fairly accurate. For counties with rapidly increasing population, it is more difficult to approximate that part of the total inhabitants who were entitled to vote. It is almost impossible to determine the number for counties that were subdivided during the period, so none of them will be considered here. Dinwiddie County kept the same boundaries from 1755 on. From 1755 to 1790, the white males above 16 had increased from 784 to 1,790, which is nearly 29 a year on the average. If the increase was steady, there would have been 1,016 in the county for 1763. In that year 650 had freeholds. If the hypothetical number of white tithables is approximately correct, a fair percentage could vote—about 65 percent. Hanover, Patrick Henry's county, had 1169 in 1755 and 1637 by the time of the first federal census, an increase of 487 or a little more than 13 per year on the average. With gradual, steady increase, the county should have had 1273 white men by 1763; in that year 760 paid quitrent—59 percent. Spotsylvania doubled her population in the thirty-five years after 1755. Her white males went from 665 to 1361, an increase of almost twenty per year. One hundred sixty should have been added to the 665 before 1763 to make 725. That year, according to Blair's report, 450 freeholders lived in the county, or 62.07 percent. Using the same system of computation, Princess Anne's percentage of freeholders was 56 and Prince George's 60. To balance the picture, however, Norfolk had more than doubled her population and, by the method used above, had only 38 percent of her white males paying quitrents. While no claim is made that the foregoing percentages are absolutely correct, it does appear that the people who had the right to vote made up considerably more than 50 percent of the adult white men.

The question of how many colonials actually voted has plagued scholars for years. Professor J. F. Jameson discussed the problem in a provocative article published in *The Nation,* April 27, 1893.[41] After examining the election returns for Westmoreland, Frederick, Fauquier, and Surry Counties, he concluded that at least six percent of the white inhabitants actually went to the polls. Dr. Jameson was answered by Dr. Lyon G. Tyler, then editor of *The William and Mary Quarterly,* who believed, on the basis of information not accessible to Jameson, that an even greater percentage voted: in Elizabeth City (1758), eight percent; in King George (1758), ten percent;

57

and in Westmoreland, ten percent.[42] Both Jameson and Tyler based their figures on Governor Dinwiddie's 1755 list of tithables.

Since the time when these two scholars wrote, seventy-odd years ago, more election returns and other information have been made available. In considering the percentage of freeholders who actually participated in voting, we are on much firmer ground than in making estimates of residents who were freeholders. Of the existing sixty-four polls, ten are for 1755. Therefore it is easy to compare the number of voters with Dinwiddie's list of tithables. Eleven more polls are for 1761 or 1765, and one of them can be checked against Blair's list of freeholders. Five polls are for 1771, two years before the 1773 list of tithables. The information contined in these lists should either substantiate or disprove the conclusions of earlier studies.

Accomac County, so Dinwiddie reported, had 1506 white tithables in 1755. That year 540 freeholders cast votes for nine candidates. This makes 35.1 percent of all white men above 16 or, using Jefferson's method for arriving at the numbers of voting age, 48.8 percent of all white men 21 or above. In the same year, 353 Essex County residents, out of 889 white tithables, voted: 39.7 percent of all white tithables. In other counties for which there are election returns for 1755, 26.6 percent of the white tithables went to the polls in Fairfax; 13.6 percent in Frederick; 33.7 percent in King George; 29.2 percent in Lancaster; 27.4 percent in Richmond; 31.4 percent in Spotsylvania; and 39.9 percent in Westmoreland County.

By using Dinwiddie's figures for arriving at the total of all whites (four times the white tithables), the percentage of actual voters in the total white population for the nine counties for which there are 1755 election returns is as follows:

Accomac	8.9
Essex	9.9
Fairfax	8.9
Frederick	3.35
King George	8.4
Lancaster	7.3
Richmond County	6.8
Spotsylvania	7.9
Westmoreland	8.9
Average	7.82

These figures take into consideration all white men, women, and children. The average participation was of course very low. To look at it from another angle, let us use Jefferson's suggestion that the men of voting age were three-fourths of the white tithables. Again using the same nine counties, we find the following percentages for men of voting age actually participating in elections:

Accomac	47.8
Essex	52.5
Fairfax	39.1
Frederick	18.9
King George	45.0
Lancaster	39.1
Richmond County	36.6
Spotsylvania	41.8
Westmoreland	47.74
Average	40.95

Essex County is the only one included in Blair's list of freeholders in 1763 for which there is also an existing poll for 1761. In that year 369 out of 620 or 59.5 percent of the freeholders voted.

The 1773 list of tithables makes no distinction between whites and blacks, but it may be assumed that the ratio between the races was still about what it was in 1755. Therefore we can determine the approximate number of white men above 16 in Essex, Northumberland, Richmond, Spotsylvania, and Surry Counties, for which there are election returns for 1771. In 1755, Essex County population was divided about one to two between the white and black tithables; the whites made up 34.19 percent of the total. Applying that ratio to the 1773 totals, 974 out of 2850 would have been white. At the election for burgesses on November 22, 1771, only 241 or 26.7 percent cast their votes. Of the tithables in Northumberland 40.6 percent were white; therefore 1006 of the 2922 in 1773 should be white. Three hundred forty-one or 33.9 percent of them voted on December 4, 1771. The percentage of tithables in Richmond County who voted in that year is lower than that in neighboring Northumberland. Only 259 out of a possible 934 tithables went to the polls—that is, only 27.7 percent. In Spotsylvania, 286 out of a possible 782, or 36.4 percent, participated in the election. In Surry the percentage ran higher—286 out of 720, or 39.7 percent. It must be emphasized that the number of white tithables used here is derived from the total tithables at the ratio of 1755. It must also be borne in mind that all white men sixteen and above are included and not just those of voting age.

To date the most exhaustive work on voting in Virginia has been done by a husband and wife team, Robert E. and B. Katherine Brown. After examining not only the polling records but also quitrent and tithe lists, wills, testimony from various sources, and every bit of other available evidence, they conclude that most white men, not only freeholders but many tenants, apprentices, artisans and townspeople of small estate, "either had or soon acquired" enough property to meet the voting requirements.[43]

To sum up, according to the most accurate information we have, between 55 and 60 percent of all white males above 16 years of age were freeholders in 1763 and therefore had the necessary property to vote. It may be assumed that the ratio was essentially the same during the whole 1750–1774 period. In nine counties, 7.4 percent of *all* whites, or 39.07 percent of all white men of voting age, actually went to the polls in 1755. The average participation in the 1771 election (in five counties) was even higher—32.55 percent of white tithables or 44.8 percent of white males of voting age. One must conclude that more than forty percent of the potential voters were taking an active part in electing their burgesses. This analysis of population and election statistics indicates that Jefferson either was mistaken in his belief that a majority of the white men had no voice in their government, or that conditions had changed after Independence; and that the situation Professor Main found in the 1780's was quite different from what the present study has found to be true in the late colonial period.

Issues and Personalities

On the advice of the council, Dunmore, when he arrived in 1771, dissolved the old assembly and called for a new election. He saw no good reason for doing so, and he personally was adverse to it because he observed that much riot and disorder came from allowing people to go to the polls. But it was customary in the province, and he was told (presumably by the council) that an election would be a "pleasure to the people, who are no doubt fond of the exercise, which makes them feel their own consequence."[44]

Why did Virginians go to the polls? Were they merely fond of exercising abstract power, or were there issues at stake which they wished to settle? It need not be demonstrated again that there were many hot political races in the Old Dominion. What motivated them? In searching for the answer, we learn much about the nature of politics in Virginia. Despite all the noble and patriotic sentiments expressed in petitions, pamphlets, the *Gazette,* and innumerable private letters, Virginians said almost nothing about the leading issues in their political campaigns. From the widespread concern about the Stamp Act and the Townshend Acts, it seems likely that they figured largely in the elections of 1765 and 1769, especially since some plain spoken resolves opposing them had been the cause for dissolution of the assembly. Less than three weeks before the 1765 election, an unidentified but patriotic friend of Richard Henry Lee was exhorting all Virginians to unite "to convince the world that we are firm and unanimous in the cause of liberty as so noble and exalted a principle demands." There is little

60

further evidence, however, that this issue or any of the other issues in which people of all parts of the colony were interested—frontier defense, paper money, or even taxation—had an influence on elections. What evidence there is suggests rather that campaigns were won or lost by appeals to local or personal interests.

In Robert Munford's satirical drama on Virginia politics, *The Candidates,* one of the men aspiring to be a burgess promised to move mountains, make rivers navigable, and "bring the tide over the tops of the hills for a vote."[45] Candidates in the flesh were no less extravagant. One candidate who opposed George Washington, a friend who had electioneered actively for him earlier, "trumpeted" about Frederick County that he would "reduce to practice" the "shining virtues" of disinterested public spirit and generous commercial schemes which were to "diffuse gold and opulency through Frederick and prove . . . a sovereign remedy against poverty." And however "strange and chimerical these non-entities" may have appeared to common sense, there were many, particularly the "plebeians of unstable minds," who were "agitated" by the "breath of novelty, whims and nonsense."[46]

Not all campaign promises offered "pie-in-the-sky"; some of them were concrete and practical. In Lunenburg in 1758, for example, Matthew Marrable favored dividing the county, which was very great in size and very injudiciously wrote a letter to David Caldwell agreeing that if he were elected, he would "do something extraordinary" for the freeholders in the upper settlements, or forfeit a large sum of money, five hundred pounds to be exact.[47] Henry Robinson, in 1752, complained that John Chiswell and John Syme of Hanover promised to oppose a division of the parishes; the promise reportedly was made *after* the election writs were published. Dissenters, who were numerous in that county, opposed any multiplication of parishes because the taxes would be increased, and voted in considerable numbers for Chiswell and Syme. Robinson believed that the promise unduly influenced the freeholders. In comparison with later electioneering methods this looks innocent enough, but the House decided that the two returned members from Hanover had broken the part of the election law that prohibited promises after an election was set. Consequently, the election was thrown out and a new one ordered. Landon Carter, serving his first term in the House, could not "forebear saying with others that the petitioners being allied to the chair had great weight" in settling the matter. In his opinion, constituents had a right to exact promises from candidates if they chose.[48]

A similar case was decided in favor of the defendants. James Littlepage, who was opposed to the tobacco inspection law, made the promise that he would work for its repeal and wrote several freeholders, soliciting their votes. "My plan, sir," he wrote one of them, "is to serve the people that's now injured by the damned inspecting law. . . . You may depend I have interest enough to have that taken off, and I want to have the inspectors chosen every year by the freeholders of the county. I will be at your church tomorrow se'ennight and to your house." The election was held in midwinter, and Littlepage invited the freeholders who lived in the northern part of the county, fully twenty-five miles from the courthouse, to spend the night before the election at his house. This they did, and "several were pretty merry with liquor" when they arrived, but they had chiefly cider during the night. The extensive testimony convinced the House that the treating had been early enough to comply with the law, that liquor had not been served at the polls until after the election, and that Littlepage was wholly within his rights.[49]

The location of the capital was the topic of much heated debate in the early 1760's. It had long been recognized that the seat of government should be nearer the center of population; but Speaker Robinson, who favored removal, had been unable to get an appropriate bill passed. In 1761, such a measure failed again but by only a single vote and then because the legislators could not agree on a new site. Whether the "great struggle" was for "other reasons than to integrate themselves for the approaching elections," Governor Fauquier was not sure, but the arguments offered by both sides appeared to him very trifling.[50]

These cases are the only ones that have been discovered in which real issues were at stake. It should be noted that only the promises to get the tobacco inspection law changed and the capital moved could in any way be classed as colonial; the others applied to local situations only. In all probability the average candidate promised little more than to "make it a point to dispatch the business" and to "study to promote the good" of his country.[51] From this meager evidence, the student must conclude that issues seldom played an important part in a campaign.

Nevertheless, heated races did occur, apparently the result of personal rivalry. It seems not to have been so much a question of *what* as *who*. In some counties, unknown men stood for election; but almost always the real race was between men of equal wealth, position, and public experience. How then were the freeholders to choose between them? Family influence was always of value; many a father-in-law used his official position and wide acquaintance to get a seat for his daughter's husband. Even this was not enough to assure victory because the leading families were so intricately interrelated that it was a rare candidate who was not kin to his opponents. It remained, therefore, for the candidates to make direct appeals to the freeholders in whatever way they thought was the most effective means of getting votes. Electioneering was practiced in every part of the colony.

Electioneering was not always delayed until an election was imminent.

There seem to have been some men in public office who campaigned much of the time, men like Benjamin Waller, the most popular man Landon Carter knew, who "harangued a great deal to please the humour of the plebeians." Waller was not an isolated example; at the time of the vote on the stint law in 1755, "the worthy gentlemen" were so bent on pleasing their constituents that Landon Carter found it "most remarkable" to note the contrast between their public and private utterances, "exclaiming against" it out of doors, yet "plumb for it on every motion within."[52]

Electioneering

The best contemporary description of electioneering methods is found, not in the *Gazette* or political pamphlets, but in the play already mentioned, *The Candidates, or the Humours of a Virginia Election,* a comedy in three acts by Robert Munford. The author, a burgess of Mecklenburg County from 1765 to 1775, wrote the play shortly after the death of Governor Botetourt on October 15, 1770. It is probably America's oldest native drama. The plot of *The Candidates* was simple. *Wou'dbe,* an honorable gentleman, was seeking reelection to the House of Burgesses. *Worthy,* his partner in past elections, refused to run again. Three new candidates entered the race when they heard of Worthy's decision. They were *Sir John Toddy,* a convivial sot; *Strutabout,* a conceited, silly fop; and *Smallhope,* a gentleman whose chief distinction came from his devotion to horses and the turf. The action of the play centered around the antics of these three candidates in wooing the freeholders into voting for them. There was a whispering campaign that backfired; ridiculous situations when the candidates pretended to know the names of all their potential constituents; and slapstick comedy when the voters drank too much free toddy. When *Wou'dbe* refused a dishonorable alliance, a joining of interests with either of the three opponents, *Worthy* came out of his retirement and saved the election for *Wou'dbe*— and himself. The comedy ends with a quatrain:

Henceforth, let those who pray for wholesome laws,
And all well-wishers to their country's cause,
Like us refuse a coxcomb—choose a man—
Then let our senate blunder if it can.[53]

Politically minded Virginians loved a good campaign; it broke the monotony of rural existence. "We have dull barbecues," wrote George Washington's former secretary, John Kirkpatrick, during the 1758 campaign, "and yet duller dances. An election causes a hubbub for a week or so and then we are dead a while." While the hubbub lasted, the "flame of burgessing entered every heart" and elections took up the "whole talk."[54] Campaign ballyhoo is largely the invention of a later age; paid political advertisements, printed or well-formulated platforms, even editorials, all of which eventually became parts of every campaign, were all missing until the very eve of the Revolution. There were a dozen or so pamphlets published in the colony, but otherwise the published political literature was confined to the *Virginia Gazette,* chiefly in letters to the editor. Now and then an anonymous poem appeared with obvious political purposes. Generally speaking, however, the candidates preferred more direct methods of electioneering.

Treating was an accepted phase of a political campaign, and the sum expended for liquid refreshments was undoubtedly the largest item in electioneering expenses. George Washington, who probably was no more generous than other candidates, spent £39.6.0 at the election of July 24, 1758, and ten years later put up a smaller, yet considerable, sum of £25.12.7-1/2 for the election of 1768.[55] John Bannister of Battersea, Dinwiddie County, was "very much engaged" after the dissolution of the assembly in the spring of 1765 "in swilling the planters with bumbo" and by midsummer was sure that "every man of the least distinction" in the county was for him.[56] Care had to be practiced in timing treats of any kind, or they were grounds for throwing out the election.

Handshaking was as important to the politicians than as now. County court offered a good opportunity to see a great many freeholders in a single day; church, sales, and militia musters were equally good. Some candidates tried to visit all the churches in their counties, both Anglican and dissenting, as time permitted. The support of the leading citizen and of large blocs of freeholders was important. Before the end of the colonial period, the dissenters, and especially the Quakers, were numerous enough to require special notice.

Personal friends were of inestimable value during a campaign, especially if the candidate lived any great distance from the county where the polling was being done. They felt the public pulse, reported the chances of a candidate, and suggested tactics necessary for winning. It was considered desirable to make personal appearance in as many places as possible and almost imperative to be present at the courthouse on election day. Political supporters of George Washington in Frederick believed that it would clinch the victory if he could but "show his face" at the polls. But since he was busy fighting the Indians and, therefore, unable even to attend, Gabriel Jones, John Kirkpatrick, Adam Stephens, and others carried on an active and successful campaign for him.[57]

In the foregoing pages, we have examined elections in Virginia in the quarter-century before the Revolution: the laws under which the colonists voted, their methods of getting out the vote, procedure at the polls, and the numbers who could and did vote. There still remains the question of who was elected under such a system. What, for example, was the social status of the burgesses? Were they average farmers or great planters? What were their interests other than making a living? In what other capacities did they serve their country?

The answers to these questions are not easy. One difficulty arises from the fact that Virginians said very little about social distinctions in their writings. Another is that, while there is much available information about Virginians, it is concentrated on a few families. Furthermore, most secondary works are so filiopietistic in nature that they are of little use to the historian. Therefore, before we can generalize about the burgesses, we will have to examine some of them at close range. We will use for our study seven representative counties: two in the Tidewater, two on the frontier, and three in the interior. Although I could use almost any or all of the counties because of the vast amount of Virginia local history, these choices are not entirely arbitrary. I chose them for their representative geographical location and because of their extensive political records, particularly of their elections.

4

RICHMOND AND ESSEX COUNTIES
ON THE RAPPAHANNOCK

In the preceding pages, we have been examining the political structure, governmental institutions, and election practices of colonial Virginia. From the governor down, every officer, except the burgesses, was appointed by someone—the king, the governor, the secretary, or the justices. In the election of burgesses alone did the freeholders exercise the right of suffrage; and, judging from the interest exhibited in every part of the colony, the freeholders considered the choosing of their representatives an event of major proportions. Whether or not they thought of it as a "democratic" process, they did value the right to choose the members of the branch of government that they were coming to regard as the only body with extensive power over them.

To see at close range how Virginians chose their representatives and what kind of men they chose, let us turn to some representative counties from all parts of the colony and examine them in detail. Of the seven counties selected for that purpose, Richmond and Essex are in the Tidewater, Augusta and Frederick on the frontier, and Henrico, Albemarle, and Amelia in the Piedmont or on its border.

Richmond and Essex counties had once been one county, Rappahannock —"Old Rappahannock" it is usually called, because it ceased to exist in 1692.[1] That year it was divided into Richmond to the north and Essex to the south. The river which had once united it now divided them. Geographically and ethnologically, the two are very similar; it would be logical to assume that their politics was much the same. But this was not the case.

Elections in Richmond

Richmond County may be considered typical of the more staid Tidewater plantation counties. The area had long been settled; all available land was taken up, and most of the residents were direct descendants of those who had received land from the king by patent. There was little place for the newcomer in the economic or political life, and, one suspects, in the social life. During the period 1750–1774, the county had only five burgesses; and one of them, Thomas Glasscock, served only in the brief assembly of 1769.[2] John Woodbridge and Landon Carter were the county representatives until 1769 and 1768, respectively. Carter's son, Robert Wormeley Carter, and Francis Lightfoot Lee, son of President Thomas Lee and brother of Richard Henry Lee of Westmoreland, were elected in September 1769. These two young men would serve the county at the capital during the remainder of the colonial period.

The number of unsuccessful candidates, in comparison with some counties like Accomac where eight to ten were always in the race, was also small. According to the six extant polls for Richmond County (1752, 1755, 1758, 1769, and 1771), only five men, besides the successful candidates, ran for office. In 1752, Capt. John Smith ran last in a three-man race, polling 120; Capt. John Woodbridge received 231, which made him the senior burgess; and Landon Carter, 176.[3] Mr. Robert Mitchell received only 55 votes on December 5, 1755; Landon Carter, Esq., and Capt. John Woodbridge polled 189 and 173 respectively.[4] Colonel Tarpley, with 114 votes, and Mr. William Glasscock, with only 24, were the unsuccessful contenders at the July 20, 1758 election.[5] Col. William Peachy (with 19 votes), and Smith again (but this time with 124, which was only eight less than Landon Carter's 132) participated in the 1761 election; Woodbridge polled 196.[6] Thomas Glasscock, on September 22, 1769, and Hudson Muse[7] in 1771 are the only men that we know who ran successfully against the Lee-Carter combination.[8] The total votes polled by all the unsuccessful candidates in the six elections was only 710 as compared to 2106 for the men who went to Williamsburg.

With four men dominating public office, and having little more than token opposition, it would appear at first glance that politics followed a set pattern, and life was serene. But this conclusion is far from the truth. Candidates used campaign tactics more like those we associate with the twentieth century than the eighteenth; and political life was often turbulent. What made it so was the burgesses themselves.

The Burgesses of Richmond

John Woodbridge. Little is known about John Woodbridge except that he was born in the county on November 24, 1706, the son of William and Sarah Woodbridge of Farnham Parish. He had been in the House since 1734; and although only three years older than Landon Carter, his new colleague in 1752, he was a veteran of eighteen years' experience. He was on the committee of Propositions and Grievances from 1752 on; but he was never a chairman of any committee or, it seems, more than a faithful, if unspectacular, member of the House.[9] In 1767 he headed the court of Richmond County and was doubtless a public-minded citizen.[10] He had contemplated retiring as early as 1765 but for some reason ran again that year, and was reelected then and twice thereafter. He drafted a public statement, dated July 1, 1765, in which he thanked his constituents for their past favors. "To my Good Friends, the Freeholders of Richmond County," the paper began.

> At the same time I declared my intentions of not being a candidate at the approaching election, I might justly incur the hateful epithet of Ingrateful should I omit to justify my great regard for favors past. Permit me, therefore, to return to the dutiful, sincere acknowledgement, the slender but just returns of a heart truly susceptible to the deepest impressions of gratitude for the many public demonstrations of esteem and confidence you were pleased to repose in me so often as you did me the honor with that unanimity of nominating me one of your representatives in the General Assembly, and such is my regard for the country, the place of my nativity, that I can earnestly wish you may elect one to succeed me who with the same purity of intention and attestation of conscience, unbiased and unprejudiced, will discharge the important trust.[11]

So far as we know, this paper was never printed, nor is it certain that it was ever circulated. In fact, it may have been only a trial draft which Woodbridge submitted to Landon Carter for his opinion. Be that as it may, he had four more years to serve. Death, rather than retirement, ended his career.

Landon Carter. Woodbridge, whatever he was in private and public life, was overshadowed by his colleague, Landon Carter, Richmond County's leading citizen. Paul Carrington, a fellow burgess from Charlotte, considered Carter one of the seven leaders of the House of Burgesses; but unlike Richard Henry Lee and Edmund Pendleton, who were men of superior ability, he "derived great influence from station, wealth, and connection," not from personal talents.[12]

Carter, who inherited an ample fortune in land and slaves and added to it by patent and purchase, apparently had few financial worries.[13] As a resident of the Northern Neck he was tenant to Lord Fairfax to whom he paid at intervals—and only under pressure—quitrents. In nine years (1743–1752) the sum due to the proprietor was £797.5.9; that due in April, 1760, was £433.5.9. At this latter date, Carter paid rent on thirty-five thousand acres.[14] A good businessman, he was not loathe to take a chance to make an honest pound, but money-making was not the main purpose of his life. His economic interests were centered in land and planting; he worked to improve the breed of horses and to foster the cultivation of the vine in the colony.[15] At his death in 1778, the inventory of his estate showed he had a total of 401 slaves on estates in seven counties.[16] His manor plantation was Sabine Hall.

Working out the intricacies of kinship for Virginia families is primarily a task for the genealogist, not the historian. But it is impossible to understand the structure of politics without some knowledge of these interrelationships. Landon was the fourth of five sons of Robert "King" Carter. The oldest was John, secretary of the colony from 1720 until his death in 1743; the second was Robert II, the father of Robert, the "Councilor";[17] the third son was Charles, the master of Cleve in King George County and burgess for twenty-eight consecutive years.[18] All these sons were educated in England. The daughters of Robert "King" Carter all married into prominent families. Elizabeth, the oldest, married twice, first to Nathaniel Burwell, by whom she had four children: Lewis, Carter, Robert, and Elizabeth. When they reached maturity, Lewis and Carter represented James City County and Isle of Wight County in the House. Elizabeth Burwell, the granddaughter of Robert "King" Carter, became the wife of President William Nelson and was the mother of Thomas Nelson, Jr., burgess from York and later governor of the Commonwealth. After the death of her first husband, Elizabeth Carter Burwell married Dr. George Nicholas, a native of England, and had three sons, two of whom were leaders in the colony: John, burgess from Albemarle and Buckingham, and Robert Carter Nicholas, burgess and treasurer after 1766.[19] Judith Carter, the second daughter of Robert "King" Carter, married Mann Page of Rosewell in Gloucester and had at least two sons who were prominent in the affairs of the colony: Mann, burgess from Gloucester, and John, the representative of the College in the assembly, until he became a councilor in 1773.[20] The third Carter daughter, Anne, married Benjamin Harrison of Berkeley, Charles City County; their son Benjamin, burgess from his home county, was a signer of the Declaration of Independence; and their daughter Elizabeth married Attorney General (and later Speaker) Peyton Randolph. Carter Braxton, another "signer," was the son of Mary Carter (the fourth daughter) and George Braxton of Newington, burgess from King and Queen. On the Carter side, therefore, Landon was brother, brother-in-law, uncle, or cousin to a goodly number of the powerful leaders in Virginia.

By marriage he was connected to about as many more. Landon Carter was married three times; each wife was from a prominent family that had important political connections. The first was Elizabeth Wormeley, daughter of John Wormeley of Rosegill, Middlesex County. The Wormeleys were probably the leading family in that county and had furnished burgesses and councilors for years. The second wife was Maria Byrd, daughter of William

Byrd II, who in many respects was the counterpart of Robert "King" Carter in wealth and social position and even his superior in education and literary skill. Anne Byrd, Maria's elder sister, married Charles Carter of Cleve, and thus Landon became his brother's brother-in-law. Another sister of Maria's, Jane, married John Page of North End, Gloucester, another burgess.[21] It must be remembered, too, that William Byrd III was burgess from Lunenburg before he became a councilor at the death of John Lewis.[22] The third wife of Landon was Elizabeth, sister of Captain William Beale.[23]

Though a leading citizen, Landon Carter was not above criticism; indeed, his place of preeminence seems to have been the cause of jealous attacks. The political picture of the county would be clearer if we knew the name of the rhymester who lampooned (or praised?) Carter on more than one occasion. There is no reason to believe that the author of this homespun verse was one of the known candidates, but it must be admitted he was interested in the political scene. It is not even certain that one person wrote all of them; although the style is the same, some became scurrilous to a degree not reached by others. One of these, in manuscript, is in the Sabine Hall papers and is dated November, 1768. It is entitled "Verses relative to Col. Carter inclosed to Col. Tayloe a little before the Richmond election. An answer is now subjoined to them." And by whom the answer was appended is as much a mystery as the author of the original piece. It may have been Col. John Tayloe to whom the first part was directed; if so, he copied the style of it accurately.

Since the original verses circulated as campaign literature and also tell a great deal about Carter's personality, they will be given here in full.

When Carter cooly does his thoughts rehearse
How smoothly glides the soft harmonious verse
Our fancies stops nor knows by which its caught
The even numbers or the happy thought
His stern behavior gives no more offence
We praise his diction and admire his sense
Pleased with [   ] his amicable plan
Forget the cynic and admire the man
And with such thoughts how might he be rever'd
Would he strive rather to be loved than feard.
Such is the nature of the human soul
Fear may command a part, but love the whole
But forced submissions is mere family pain
Ripening with discord unto potent man.
Thus Burgesses in reputation fell
And Carter dwindled by not ruling well

70

For what but that could opposition raise
Against the man that [   ] contrive to praise?
With rich and poor when are the question's put
To all their praise they add one fatal but
That but removed for the time to come
Let him relax and we are all his own.

The reader is as confused as the writer of the answer about the viewpoint of the author.

THE ANSWER

How hard the task to censure or commend
This poet may be either foe or friend.
Praise tuned so high must mean a stroke severe
Contrived perhaps to catch the slavish ear.
What stern behavior ever gave offense
To men admiring if they judged with sense
Admiring what? Tis stupid to suppose
Man fancies man for what he only knows
What arts should duty recommend
To court the love of those who will offend
Must justice pine or Right give up its whole
To purchase love, so painful to the soul?
Why then misuse that nobly written line
That meant alone parental love t'enjoin?
Say what submission ever was his thought
Who practices Justice, though he lose a vote?
Is this the force that gives such fam'ly pain?
If discord ripens, 'tis with foolish man
Such reputation ne'er could lose a friend
Less would be ruling to no useful end.
Your question then for oppositions cause,
(Though raised on high from Carters great applause)
Must search its answer in some bosom mean,
Where envy rankles though it can't be seen
That foe to merit which it cannot taste
And therefore lessens by some poisonous blast
No mortal man can ward your dreadful *but*
With rich or poor when such a questions put.
Besides there is something in a good estate
Which those who don't enjoy will ever hate
By prudent passions e'en common sense will grant

71

One man may purchase what the lazy can't
Then mark the idle fool who e're he be
You'll find that envy's half his misery.
Till want instructs him to evade just laws
And by mere plunder he'd subsistence draws
Thus feeds his neighbors verdant fields
With horses, cause his own no pastrage yields
Each Benfo's [?] birds or hogs devour those lands
They never shared their cultivating hands
And lazy rapine makes its growling noise
Because his neighbor cannot sacrifice
All property to inconsistent yell;
Then calls it dwindling by not ruling well.
To this the praise desired, your but to shun
Twill be relaxing till their's nought ones own,
Should Carter purchase such a dear bought rule
He might be R_____ or any stupid fool.
He ne'er can merit who his interest buys
An ass must [   ] before the slavish voice
But when you want to [hurt] your country's cause
Let him [   ].

It is unlikely that this poetic effort was ever put in print, but two others
very severe in tone did appear in the *Gazette* in 1767, one in January and
the other in June.[24] After comparing Carter to asses, bugs, hairy beasts, and
a host of other repulsive creatures, the author closes a long poem of fifteen
stanzas with these lines:

The laughing power Great Jove obeyed
(No god neglects great Jove's request)
Admiring Landon's skill, displayed
In characters of man, bug, beast
Yet owning with particular grace
He filled the character of [   ][25]

There can be no mistake that the purpose of the first stanzas was to blast
Carter, but these closing lines, like the earlier quoted piece, are so be-
muddled, and the figures so mixed, that one wonders if the author was very
clever in concealing his true purpose, or merely blundering.

This propaganda had the obviously desired effect—Carter was defeated
by Thomas Glasscock in 1768. He had earlier expressed a wish to retire.
"I yet hope, my friend," wrote Richard Henry Lee to him in June, 1765,
"that you have only thought, not determined, on declining to take a poll

at the ensuing election. When the cause of our dissolution is known, will ministerial cunning fail to suggest that the people of Virginia disavow their Burgesses' claim to freedom, if a considerable change is made by them in their choice of new representatives?"[26] John Woodbridge announced his own intention to retire ten days after this letter, so it may be that they were planning to step aside together. But the threat of what use "ministerial cunning" would make of this proposed resignation may have persuaded them to stand again. At least both of them did. The campaign to defeat Carter, as we have seen, ran on for more than a year before the next election. We have no copy of the poll for 1768; but Carter, some eight years later, recalled in his diary the experience. "I can well remember when I was turned out of the H. of B. It was said that I did not familiarize myself among the people."[27]

Carter's defeat cannot be attributed to his views on the current issues. He upheld the popular view in the affairs resulting from the Two-Penny Act.[28] In the fall of 1759, the Rev. John Camm entered a suit against his parish in York County for the recovery of his salary in tobacco. Upon hearing of this the Committee of Correspondence, of which Landon Carter was a member, decided that the cause of this particular parish was the cause of the whole colony and recommended the matter to the consideration of the House of Burgesses.[29] Carter and Richard Bland were leaders in the fight against the clergymen's cause. They felt that justice to the people and charity to the poor justified their action in disregarding the mandates of the king.[30]

Carter's position on the Stamp Act was equally in keeping with the popular feeling. Second only to Richard Bland as a pre-Revolutionary political writer, he wrote Josiah Green in November, 1765, denouncing a parliamentary act, which he did not identify, because he had "as great an aversion to all acts of Parliament of that kind" as to the Stamp Duty Act. They were, he felt, as much a violation of the Englishman's rights in the colonies as the other was, as they were not considered or framed by any representatives of the colony.[31] Shortly thereafter in a long piece for the press, he was saying much the same thing, that any law (he did not say revenue act) by any body in which the colonies had no representatives could not be binding under the British Constitution.[32] Having been a member of the committee which in 1764 took the first notice of the Stamp Act and a leader in the opposition, Carter was recognized as an authority on the matter. An old gentleman, a member of Parliament who was making a tour of America for Lord Shelburne, was dining at John Tayloe's. His host invited Carter to be present because "Col. Lee says you are so well acquainted with the points in dispute that you may perhaps make an impression of great service; therefore I entreat you to come."[33] In fact, in later years, Carter claimed that it was he "who gave the first breath for liberty in America," and not Patrick Henry who "only assisted in the resolves after the Stamp Act came in by the advice of another."[34]

As was becoming for an eighteenth-century gentleman, Carter dabbled in science and medicine. As early as the Dinwiddie administration, he had been on a House committee to consider a report by one Richard Bryan that he had a "compound medicine" which his father had found "effectual in curing the Dry Gripes." This recipe had been communicated to the son, who had used it successfully on patients seriously ill and "deserted by other doctors as incurables." He was willing to divulge the secret of this remarkable remedy for a suitable reward from the government.[35] In April, 1774, Carter became a member of the "Society for Propagating Useful Knowledge"; he acknowledged his election in the *Gazette* and then proceeded to discuss for three columns his treatment for persons struck by lightning.[36] He wrote treatises on grain weevil and other farm problems. Seemingly unique in Virginia was his proposal for the establishment of a "Patriotic Store" with a capital stock of sixty thousand pounds sterling to be raised by public subscription. This eighteenth century version of the farmer's cooperative would help keep the "industrious planter out of debt."[37] He was, in short, one of the most literate of the burgesses, writing long pieces for the paper on varied subjects. Editors Rind and Purdie, although complaining of an oversupply of material for their publications, were glad to have contributions from him.[38]

Carter served his country well and in many capacities. A justice of the peace and "of the quorum" as early as 1734, he presumably remained in the county court the rest of his life.[39] He was active in the affairs of the various non-importation associations and was sorry not to see his "son John's hand to the association (of May, 1774) as many not burgesses had also signed it."[40] Having served as county lieutenant under Gooch, Dinwiddie, and Fauquier, he hoped to continue in the same office under Botetourt, and presumably did.[41] He approved the resolution for a day of fasting and prayer for Boston and bitingly observed that that was "the very first time the praying that His Majesty and his Parliament may be inspired from above with wisdom, justice, and moderation was ever thought derogatory to the honor of either of them," especially in an established church, whose liturgy proposes collects for that very purpose and in words almost identical. "I think," he concluded, "the Gazette should have published the resolves for a fast to show the reason for the dissolution."[42]

Although an ardent champion of American rights, Carter was not ready for independence when his countrymen sought it. It was, as he phrased it, only jumping from the frying pan into the fire. *Common Sense* was the most "nonsensical" of all pamphlets. Yet he clearly foresaw that the struggle between Great Britain and her colonies must eventually lead to trouble, and he had "never been moved with the least fear or apprehension as to the success of the dispute."[43] Old, ill, and out of sympathy with affairs after 1775, he nevertheless stayed on good terms with George Washington, whom he called his "Chum," writing him garrulous, nostalgic letters about public events and prominent people, complaining peevishly of the trends toward more democracy and less discipline among the common folk.[44]

Robert Wormeley Carter, who became a burgess in 1769, was prospective heir to half of his father's estate. That included lands in Northumberland, Richmond, Westmoreland, and Stafford counties. In 1788, ten years after Landon Carter's death, the son was listed as one of the hundred wealthiest men in the state with a total of 10,533 acres in six counties (besides two lots in Williamsburg), 164 slaves, 23 horses, and 141 head of cattle.[45]

Young Carter, a diarist like his father, kept records for most of his adult life from 1764 on. The most frequent entries concern winnings or losses at cards; yet his observations on the political scene are valuable. There is further light, for example, on the campaign of 1769, in which his father thought he had humiliated himself before the people. On July 14, Robert Wormeley notes that he returned home that day "from among the free-holders where I have been four days." The next day he went to a muster at Reid's Old Field where he saw "a good many freeholders." Two weeks later he attended the sale of the John Woodbridge estate, where he treated Captain Peachy's and Captain Griffin's companies. The treat used twenty gallons and a quart of rum plus the necessary sugar. At the back of the diary he stated, but incompletely, his "burgessing Expenses," from June 1 to October 2. The recorded expenses total £7.14.6, all paid to individuals, presumably, for liquor or services at the polls. The largest sum went to Vincent Garland, who was paid £4.10.21 on June 1. It is interesting to observe how soon after the dissolution of the assembly on May 17 active campaigning began. Little of the necessary local business had been attended to, so it was certain that writs for a new election would be issued before many months. Such writs were published in the *Gazette* on August 10.[46] On September 22, Carter wrote, "This day came on the election. I was returned first by a majority of nine votes; Col. F. L. Lee also returned." These two men stayed in office until 1776. There is ample reason to believe that they served their country well and that their constituents approved their actions in the Assembly.

But popularity is a fickle mistress. At the 1776 election, both men were defeated at the polls by Hudson Muse and Charles McCarty. This was a rude shock, and both Carters made lengthy comments about it in their diaries. "Come on the election of Delegates," the younger Carter began his entry for April 1, 1776, where Col. F. Lee and myself, after near seven years of faithful service were most shamefully turned out by Muse and McCarty; it was a bad day, and but little more than half the freeholders attended, and those picked, determined men; surprising that Col. Lee, who was judged by Convention a proper person to go to Congress should be rejected by Richmond County as not fit for Convention. As for myself, I never asked but one man to vote for me since the last election, by which means I polled 45 votes, an honorable number.[47]

Remembering his own defeat in 1768, Landon Carter said acidly, ". . . I may say for the honor of Richmond that she is no changeling." Having turned out father, she now turned out son. This happened in spite of the fact that

the first (R. W. Carter) has not only kissed the ———— of the people, and very seriously accommodated himself to others, and yet has been shamefully turned out. Notwithstanding Lee was at the Congress, an honor not easily obtained, and the Colonel, his father-in-law, did everything that a gentleman ought to do, he has been also turned out of Convention, although to the disgrace of his seat in Congress, and that by a worthless, impudent fellow, and a most silly, though good-natured fool.

To Landon Carter, however, the worst discovery of this election day was the "unsteady, lukewarmness of even gratitude itself . . . and even relations as well as tenants all voted against the showy professions of their principles." But, he philosophized, such is the nature of popularity; he had long since discovered her to be "an adultress of the first order."[48]

Francis Lightfoot Lee, who went down in defeat with Robert Wormeley Carter, had begun his political career in Loudoun which he represented from 1758 until 1768. The part of his father's estate which he had inherited was in Loudoun, but apparently he never lived there. Election laws did not require residence; and, since he was unmarried during those years, he probably continued to live at Stratford Hall with his oldest brother, Phillip Ludwell Lee. Shortly before his marriage, he built Menokin and moved to Richmond County.[49]

In March, 1769, he married Rebecca Tayloe, daughter of influential John Tayloe of Mt. Airy, a member of the Council.[50] The bride, a young lady "whose many amiable accomplishments and inestimable virtues render her a very worthy pleasing prospect of happiness in her married state," also made Lee, already related to the Corbins, Ludwells, and other prominent people, kin by marriage to several more leading families. The Tayloes themselves were equal to the Carters and Lees in prestige, and their daughters (John Tayloe II, father of Rebecca, had only one son, John III, among his nine children) married into the Beverley, Carter, Washington, Page, and Lomax families. This Tayloe connection was responsible for Lee's election from

76

Richmond in 1769. John Woodbridge, a burgess since 1734, had died some time before June of that year, leaving a vacancy that Tayloe desired for his new son-in-law; it was by Tayloe's "asserted interest" that Lee carried the election.[51]

Unlike his brothers Richard Henry, Thomas Ludwell, and Arthur, who received English educations, Francis Lightfoot was trained at home by the Rev. Mr. Craig, "who not only made him a good scholar, but imbued him with a genuine fondness for the study of the classics and for literature in general."[52] "Brother Frank," whom his brother William addressed as "calmness and philosophy itself," seems to have been a great favorite with his contemporaries; acquaintances found "the sternness of Cato or the eloquence of Cicero" of his brothers less to their tastes than "the gay good humor and pleasing wit of Atticus."[53]

In spite of love for literature and fondness for good companionship, Lee was essentially a businessman. His extant correspondence is mostly with his brother William, merchant and politician in London, and about tobacco, the new fulling mill, the Mississippi Land Company, and improvements in agriculture. Arthur and Richard Henry could discuss politics and philosophize about the world in general, but Francis and William took greater interest in economics than did their other brothers.[54]

This, however, is not a complete picture of Lee. He was, as Benjamin Franklin described him, of "inflexible purpose in the cause of his country." Like his brother Richard Henry, he was outspoken about the Stamp Act and, when the controversy was going full blast, went so far as to insert an advertisement in the *Virginia Gazette,* asking all his acquaintances never to take a letter directed to him out of the post office, for he was determined "never willingly to pay a farthing of any *tax* laid upon this country in an unconstitutional manner."[55] Lee, along with his brother Richard Henry, Dabney Carr, Patrick Henry, Thomas Jefferson, and a few others who met frequently at the Raleigh Tavern to discuss public affairs, was one of those who drafted the Boston Fast Day Resolution. Elected to Congress to replace Richard Bland, too old and ill to serve his country longer, Lee signed the Declaration of Independence, of which he heartily approved. He was, in fact, active in every measure of defiance against Great Britain from the Westmoreland Resolves on the Stamp Act (February 27, 1766) until the end of the colonial period. Although he was replaced as burgess from his county, he continued to serve Virginia in Congress from 1775 until 1780. Preferring the quiet of Menokin to the mad scramble of Philadelphia, he retired to his plantation voluntarily. His public career was not over, however, for he was elected to the state senate and served at least four years.[56]

Eight men represented Essex, just across the river from Richmond County, in the 1750–1774 period; only one, Thomas Waring, who died in office, had less than two terms; and only one, Francis Waring, had more than three. Unlike Richmond, where there were few candidates, Essex had numerous aspirants for office. The poll on January 15, 1752, was taken by William Upshaw Davis for Francis Waring, sheriff, who may have relinquished the duty to his deputy because his father, Thomas Waring, was one of the leading candidates.[57] Besides the elder Waring, who polled 206 votes, the other successful candidate was Maj. Francis Smith, who, with 210 votes became the senior burgess. Running third was Col. John Corbin, who polled 119. Capt. John Livingston (49 votes) and William Daingerfield, one of the incumbents, with 31 votes, may have been running mates. Five others who received votes got so few that they can hardly be considered candidates: Capt. William Round (or Bound or Brand?) 3, Thomas Atkins 3, Captain Wingo Roy 1, Captain Sam Hipkins 1, and James Moseley 1. Although these last five polled very few votes, they cannot be dismissed as nobodies; their titles indicate the offices in the militia that were reserved for gentlemen.

Four men ran strongly in 1755. At the election of December 4, William Daingerfield, who had served out Thomas Waring's unexpired term, was again a candidate, polling 188 votes, which made him the senior burgess. Francis Smith, likewise running for reelection, received 173. Capt. James Garnett ran third with 158, and Mr. John Upshaw, who was to win the next election, ran fourth with 137. Capt. William Garnett ran a very poor fifth with only 39. Francis Waring, now out of the sheriff's office, made an even poorer showing with only five votes. Major Roane (presumably William Roane who was elected in 1769) had only four; and John Jones and John Covington, one each.[58]

The election of July 26, 1758, was a political upset. Daingerfield and Smith, although both receiving votes and therefore presumably candidates, were defeated, getting 3 and 170 votes respectively. Upshaw (209) and Francis Waring (208), now a colonel, were the victors; Capt. John Lee received 111.[59] What caused the constituents of Essex to turn out the men they had elected only three years before is not known, but Daingerfield and Smith did not again represent the county at Williamsburg.

When the freeholders voted next on May 6, 1761, Francis Waring was defeated in a strong three-man race, in which the votes stood:

John Upshaw	276
John Lee	243
Francis Waring	211[60]

But the next time (July 9, 1765) Francis Waring made a comeback, running second to John Lee; Lee's vote was 300; and Waring's, 283. John Upshaw, who for some unknown reason was not an active candidate, received only one vote; Robert Beverley, who seems to have made here his only real bid for representation, 138.[61]

New burgesses were again elected on September 15, 1769 in what appears to have been a three-man race; if there were minor candidates, they are not listed in what may well be only a partial return. William Roane (231) and James Edmondson (161) were elected over Meriwether Smith (124).[62] These two gentlemen were reelected on November 2, 1771, when John Upshaw was sheriff.[63]

Essex County election returns are more complete than those for any other county after 1750; only the polls for electing a burgess in 1754 to replace Thomas Waring,[64] deceased, and for 1770, when William Roane was returned at a by-election, are missing. As shown in this account, there was frequent change in representatives. Richmond, facing Essex across the Rappahannock, had made only two changes in the same period. What made the difference? The answer is not clear, but there is some clue in the careers of the men involved.

The Burgesses of Essex

Thomas Waring. The Warings lived at Goldberry in St. Anne's Parish, near Hobbes Hole. Thomas Waring had migrated from England and settled there late in the seventeenth century. He had married Lucy Cocke, the daughter of William Cocke and member of a numerous clan, and had evidently settled down to be a gentleman planter. He had been named sheriff on June 11, 1742, and had served his country on the county court and his parish on the vestry. He had also been in the House one term, from 1734 to 1740, where he had been on the standing Committee of Privileges and Elections, temporary committees to draw up a bill regulating the fees of physicians "and other practicers of Physic," and to draw up an order requiring naval officers to report accounts of slaves imported into the colony. He had been asked to form a committee to carry a message to the governor to arrange a conference with the council, and in general had been a useful and responsible member of the House.[65] He died in 1754, too early in the period under consideration to have had much influence on public affairs, but he left two sons and three daughters who directly or indirectly continued to have a voice in the course of events.[66]

Francis Waring was born July 23, 1717, and was therfore nearly thirty-seven when his father left him the bulk of his estate; he died in 1771.[67] In 1761 he was defeated at the polls; in July, 1765 he was again returned; in

1768, he was senior burgess, and after that we hear no more of him. Since he died in 1771, he may have been in poor health and entirely out of public affairs. In the House he was on the committees of Public Claims and of Trade.[68]

Francis Smith. Little is known about Francis Smith beyond his polling record and his family connections. His will, however, made on March 19, 1760 and proved March 15, 1762, shows that he had considerable property in land, slaves, horses, and household articles.[69] His wife was Lucy Meriwether, hence the name of their son, Meriwether Smith; his second wife was Anne Adams, sister of Richard Adams, burgess from New Kent and Henrico. His home was in South Farnham Parish where he was vestryman, justice of the peace, major, and later colonel of the militia;[70] he had not been in the House before 1752 and his career ended with his defeat at the polls in 1758. In 1761, six of his friends cast votes for him, but the fact that he had already made his will and would die before another year was out may indicate that he was a sick man.

William Daingerfield, who was returned in place of Thomas Waring at a special election in 1754, lived at Belvedere, which was "very pleasantly situated" on the banks of the Rappahannock some seven or eight miles below Fredericksburg. His mother was a daughter of Colonel William Bassett of Eltham, New Kent County, who was closely related to Martha Washington. Daingerfield "had his education in England and was a very smart man," who maintained a lively interest in books. Primarily if not exclusively a planter, he raised wheat and corn rather than tobacco.[71] Like most of his class, he took his turn as vestryman and churchwarden, handling the affairs of the parish.[72]

Daingerfield's career in the House began in 1748 when he replaced James Garnett at a by-election; he was a candidate at each election until 1765, but was elected only at the by-election in 1754 and at the general election in 1755. He held a place on the standing Committee of Claims and was often a member of a subcommittee to investigate claims against the House; at least once he was on the body that prorated the public levy.[73]

John Upshaw was senior burgess by one vote in the political upset in 1758. His record of public service reads like that of many another of his contemporaries: vestryman, justice of the peace, sheriff, tobacco inspector at Hobbes Hole, signer of the Westmoreland Resolves, February 27, 1766.[74] He did not appear as a candidate in 1765 or at any time thereafter.[75] He was, however, active in the affairs of the county and especially in the enforcement of the Associations. In February, 1771, he was on the committee to examine the papers of Meriwether Smith and to decide if he were guilty of violating the spirit of the association.[76] Five years later he was chairman of the committee which pronounced the Fowler brothers, John and George, guilty of the same offense for which Smith had been exonerated.[77] In addition to this, he was county chairman of the Committee of Correspondence, which included nineteen of Essex's leading citizens; he moderated a meeting in his home county which was called "to consider the present danger" in July, 1774, and collected relief for Boston from the upper end of South Farnham Parish.[78] If he was out of office, it was not due to his lack of interest in public affairs.

John Lee, like Thomas Waring, died in office. Lee, the second son of Henry and Mary Bland Lee, was a brother to Richard Lee, burgess from Westmoreland, and Henry, burgess from Prince William. These three Lee brothers were first cousins to the other trio of Lees in the House; Thomas Ludwell, Francis Lightfoot, and Richard Henry.[79] Having married Mrs. Mary Smith Ball (widow of William Ball) in 1749, he was connected with both the Smiths and the Balls. All that is known of his other public life is that he was clerk of the court in Essex from 1745 to 1761.[80]

William Roane and *James Edmondson,* elected in 1769, were to be the last of the burgesses from Essex; both also were chosen by their constituents as delegates to the conventions of 1774 and 1775; both were active in the Associations; both were on the Essex County Committee requested by the Continental Congress to take cognizance of the state of affairs. About the time of his election in 1769, Roane became deputy attorney for the king in the county; and, as the law required when a burgess accepted an "office of profit" in the crown's bounty, he resigned. His constituents nevertheless returned him to the House at the next election.[81] Roane was on the Committee of Propositions and Grievances, of Public Claims, and (in the 1772 session) of Privileges and Elections.[82] Edmondson's service on a standing committee was confined to that on the Courts of Justice, but he was on the temporary committee of which Richard Henry Lee was chairman to inquire into what laws would expire at the end of the 1772 session.[83] Both Roane and Edmondson were on a committee to investigate the claims of one William Ayre (Eyre) that he had a medicine for the flux that had healed every patient who had used it. Although Roane, as chairman, made a favorable report and recommended a suitable compensation for the prescription, the House voted it down.[84]

Little is known of these two men besides their public careers. Edmondson was married to Elizabeth, daughter of John Webb; his place near Tappahannock was known as Charlton Hill; he died some time between July 4, 1791 and April 16, 1792, leaving no children.[85] Roane's mother was an Upshaw and his first wife a Ball. John Upshaw witnessed the will of William Roane, Sr., in 1757 and may have been either father or brother of Mrs. Roane.[86]

This is the known record of the men who represented Richmond and Essex counties in the General Assembly after 1750. Richmond County

81

politics was dominated by four strong individuals, three of them sons of prominent men. John Woodbridge died in office; Landon Carter was defeated at the polls. The opposition that elected Thomas Glasscock in 1768 turned him out in less than a year. Three of these men—the two Carters and Lee—were of more than local importance. With the possible exception of Woodbridge,[87] the Richmond burgesses were allied by blood and marriage to the leading families of Tidewater Virginia. Like Robert Wormeley Carter in Richmond, Francis Waring in Essex followed in his father's footsteps; but to carry the analogy further, neither was elected to succeed his father; in both instances an assembly had intervened before the sons were sent to Williamsburg. There were eight successful and a total of thirty unsuccessful candidates in Essex County.[88] Once, in 1758, both incumbents were replaced; in nearly all the elections there was a strong third candidate. Beyond the fact that two men died in office, we have almost no information that explains the frequent changes at the polls. If there were campaign issues or personality clashes, we have no records of them. In the absence of any evidence to the contrary, it may be concluded that Essex County, less dominated by a few families, had greater freedom at the polls than its neighbor. With a better chance of success, more candidates offered themselves; and, with greater freedom the freeholders changed their representatives at frequent intervals.

5

AUGUSTA AND FREDERICK
ON THE FRONTIER

In 1750 two counties, Augusta and Frederick, embraced all of Virginia west of the Blue Ridge Mountains. These two political units, which had been created in 1745 and 1743, respectively, included what is called the Valley of Virginia and extended westward from the crest of the Blue Ridge Mountains to undefined limits. It was generally assumed that their west reached the Ohio country and the "western waters." Beyond the valley lay a vast domain, uncharted, unexplored, and unknown.

Augusta County was by far the larger and in some respects the stronger of the two. All the west had once been Orange County, but in the 1740's the land beyond the mountains was separated from the mother county and made into two new counties, divided by a line which ran from the "head spring of Hedgman River to the head spring of the River Potomac." Frederick County was to have all territory lying on the northeast of this line beyond the top of the Blue Ridge. The Potomac in a vast arc was the northern boundary. Thus, Frederick had definite boundary lines. On the other hand, Augusta included all the land "northerly, westwardly and southerly" beyond the crest of the Blue Ridge "to the utmost limits of Virginia."[1] In 1749 it was estimated that Augusta had 1,423 tithables; six years later Dinwiddie reported the tithables at 2,273, and the vestry book of Augusta Parish which included all of the county gives the number as only slightly less—2,227. In spite of losses of territory and citizens to Hampshire and Botetourt Counties, the vestry book gives 3,043 in 1773 and 2,845 in 1774 as the tithable population of the county.[2] These of course were only a part of the populations since tithables were white men sixteen years of age and upward and all Negroes, both men and women, in the same age group.[3]

The valley was considered a land of opportunity and was being filled with settlers of two general groups: Virginians from the east, and Scotch-Irish and Germans from the north. Here sons of Irishmen and "Virginians from below the mountains fought and bled in a common cause."[4] By nature and past experience the Scotch-Irish, who made up a large percent of the total population, were a lawless breed; and the constant threat of Indian raids, steady French encroachments, and the daily struggle of frontier living did little to tone them down.

Elections in Augusta

Augusta elections and politics in general were as turbulent as the times and environment from which they sprang. There are no polls for the county, but there is the account of a brawl of major proportions at the election of 1755. Furthermore, most of the eight men who went to the assembly were colorful figures and strong personalities. From various sources it is possible to reconstruct a picture of the practices and malpractices perpetrated in Augusta County. The burgesses were: John Madison, 1752–1754; John Wilson, 1752–1771; James Patton, 1754–1755; Gabriel Jones, 1756–1758, 1769–1771; William Preston, 1765–1768; Israel Christian, 1758–1765; Charles Lewis, 1773–1774; Samuel McDowell, 1772–1774.

December 17, 1755 was election day at Augusta Court House. Sheriff James Lockhart in obedience to a writ from the governor had, in the time honored phrase, "summoned all the freeholders of the said county to meet . . . and freely and indifferently to elect two of the most able and discreet persons in the said county to serve as burgesses." Affairs, however, went anything but smoothly. In a sworn statement the sheriff reported, "I used all the means in my power to comply with the said writ, but the people were so tumultuous and riotous that I could not finish the poll; for that reason no burgesses could be returned. . . ."[5] Upon hearing this report, the House decided to summon the sheriff for further questioning. Under examination he said that Richard Woods, David Cloyd, and Joseph Lapsley were the "chief movers of the said tumult and riot." This was a serious breach of both the peace and ". . . of the privileges of this House," a subject on which the burgesses were very sensitive. It was decided, therefore, that the three alleged culprits should be brought before the bar of the House. Peyton Randolph, chairman of the Committee of Privileges and Elections, was authorized to ask the governor for a new writ of election for Augusta, since no burgesses had been returned.

On April 23, 1755, Woods, Cloyd, and Lapsley appeared before the House in the custody of the sergeant-at-arms.[6] They entered a petition that they were "altogether innocent" of the matter with which they were charged. Not only was he not guilty, Woods asserted, but, on the contrary, he also had "often applied to the sheriff, desiring him to command assistance to suppress the tumult and offering his own assistance therein."[7] The truth of their allegations the trio could prove by many witnesses "whose depositions" were "taken and sworn to before a magistrate of that county." Because of the great distance from their homes to the capital and the peril of leaving their families "exposed to the dangers of the enemy in their absence" they said they had hoped sworn testimony would be sufficient for their cause. The petitioners asked, of course, that they be discharged without further ado. The matter was nevertheless referred to the proper committee of the House.

The next day the attorney general, chairman of the committee, reported the deposition of one William Lusk that he saw Woods, Cloyd, and Lapsley go peaceably and quietly into the courthouse and give their votes and then come out again, and that he saw no misbehavior in them during the poll; the deponent should know whereof he spoke because he had been appointed by the sheriff to stand at the bar to keep the voters from crowding in too fast.[8]

The case was reopened on April 17, 1757,[9] with Woods, Cloyd, and Lapsley entering the plea of innocence and offering proof that at the election they had tried to be of assistance in quelling the disturbance. On May 2, the committee was ready with its report; it admitted, however, there was "great contrariety" in the testimony of the two sides.

> On the 17th day of December, 1755, the day appointed for the election of burgesses . . . for the county of Augusta, . . . [the deposition of the three petitioners began] the poll was taken till toward the evening when the people crowded into the courthouse and pressed upon the sheriff who struck several of the freeholders with his staff on the shins and pushed them with the same in the breast and other parts of the body and threatened to push it down their throats if they did not keep back. . . . He desired to summon a guard to keep the crowd off and that the petitioner Woods offered to be one of the guards. . . . The sheriff whispered to several freeholders as they came to vote to know who they were for and then refused to take their votes. . . . He several times during the election left the Court House which stopped the same while he was out. . . . After candles were lighted the petitioners Lapsley and Cloyd came to give their votes and the sheriff seized Lapsley by the breast and pushed him backwards on a bench, upon which Cloyd, with some warmth, said "Collar me too, Sir". . . . Lapsley and Cloyd then gave their votes and the poll was continued some time afterward.[10]

From the deposition of the sheriff it appeared that the three defendants were as guilty as they were accusing the officer of being. While the poll was being taken,

> Petitioner Lapsley pulled out his purse in the court yard and offered to wager that Mr. Preston and Mr. Alexander, two of the candidates, would go burgesses and that he and his party would carry the day. Petitioner Woods was

noisy and loud in the interest of Mr. Alexander and offered to wager as Lapsley did. . . . When the crowd pressed on the sheriff he endeavored to keep them back in a civil manner by putting his stick across their breast and summoned a guard to assist him which was broke thro. . . . A person came out of the Court House and said to Cloyd, "The election is going against us," who answered, "It should not, if we cannot carry it one way we will have it another. I will put a stop to the election," and immediately the crowd increased. . . . When Lapsley pressed thro the crowd to give his vote, the sheriff desired him to keep back, but he pushed on and seized the sheriff and pushed him against the table. . . . After Lapsley and Cloyd had voted, the sheriff desired them to withdraw which they did not do and in short time afterwards the candles were struck out by the petitioner Woods and the riot began which put an end to the election, the sheriff being thrown on the table which was broke under him and the clerks fled to the bench, and during the tumult Lapsley called out, "Lads, stand by me. I'll pay the fine, cost what it will. You know that I am able."[11]

From the vantage point of two centuries, one story sounds as convincing as the other, but the House decided that the petitioners "had not proved the allegations of their petition." Instruction was sent to the Committee of Claims to allow Sheriff James Lockhart "his reasonable charges and expenses in attending this House to defend himself against the petitioners of the said Woods, Cloyd, and Lapsley." If any punishment was meted out to the trio, there is no record of it. Regardless of who was right, one thing is unmistakable: election day was rough.

Burgesses in Augusta

There is much about this election that the testimony does not tell. Who, for instance, were the candidates? "Mr. Preston and Mr. Alexander" were two of them; presumably there were others. Preston, in all probability, was William Preston, who was elected ten years later; but Alexander was a name too common to be identifiable. John Nash may have been one candidate. There is a puzzling letter from Clement Read to Col. John Buchanan of Augusta that speaks of a petition filled with complaints of undue election and return of "Col. Nash (tho' he was chosen by the unanimous voice of the Augusta men . . .)." Such a petition, however, would not have been sent to the council, as he said it was, but to the House, and there is no record of it in the *Journal*. John Nash was elected from Prince Edward, being one of its first burgesses, in 1754. It was possible, as in the case of Dr. Thomas Walker, who was returned from both Louisa and Hampshire at one time, for a man to be elected from two counties simultaneously. In such cases he had to choose which he would serve. But there is no record that this happened in the case of John Nash. On the other hand, the major portion of the letter from Read is about an abortive expedition against the Shawnees in which Col. John Nash, Col. Richard Callaway, and Obediah Woodson (who are mentioned in the letter) took an active part. This election may have been to a military post, although generally these positions were filled by appointment.[12] John Wilson and Gabriel Jones were returned when the election was held again some months later, so they may have been the leading candidates on December 17, 1755. This is the total record of elections. It is not, however, all we know about those who were elected.

James Patton. The stormy petrel of Augusta County until his death at the hands of a scalping party in 1755 was James Patton. Having held practically every possible office in the county, he climaxed his career with a term in the assembly. He may have been a candidate earlier, but it was not until John Madison vacated his seat in the House to become coroner in 1754 that Patton was elected.[13] Born in Newton Limaddy, Ireland, in 1692, he had migrated to the new world in 1738, but only after he had crossed the Atlantic "quite twenty-five times," bringing Irish and German redemptioners and returning with cargoes of tobacco. He was primarily a shipmaster and merchant, but his trade with the west (Hobbes Hole on the Rappahannock was his port of entry) convinced him of the opportunities to be found in land. Consequently, he acquired large tracts—Koontz says one hundred and twenty thousand acres—by patent in Augusta and was largely responsible for settling the area south of Staunton. In addition to the redemptioners, he brought with him several of his near relatives—the Prestons, the Buchanans, the Breckenridges, and probably others.[14]

It was not conducive to peace and harmony on the frontier that James Patton and John Lewis, leaders of rival factions in the county, were both members of the Tinkling Spring Presbyterian church, "the most numerous and richest" of the Reverend John Craig's churches. These men, "proud, self-interested, contentious and ungovernable, all of them close-handed about providing necessary things for pious and religious uses," for years could not agree on a "place or manner where or how to build their meeting house." This state of affairs gave Craig, who was also a Scot and probably had his own share of stubbornness, great trouble in holding his congregation together. Rivalry between Lewis and Patton "as to which of them should be in the highest in commission and power which was hurtful to the settlement" and embarrassing to their pastor had been going on for years. They were jealous of Craig's "interest with the people to such a degree that he could neither bring them to friendship with each other, nor retain their friendships at once. . . ." They both had "good interest with the people of their own party and one of them always bitter enemies" to him "which was very hurtful" to his peace and interest. By turns they watched his every step for flaws in his character. This state of affairs continued for thirteen or fourteen years until the death of Patton in 1755 during a time when he was "at peace" with his pastor.[15] With his old rival in the grave, Lewis forgave Craig for what he must have considered strange taste in friends, and remained on good terms with him until his own death in 1762.[16]

By and large, ministers of the gospel took little active interest in politics beyond their own parish.[17] Clergymen were prohibited by law from holding public office and apparently no son of one offered himself as a candidate. The dissenting clergyman, of course, had more at stake in elections than his fellows in the Established Church, and from the scanty information, churches on the frontier seem to have taken definite stands on public issues, while eastern churches did not. The Rev. John Brown, Presbyterian divine whose congregation "appear . . . to be on the roving and Holston is their retreat," wrote to William Preston, former burgess, regarding the forthcoming election (1771) in Augusta.[18] "The sixth of next month is appointed for our county to elect burgess. No doubt Father [John] Wilson will go for one. The contention will be betwixt my friend Lewis and Mr. [Samuel] McDowell. I have not consulted the moods of my congregation as yet, but Wednesday next being a lecture day, I shall know how their pulse beats. I have no doubt that L. will carry. . . ."

John Wilson. Whether Wilson was Patton's father-in-law, or whether "Father" was a term of respect for a venerable man is unknown. Honest, homespun Wilson had been in the House since 1746, when he and John Madison became the county's burgesses.[19] He had served faithfully on the Committee of Claims and numerous subcommittees which handled cases of militia pay and claims from war victims asking for disability compensation. He reached the peak of his usefulness as a legislator in the 1760's when there were many claims from the French and Indian War.[20] When Brown wrote the above letter, Wilson's days were numbered; on March 4, 1773, an election writ was requested for Augusta to replace him; he had died after the last session.[21]

Charles Lewis. Brown's "friend Lewis" was probably Charles Lewis, who was elected, not at the regular election as the clergyman hoped, but at the by-election to replace Wilson. Lewis was brother of Andrew Lewis of Botetourt and the younger son of John Lewis, Patton's old rival. He was reported to be the most skilled of the frontier fighters. His life as a burgess was very short; for, in October, 1774, he went down fighting at Point Pleasant at the mouth of the Great Kanawha; his brave death was widely heralded and universally regretted.[22] A friend observing the "general grief of the occasion" was inspired to attempt an elegy which appeared in the *Gazette.* Written in the popular couplet, it began thus after the usual appeal to the muses:

For Lewis, muse thy artless numbers raise
Superior worth demands superior praise
In him the Christian and the Warrior joined
The son obedient and the brother kind.

The concluding stanza:

Grateful Augusta, as a tribute just
With tears hath watered thy beloved dust
Virginia's sons should long revere thy name
Whose bright example leads to deathless fame.[23]

Samuel McDowell, as Pastor Brown suspected, was a candidate in 1771 and was elected. He was as typically of the frontier as Patton, Preston, or Lewis. He was a Scotch-Irish Presbyterian; he was orphaned early (1742), when his father was killed by Indians; he was an Associator in 1769 and 1774; he was in the Second Convention that sent delegates to the Second Continental Congress with instructions to vote for independence; he was a colonel in the Revolutionary War. When Thomas Nelson, Jr., became governor in 1781, McDowell became a member of the Council, which, under the new state government, was an elected body. At the end of the war (1784), he moved to Kentucky where he continued to be active in public affairs; he was chairman of the conventions called to consider separation of that territory from Virginia; finally, when Kentucky became a political entity, he was president of the Constitutional Convention of 1792.[24]

William Preston. Another Scotch-Irishman to represent Augusta was William Preston, who migrated with his father in 1749 when William was eleven years old; his mother was a sister of James Patton. Preston was burgess from Augusta from 1765 to 1768 and, as after 1761 he had lived in the area that became Botetourt, represented it upon its separation from the parent county. He seems, however, to have had little interest in the legislature. Although he was a member of the House for six years, there is evidence that he attended only the November 1766 session. He served on the Committee of Claims with the veteran John Wilson. The only special attention he received in this term was a charge that he had been responsible for election writs not reaching the sheriffs of Frederick and Hampshire Counties in time for an election. Preston, who was at the capital when the writs were issued, offered to deliver them to these two counties. On his way home, his "travelling chair" broke down, and he was delayed for repairs. However, he sent the two packages containing the writs by Thomas Bowyer, a resident of Staunton, who in turn tried to send them on to their destination by Gabriel Jones. Jones was going in neither direction, and Bowyer had to wait until someone came along who could deliver them. Somewhere the writs were lost. The House decided that it was by accident and freed Preston and Jones of any guilt in the matter.

Preston was primarily a frontiersman and soldier who gave his whole life to the service of the country. He was captain of a company of rangers in 1755–56 and again in 1757–59 in the war against the French; he was repeatedly in action against the Indians; he constructed several forts on the frontier and used his own house as a garrison when the need arose. With the coming of the Revolution, his duties were increased. He was county lieutenant of the newly organized Montgomery County (1776) and his home, Smithfield, became unofficial headquarters for the defense of the Southwest; in 1780 he led an expedition against the Cherokees. Before his death in 1783 he had lived in and held office in four counties: Augusta, Botetourt, Fincastle, and Montgomery; and his military exploits had taken him into all parts of the frontier.[25]

Israel Christian, a burgess from 1758 to 1765, was a merchant and trader by choice and a soldier by necessity. He had an extensive Indian trade in which at times the colony's affairs and his own merchandise became so involved that on one occasion he was charged with being a "Rogue, Cheat, and Rascal."[26] When he was commissary for Col. William Byrd's Regiment during the French and Indian War, he moved to the Roanoke, where he established a community store in his own stone house. This was only one of many stores he had in the back country.[27] His services for the colony in dealing with the Indians were extensive, and the council once overruled a disallowance by the House when the council approved a demand of Christian's for £182.15.16 "for his services respecting the Indians."[28]

As a legislator and the colleague of the venerable John Wilson, he attended all but two of the eight sessions of the assembly that were held during the years he was a burgess, which in view of the distance from Augusta to Williamsburg is a better record than some of his fellows made. He was on the standing Committees of Public Claims and Trade and many others for local legislation. He and John Wilson, for example, drew up the bill to create the town of Staunton out of Beverley Manor; these same two drafted a bill to survey and build a road over the mountains from Rockfish Gap; and they handled the numerous petitions from soldiers praying for compensation for wounds received in His Majesty's service.[29]

As a military man Christian was a captain in the French and Indian War; as a public citizen he was on the county courts of Augusta and Botetourt Counties successively, and took his turn as sheriff.[30] In 1773 he advertised that he was moving farther west to Fincastle County, where he died in 1784.[31]

Gabriel Jones was the "Valley Lawyer." His whole interest seems to have been in law and lawmaking and law practice; there is no evidence that he speculated in land, traded with the Indians, or fought against the French. Unlike some of his contemporaries who read law under Virginia lawyers, he had an English education. He was born in 1724 near Williamsburg of English-Welsh parentage; but, shortly after his father's death, when Gabriel was still a small child, his mother went back to England and put her son in a boys' school. He later served an apprenticeship in law under one John Houghton. Returning to America sometime in the 1740's, he qualified as king's attorney and began practicing in the newly created Augusta and Frederick Counties; he was to spend his life in those two counties and in Hampshire County. When he was less than twenty-five years of age (in 1748), he was elected to the House by Frederick County constituents. Except for a brief period in 1753–54 when he was coroner, he served continuously as burgess until 1771, until 1755 for Frederick, in 1756–58 for Hampshire, and after that for Augusta. As was fitting for a lawyer, he served long periods of time on the Committee for Courts of Justice. He was clerk of the Hampshire County Court and practiced before the General Court in Williamsburg; he was a trustee for the Staunton Academy; he signed the Association of 1769. Yet he was lukewarm about independence; and, although elected by his fellow citizens to Congress and to the new state assembly, and appointed as the head of the new court system, he refused to take any part in the new government. After the Revolution, his only political activities beyond his home county were one term in the legislature (1783) and participation in the convention of 1788, which ratified the federal constitution. Generally he was opposed to popular government, not because it was elected, but because it was weak. He died in 1806, but stories of his eccentricities, fiery temper, and profane language lived much longer.

By his marriage to Margaret Strother, Jones was a brother-in-law of John Madison who sat in the House for Augusta while he was for Frederick. Thomas Lewis, one of John Lewis' sons, married a third Strother sister. So again the ties of blood and marriage were tightly entwined.[32]

Frederick, the other frontier county in 1750, was wholly within the bounds of the Northern Neck Proprietary Grant, or as it was familiarly called, the Fairfax Grant. Originally the patent was issued not to a Fairfax at all, but to six associates of Charles II in 1649. One of these was John Lord Culpeper, whose descendants became sole owners by 1681. Thomas Lord Culpeper succeeded Sir William Berkeley as governor after the Bacon Rebellion and, being on the spot, could and did do much to consolidate and strengthen his claims in America. At his death, his only legitimate daughter, Catherine, became owner of the Northern Neck. When she was twenty (1690), she married Henry Lord Fairfax, a nobleman with an honorable title but a depleted fortune. Through this marriage, the Culpeper interests in the Northen Neck passed into the hands of the Fairfax family.

The Fairfaxes took no great interest in their American lands until the 1730's, choosing merely to intrust their affairs to the hands of an agent. Daniel Parke, Nicholas Spencer, Philip Ludwell, Robert "King" Carter, Edmund Jennings, and Thomas Lee had been successively in the employ of the proprietor, but seem to have served their own interest as much as those of Fairfax. Carter alone acquired upwards of two hundred thousand acres of choice land in the area in the years between 1724 and his death in 1732. The chief duties of the agent were to issue patents to land, preferably in large tracts, and collect the quitrents which, in the rest of the colony, went to the king. Even before Carter's death, the current Lord Fairfax had come to the conclusion that all was not well with the administration of his estates. When the agent died, he persuaded his cousin William Fairfax, then residing in Salem, Massachusetts, to move to Virginia and take charge of his affairs; Thomas Lord Fairfax himself went to the colony within two years. Thereafter, the Northern Neck was administered by the Fairfaxes themselves.

Neither the governors nor other officials liked having this anomalous district within the limits of the colony. For one reason, they never knew exactly what powers were given to the proprietors. From time to time the patent was changed and the powers altered, but the terms were kept secret. Only later was it revealed that the only rights that were held by all the proprietors were the exclusive ownership of all the land with the right to dispose of it any way they chose, and the right to collect quitrent from it. There is no evidence that they attempted in any way to establish a civil government for the area. By this arrangement, inhabitants of the Northern Neck were tenants of Lord Fairfax but also citizens of their respective counties. The laws of the colony, except those regarding quitrents, applied to them as they did to all other Virginians.

A second cause for uneasiness was the indefinite western boundary, which the early patent had set as a line running from "the head of the Rappahannock to the head of the Potomac." When a new grant was made to Lord Culpeper, the wording was changed from mere "head" to "first heads or springs." In 1649 no one cared about the western boundary; but two generations later, when settlements had moved up river, the matter became important. There was little question about the upper reaches of the Potomac; but, ten miles above the falls of the Rappahannock, that river forks; the northern branch is called the Rapidan, the southern branch the Rappahannock or the Hedgman. Which was to be used as the southern limit of the grant? The proprietor claimed the southern branch, while the royal authorities insisted on the northern. There was a difference of some half million acres, an area worth quarrelling over. In an attempt to settle the dispute, a commission consisting of Fairfax and certain colonial representatives was appointed to survey the area. While this survey was under way, Lord Fairfax, for reasons best known to himself, slipped away and boarded a man-of-war for England, where he presented his case to the Privy Council. In exchange for the southern boundary he promised to: first, confirm all royal titles in the disputed area; second, waive all past quitrents due him within the extended proprietary; third, yield to the crown all arrearages of such rents due under royal grants, provided he was allowed all these rents in the future. On this basis the Privy Council decided the case Fairfax vs. Virginia in favor of the proprietor. That was April 6, 1745; the agreement stood until it was ended in 1785 by statehood and independence.[33]

It is not surprising that Fairfax influence was felt in the politics of the Northern Neck. In Fairfax County alone, two relatives of Thomas Lord Fairfax were elected burgesses: George William, son of the proprietor's cousin William who came from Salem to manage his affairs and the financial agent for the proprietor; and Thomas Bryan Martin, nephew of Lord Fairfax. Both these men represented two counties successively, and George William became a member of the Council.[34] George Washington was more than a mere surveyor for Lord Fairfax; he was an intimate of the family: George William was one of his best friends and Sally Cary Fairfax his confidante. Anne Fairfax, sister to George William, was married to Lawrence Washington, George's elder half-brother. It is a truism that Fairfax interest and support launched the youthful George on a political career.

Burgesses from Frederick County besides Fairfax, Martin, and Washington were: Gabriel Jones, who after 1755 lived in Augusta; James Wood, son of the founder of Winchester; George Mercer, son of John Mercer of Marlborough, who became collector of Stamp Duties in 1765; Captain Thomas Swearengen and Mr. Hugh West, who were elected in 1755; Robert Rutherford, close friend of Washington, who was elected in 1765 and served until Berkeley County was formed in 1773; and Isaac Zane, who was chosen to succeed him. The eleventh burgess was one Perkins, whose given name is not known and who attended only one session of the Assembly.

Elections in Frederick

Nothing is known about the election of 1752 except that Gabriel Jones and George William Fairfax were elected. In 1755 these two legislators chose to stand in other counties, Jones in Augusta and Fairfax in Fairfax; so that the field was wide open to newcomers. The successful candidates were Thomas Swearengen and Hugh West; George Washington ran a poor third with 40 votes. West and Swearengen received 271 and 270 votes respectively.[35] Washington's name was not given as a candidate until elec-

93

tion day; apparently, by some of his friends without his knowledge. His friend Adam Stephens, who had wide acquaintance in Frederick, was sure that he could have "touched on the tender spot so gently that with a week's notice" he could have brought about Washington's unanimous election. "In the meanwhile," he assured him, "I think your poll was not despicable as the people were a stranger to your purpose until the election began."[36] Washington asked for and got a copy of the poll and bided his time until another election. The opportunity came when Governor Fauquier arrived and dissolved the old Assembly.

The 1758 election in Frederick County was the most publicized in colonial Virginia.[37] This time Washington was no reluctant candidate, waiting to be pushed into the arena of politics, but an eager contestant for one of the seats held by Swearengen and West. His running mate was Thomas Bryan Martin who had decided to conduct his campaign chiefly against West, automatically making Washington the opponent of Swearengen.[38] Washington's campaign for a seat in the Assembly was hampered by another kind of campaign against the French and Indians, which required his presence at Fort Cumberland. Nevertheless, he had faithful, enthusiastic, and experienced friends at home, who gave every possible assistance to his cause. Colonel James Wood, leading citizen of Winchester, was one of his chief supporters. Gabriel Jones, first lawyer of the region, worked so hard in Frederick for Washington that he neglected his own interests in Augusta and was defeated.[39] As his friends began to make a pre-election survey of his possible strength, they were sure he would get the Quaker vote, and generally his chances seemed good. His friends would have felt much easier, however, if he could have been in the county in person. "Your presence on election day will avail vastly to accomplish your point," wrote John Kirkpatrick from Winchester three weeks before the election, when already the forthcoming poll was "the whole talk."[40] West, contrary to earlier indications, had renewed his campaigning, a fact which totally changed the picture for the Washington forces and fully convinced Wood that their own chances of carrying the election "absolutely depends on your presence that day."[41]

Generally speaking, his friends wanted him "to show his face" at the polls because they frankly had little faith in the "vulgar." "There is no relying on the promises of the common herd, the promise is too often forgot when the back is turned," was the opinion of Colonel Wood, who probably knew as much about frontier politics as anyone.[42] The voting public was questioning, probably at the promptings of the incumbents, the feasibility of a man combining military and civil careers, although the practice was common enough. The freeholders entertained "a notion of the inconvenience you lie under of attending the Assembly and defending them at the same time," reported a friend from the home front.[43] Fundamentally this was a question of absenteeism, a matter over which there was considerable concern, especially at times when a quorum could not be obtained in Williamsburg. Washington's opponents may have reminded the freeholders that at one juncture in the 1755 assembly it had been necessary to send the mace into the General Courtroom where the governor himself was sitting to round up enough burgesses to transact any business at all. Or they more probably played on the fears of the frontiersmen, fears of Indian raids and French attacks that every man among them knew to be a possibility. This was not the only issue of the campaign although it is not certain what the nature of the other was. Colonel West was himself an active campaigner, spreading tales to the hurt of his opponents. Martin accused him of "low transactions" for which he stood "condemned by some of his best friends." The whole matter, whatever it was, was to be laid open on election day. The record does not tell us if all these threats and charges were carried out, but all the factors worked together to carry the election for Washington and Martin, in spite of the fact that Washington did not "show his face" in Frederick.[44]

On election day, everyone worked according to a plan that had been formulated some time earlier, a plan by which his friends could best use their talents with the freeholders. Colonel Wood, a venerable gentleman whom everyone knew, would add dignity to the occasion and was therefore thought to be the "properest person" to sit for Washington at the polls. The undependable "vulgar" would require a great deal of attention if they were to vote "right," so Colonel Hite and Gabriel Jones worked outside the polling place among the crowd. Charles Smith was there dispensing liquid "hospitality" in liberal portions. Whether it was part of the act or not, when the sheriff opened the polls, the most important freeholder and citizen of the county, Thomas Lord Fairfax, was the first to vote, casting his ballots for Washington and Martin, as of course everyone knew he would.[45] "Dr. Burgis," wrote the exuberant Captain Charles Smith immediately after the votes had been counted, "I have the happiness to inform you that your friends have been very sincere, so that you were carried by a number of votes more than any candidate. . . ." Colonel Wood, having been his young friend's proxy, now received the victor's reward in being carried about the town "with a general applause, huzawing Colonel Washington."[46] Washington led the poll with 309 votes, Martin came second with 240, West had 199, and Swearengen only 45.[47] The shouting over, all that remained was the entertaining, which Smith did for him. The liquor for the general run of freeholders (which totaled 160 gallons or, as Freeman points out, a quart and a half per voter) and a dinner for his special friends cost him £39.6.8.[48] The winner hoped that everyone had enough and that no exception was made of anyone who voted against him.

95

He promptly voiced his thanks to Wood, Jones, and others who had been responsible for his success.[49]

The preliminaries to the May 18, 1761 election proved almost as exciting as those of the last. George Mercer stood with Washington this time instead of Martin.[50] Colonel Adam Stephens, his erstwhile friend, who had helped to elect him in 1758, now became his opponent, and there were rumors that Gabriel Jones also would be an "opposer." Captain Robert Stewart, who relayed this bit of gossip to Washington, could hardly believe it but was fully convinced that, if it were true, Jones was "actuated by the most selfish motives. . . ."[51] In spite of the rumor, Jones did not run. Washington and his friends had trouble enough with Stephens, who had a military career nearly equal to Washington's, a platform that excelled in imagination anything his opponent offered, and the common touch which both Mercer and Washington seem to have lacked. As early as February, Stephens was "incessantly employed in traversing this county, and, with indefatigable pains practiced every method of making interest with its inhabitants for electing him their representative, . . . his claims to disinterestedness, public spirit, and genuine patriotism are trumpeted in the most turgid manner. Tis said he will reduce those shining virtues to practice . . . by introducing various commercial schemes which are to diffuse gold and opulency through Frederick and prove . . . a sovereign . . . remedy against poverty and want. . . ." However strange and chimerical these wild promises appeared to common sense, "yet by his striking out of the beaten road he has attracted the attention of the plebeians whose unstable minds are agitated by every breath of novelty, whims, and nonsense. . . ." Reports of these activities gave Stewart great uneasiness until he was "certain that the leaders and all the patrician families" were firm in continuing for Washington, and it appeared that he would poll a greater majority than he had done previously; but, again, his presence in the county was urgently needed.[52] A month later, Stephens was still a great nuisance. It was reported that he intended to make use of "every method to arrive at his point du vue," but by this time nothing could raise "the most remote suspicion" of Washington's "interest being immutably established."[53] It is not known what tactics Washington employed, but the campaign generated excitement enough to bring out almost as many freeholders as had voted in 1758. Washington led with 505 votes; Mercer had 399; and Stephens trailed with 294. One vote each was cast for Robert Rutherford, Colonel John Hite, and Henry Brinker.[54] His friend Stewart congratulated him with a long and involved flourish: ". . . the joyous account of the election than the pleasing circumstances of which nothing could have afforded more solid satisfaction."[55]

In 1765 Mercer was *persona non grata,* and Washington changed the scene of his election to Fairfax; so again the field was wide open. Robert

Rutherford and James Wood were elected then, again in 1768, and 1771. At a by-election in 1773, Isaac Zane replaced Rutherford (who had become coroner) in a vote of 273 to 81—a majority of 192, the *Gazette* carefully noted.[56]

This record of elections, scanty though it is in places, is the most complete for any county outside the Tidewater. Furthermore, there is an abundance of material about some of the successful candidates that helps to round out the story of representation. Only Perkins is unindentifiable.

Burgesses of Frederick

Hugh West may have been the son of Burgess Hugh West of Fairfax, who died in office in 1754.[57] If this conjecture is correct, he was nephew to John West, who succeeded the elder Hugh West in Fairfax; and to Francis West, who sat for King William County.[58]

Thomas Swearengen, West's colleague in 1756–1758, as noted above, ran unsuccessfully for office in 1758. He had the title of captain, presumably in the county militia, and lived near present-day Shepherdstown, West Virginia. His name indicates he may have been of German ancestry, and he may have been from Pennsylvania as were the Hites of Berkeley and Hampshire counties."[59]

George William Fairfax and *Thomas Bryan Martin.* George William was the son of William Fairfax. Before the father had left New England, he sent his son George William, then only six years of age, to England for his education. The son came out to Virginia in 1746 and within two years was married to Sally Cary, daughter of Wilson Cary of Elizabeth City County.[60] His career as a burgess was cut short after two terms in the House (one for Frederick and the other for Fairfax) when he was elevated to a seat on the council to which "his family, fortune, and good sense entitled him." There was some criticism of this appointment because the Fairfax home, Belvoir, was so far away from Williamsburg that he could be of little use to the colony. William Nelson thought that, if he were in George William's place, he would have made his "most dutiful and respectful compliments for the honor" done him but would have asked to be allowed to resign.[61] Distance did not keep Fairfax from accepting the office nor from attending meetings with a fair degree of regularity. The growing tension with the mother country caused him to return to England in 1773, where his heart seems to have been always. At his departure, he made arrangements for the sale of much of his property in Fairfax County, a fact which convinced Governor Dunmore that he had no intention of returning. Fairfax lived out his life in England, sad over the rupture between England and the colonies.[62] Martin, although out of sympathy with the American cause too, did not become an expatriate but instead retired to Greenway Court (which his uncle had given him) with his housekeeper, Betsy Powers, and a few servants. There he died, leaving his manor house and a thousand acres to his faithful housekeeper and the rest of his property to his spinster sisters in England.[63]

James Wood was the son of Col. James Wood, the founder of Winchester, who had officiated at Washington's 1758 election. The son made an outstanding record as a patriot in the Revolution and was governor of the state from 1796 to 1798.[64]

George Mercer was a military hero in the French and Indian War before he was twenty-one. Feeling that his gallantry and outlay of money deserved compensation, he went to England in 1763, ostensibly going as agent for the Ohio Company, of which his father, John Mercer of Marlborough, was treasurer, but really seeking some preferment to ease what he chose to call his state of poverty. The governor, the council, and the assembly gave him letters of recommendation and sent papers by him that could be carried only by the trustworthy. He had been away from the colony twenty-two months when he was made distributor of stamps, a supposedly lucrative post coveted by Richard Henry Lee. Within twenty-four hours after his arrival in Williamsburg, he was forced to resign this office by a mob that had assembled from a wide area for the purpose. His constituents never thereafter elected him to the assembly, but the British government continued to grant him favors, giving him at least two appointments which he refused —the governorship of North Carolina and of Pittsylvania, a proposed political unit on the Ohio. Mercer made several trips to England in the interest of the Ohio Company. He died there like Fairfax, believing the movement toward independence and the resulting war were great mistakes.[65]

George Washington. Washington's career as a lawmaker has been eclipsed by his careers on the battlefield and in the president's chair. Nevertheless, he was in the House of Burgesses from 1758 until he went to the First Continental Congress in 1775, a period of approximately seventeen years.

Washington, as it has been noted, received his first votes for burgess at the 1755 election. His name seems to have been presented without his knowledge, but doubtless he approved of his friends' action. At least, he already had legislative ambitions. Some months before that election, he had asked his brother's advice about running in his home county of Fairfax. He understood that the county was to be divided and that one of the representatives did not intend to serve again, so he wrote to his brother:

[I] should be glad if you could fish at Colo. Fairfax's intentions, and let me know whether he purposes to offer himself as a Candidate. If he does not I should be glad to stand a poll, if I thought my chances pretty good. . . . Parson

Green's and Captn. McCarty's interests in this wou'd be of consequence; and I shou'd be glad if you cou'd sound their pulse upon the occasion. Conduct the whole till you are satisfied of the Sentim'ts of those I have mention'd, with an air of indifference and unconcern; after that you may regulate your conduct accordingly.[66]

Evidently the report was not encouraging; at least he did not run then; and, when he did, it was in Frederick County.

Late in 1758 after his election, Washington resigned his military commission and returned to Mount Vernon. On January 6, 1759, he married Mrs. Martha Custis. Five weeks later, he left for his first meeting of the General Assembly, which convened on February 22, his twenty-seventh birthday. There is no record of whether the new Mrs. Washington stayed at home or accompanied him to Williamsburg, but Washington's leading biographer believes she went with him and that they lived in the John Custis house there.[67]

George Washington played a useful but unspectacular role in the House. If he made speeches, there is no record of them. However, he was put immediately on the powerful Committee of Propositions and Grievances, a position he would also hold in the next assembly. In 1766 he was named to the Committee of Privileges and Elections, which had the responsibility of reviewing contested elections. He seems not to have been drawn into the Stamp Act controversy or questions of other "encroachments" by the crown. But when news of the Townshend Acts (passed in 1767) reached Virginia, Washington reacted vocally. He said, in part,

At a time when our lordly Masters in Great Britain will be satisfied with nothing less than the deprication of American freedom, it seems highly necessary that something shou'd be done to avert the stroke and maintain the liberty which we have derived from our ancestors; but the manner of doing it to answer the purpose effectually is the point in question.

He was of the opinion that "no man shou'd scruple, or hesitate" to use arms in defense of so "valuable a blessing, on which all the good and evil of life depends. . . ."[68] He joined his colleagues in many measures but most of his work was with local or private bills. Apparently he never sponsored any outstanding measure.

It might be questioned whether Washington's career as a burgess indicated in any way his later role as leader of the new nation. But what is more important is the fact that the young man learned much that was of value to him in later years. He saw at first hand the process by which the representatives expressed the will of the people—and defied Parliament. He measured his strength against some of the political giants of Virginia. He learned patience in dealing with men of differing opinions that military

99

experience alone would not have taught him. In short, he may have contributed no more than the average lawmaker, but he learned much that was of great benefit to the whole nation later.

Robert Rutherford. This study has failed to reveal anything significant about him although he was returned by Frederick County at four different elections and then by the freeholders of Berkeley when that county was formed out of Frederick. We do know that he was active in the development of the upper Potomac for navigation.[70]

Isaac Zane. Whatever Rutherford lacked in color and distinction was compensated for by Isaac Zane, who was chosen at a by-election to fill the vacancy created by Rutherford's resignation.[71] Philip Vickers Fithian recorded a meeting with him in May 1775:

> Col: Isaac Zane, Burgess for this County, came to the Store with Miss Betsey McFarland, his kept & confessed Mistress, & their young Son & Heir—Mr. Zane is a Man of the first Rank here, both in Property & Office—He possesses the noted Malbrow [Marlborough] Iron-Works, six Miles from this Town—He has many Slaves & several valuable Plantations—He is, with Regard to Politicks, in his own Language, a "Quaker for the Times."—Of an open, willing, ready Conversation; talks much; And talks sensibly on the present Commotions —He is a Patriot of a Fiery Temper—In Dunmore Shenandoah County he is Col: of the Militia—one of the Burgesses in this—But he scorns to have a Wife—![72]

Zane was originally from Philadelphia, where he had an aged father, numerous other relatives, and many friends and business connections. They were all Quakers. A historian of the Valley says that Isaac himself was a member of the Hopewell Meeting House in Frederick County.[73] His irregular personal life or the pride he took in his personal appearance (he "displaced" his own straight hair with a "flaxon full bottom" wig of respectable dimensions) would have been enough to cause the Philadelphia Monthly Meeting to censor him, but it was his election to the House of Burgesses and the subsequent oath that caused the final rupture between him and the meeting. It disowned him for having "deviated from the principals in which he was educated."[74]

Zane called himself "a gentleman and merchant," but these titles hardly described his multitudinous activities. He was primarily an ironmaster; it was iron that took him south in 1767. He soon bought out his partners and began operating the Marlborough Iron Works on Cedar Creek, a few miles south of Winchester. By 1771 he was producing weekly four tons of bar iron and two of castings consisting of kettles, bake plates, pots, and farm implements. By September of the next year, production had more than doubled and the foundrymen were wagering that, when "she comes to her height," the furnace would produce thirty tons a week of pig iron and

100

hollow ware. In spite of initial handicaps, especially low water in the summer months, and threatened disasters, his mining and smelting enterprises were very successful, and before long he opened up a second furnace and forge which he called "Bean's Smelter." He employed upwards of 150 free laborers and often advertised for wood cutters and other seasonal workers. He sold some iron locally, but sent the most of it by wagon to Alexandria or Georgetown for shipment to Philadelphia or consigned it to William Allason, merchant of Falmouth, for export to England.[75] But he was more than an ironmaster. He operated a great farm on which he raised food for his laborers; he had a retail store, a distillery, a grist mill, a saw mill, and warehouse. He was, in fact, a frontier capitalist. He lived in baronial splendor in a great stone house in the midst of a twenty thousand acre estate; his fine furniture was made by Benjamin Randolph of Philadelphia. The house was surrounded by a garden with fountains, orchards, a fish pond, bath house, ice house, the usual stables and servants' quarters, a countinghouse, and a springhouse, all built of native stone.

Zane was a man of culture and intellect. He was a member of the Philadelphia Society for Promoting and Propagating Useful Knowledge, and seemed to be at ease in all kinds of company; he numbered among his friends some of the best minds of his day. He had a substantial collection of four hundred books to which he added the Westover library of William Byrd III in 1778.[76] His letters are sprinkled with sayings reminiscent of Poor Richard and quotations from standard English poets. He had a gift for friendship and a streak of sentimentality. In his will, dated 1790, he left the bulk of his estate to his sister Sarah in Philadelphia, a spinster lady locally famous for her generosity. To Thomas Jefferson and James Madison he left ten guineas each "to purchase a memorial to our long and mutual friendship"; to Gabriel Jones he left eight hundred dollars and his horse Ranger, whose past service merited that care and attention which he was sure his friend would bestow on him.[77] In the midst of a busy life he found time to be a justice, a burgess, a delegate to the Convention of 1775, and an officer in the Revolution, which he aided very substantially by furnishing iron for ordnance. He began his will, "I, Isaac Zane of the Marlboro Iron Works, Esq., Brigadier General of the Militia of the Commonwealth of Virginia. . . ." He equalled many of his Philadelphia friends in wealth and scope of activities, and excelled many of his Tidewater acquaintances in splendor of living and cultural interests. In short, he was a flamboyant character and an enterprising industrialist, who combined financial daring, patriotic fervor, and cultural appreciation in a most colorful manner.

In these frontier counties, we have a mixture of all the elements of colonial Virginia. As shown in this examination, there were notable similarities and striking differences between the two. There was, for example, a restlessness that is characteristic of any new region. In both counties, representation shifted frequently. A few incumbents were defeated at the polls; three (Patton, Lewis, and Wilson) died in office; but many burgesses chose to stand in other counties. George Washington, George William Fairfax, Gabriel Jones, William Preston, Thomas Bryan Martin, and Robert Rutherford each represented more than one county at some time in his public career. The fact that candidates sought new fields, presumably because their chances of victory were greater in a new county, in itself bespeaks a form of restlessness. Furthermore, these were men on the go with interests far and wide. James Patton's commission for treaty-making with the Indians, Israel Christian's stores and extensive fur trade, William Preston's, Charles Lewis' and George Washington's expeditions against the French and Indians, Fairfax's and Mercer's voyages to England, and Gabriel Jones' duties as king's attorney for the whole valley all required a great deal of travelling in addition to that entailed by attendance at General Assembly.

Taken as a whole, these eighteen men formed a cosmopolitan lot. Fairfax, Jones, Martin, and Patton[78] had English educations; George Mercer attended the College of William and Mary. Washington's formal education was limited, but he had made a trip to the West Indies, where he associated with members of the ruling class and had picked up a degree of sophistication. It must be remembered also that he was related to many Tidewater families of wealth, breeding, and education, and was an intimate and frequent visitor in the homes of many of the great and near-great families of Virginia. James Patton, William Preston, Thomas B. Martin, and possibly others were foreign born; Madison, Jones, and Fairfax were sons of immigrants. All those who have left any considerable record emerge as forthright individuals and in most instances colorful personalities.

There were some differences between the counties. For example, there was the matter of the church. In Frederick County the burgesses were presumably members and vestrymen of the Established Church;[79] in Augusta, where Tidewater immigrants and Scotch-Irishmen rubbed shoulders and their families intermarried, almost as many Presbyterians as Anglicans were elected representatives. James Patton, William Preston, Israel Christian, Samuel McDowell, and Charles Lewis were all Calvinists. Patton was a commissioner (deacon) in the Tinkling Spring Church; Preston went from that congregation to the newly organized Denean Church to become one of its elders.[80] Even John Madison had the Presbyterian John Craig baptize his son Thomas, brother of James, who later became Virginia's first bishop.[81] Augusta Parish was not organized until 1747, so that the Presbyterians antedated Episcopalians in the Valley. It is presumed that men like Madison preferred to have their children baptized by a non-conformist minister than not baptized at all. The first Anglican vestry was so heavily Scotch-Irish that a petition was sent to the assembly in 1748 to have all the dissenters culled from it. The House took negative action on the petition, presumably on the ground there were too few bona fide Anglicans in the county to take care of the parish business.[82]

That Presbyterians could sit in the House of Burgesses was due to the Toleration Act of 1689, "An Act for Exempting Their Majesty's Protestant Subjects Dissenting from the church of England from the Penalties of Certain Laws." Under the act, any Protestant (but no Roman Catholic) who could take the usual "Oaths of Government Appointed by Law" was allowed to sit in Parliament, on county courts, and presumably hold any other office. The House of Burgesses recognized this fact in Augusta County, when a bill to increase the minister's salary there was under debate. Speaking against the bill, Landon Carter observed that "a majority of the people were favored by the Toleration Act"; and, though he agreed it was necessary to preserve the Established Church, he was of the opinion that it would be "cruel to load tender consciences" with greater burdens since the Dissenters already had to support their own ministers.[83]

There is a very marked difference in the direction the two counties faced. Almost without exception, Augusta men looked to the west. Preston, Patton, and Christian all had business beyond the mountains; McDowell moved to Kentucky in time to help it become a state; Jones seems to have been content to practice law up and down the Valley; Madison's clerkship of Augusta seems to have occupied his time. Except for Jones and Madison, all of them traded with and fought against the Indians; Patton and Lewis died at the hands of the red men. On the other hand, the men of Frederick who have left any extensive remains had their greatest interest to the east. Fairfax and Washington were allied by marriage and sympathy to Tidewater families; Mercer felt as much at home in England as he did at his father's estate; Martin kept in close touch with relatives in England; Zane's business was in Frederick but his market was in Philadelphia, Falmouth, and England. To be sure, Washington won fame in the west and Mercer remained the agent for the Ohio Company until it went out of existence, but they were never at home on the frontier. Some of the representatives (at least Washington and Fairfax) never lived in the county, and Zane's establishment was like something out of a romance of never-never land. As accurately as we can judge. Wood and Rutherford came nearer being a part of the frontier than the others.

Why the difference? It is difficult to say, but a partial answer may lie in the policies of Robert "King" Carter, agent for the proprietors in the 1720's and 1730's. So much attention has been centered on the extent to which Carter used his office to feather his own nest that sight has been lost of the fact that he had a fairly well defined policy for the Northern Neck. In the first place, he did everything in his power to see that accurate surveys were made, thus assuring the purchasers definite limits to their lands. In the second place, he advocated the granting of land in large tracts and thus encouraged speculation. But in the third place, Carter insisted that a manor plantation be established as soon as possible on these lands and that settlement begin. He himself was instrumental in dividing some of the frontier tracts and settling some of the Scotch-Irish farmers. Carter and other officials believed with Governor William Gooch that "without taking up large tracts upon which great improvements were necessary to be made, these counties would not have been settled so speedily as they have been, and much of that land which has been seated in small parcels would in all probability have remained to this day desolate. . . ."[84] Under such policies, the plantation system of Tidewater Virginia moved west in the Northern Neck at a faster rate than it did in some other areas no less fitted for it. Planters were leading citizens, and Virginians elected their leading citizens to represent them.

6

IN THE CENTER OF THE COLONY

HENRICO, ALBEMARLE, AND AMELIA

Henrico County was one of the original shires created in 1634 and therefore has a long history. Like all others of that date, it had been reduced greatly by subdivisions; in 1728 Goochland was made a separate county, and in 1749 Chesterfield was organized to take all the territory south of the James so that in 1750 Henrico had essentially the same boundaries it has two centuries later.[1] It lies on the border between Tidewater and Piedmont Virginia with Richmond, its county seat, at the Falls of the James. Richmond, established in the 1730's by William Byrd II, was a busy place with shipping concerns, retail stores, tobacco warehouses, lumber businesses, and other enterprises; and the high hopes of its founders to establish a commercial center were beginning to be realized.

Elections in Henrico

In spite of its long existence, Henrico County has few records; time, fire, war, and carelessness have all taken their toll. There are no election returns. There is, in fact, extensive material about only one election before statehood, the one held on December 6, 1771, following the arrival of Governor Dunmore.

That election doubtless would have been routine had it not been for the fact that Sheriff George Cox's commission was due to expire.[2] Appointed on October 28, 1769, he was sworn into office on the following November 6. The election writ did not reach him until November 4, 1771. With two days of his two-year term still to serve, he could legally appoint a polling date and send out copies of the governor's writs to the various churches. November 29 was the day set; by that time a new sheriff would normally have been appointed and sworn in; the election would have been his re-

105

sponsibility. But for some unknown reason, the county court did not meet that month.[3] Although the governor and council appointed the county sheriffs, the county courts always recommended a number of the justices from whom the new officer was to be chosen. The Henrico court, not having met, did not nominate, and the governor and council did not appoint Mr. Cox's successor, so the county was without a sheriff. The question inevitably arose, who would hold the election? The candidates attempted to get themselves out of the dilemma by agreeing to postpone the election until December 6, hoping that by that time a new sheriff would be appointed and qualified; all of the churches were notified of this change. According to Richard Adams, one of the successful candidates, Cox refused to do anything about the election dates until he was assured by all the candidates that no one of them would take advantage of any error in the proceedings. The reports do not agree as to who held the election. Adams said the old sheriff did after the candidates agreed to abide by any decision made at the polls.[4] But in any case, the election was illegal and could have been held only by common consent. Richard Adams and Richard Randolph, the incumbents, were reelected, Adams by a comfortable majority, but Randolph by only two votes more than Samuel Duval had. There is no record of the exact number of polls cast, but it was small because of bad weather, and as one suggested, "the want of notice of the day last appointed."[5] Duval was convinced that he had more "good voters" than Randolph did and petitioned the Assembly to have the poll canvassed.[6] This was, of course, the usual procedure when there was disagreement about the tally. Whether Randolph was offended by this petition or whether his legal judgment told him the whole proceeding was questionable, he decided not to "enter into that dispute" and regardless of his agreement to accept the outcome at the polls, petitioned the Assembly to have the whole election thrown out "for want of form" and to call a new one, which it did. The freeholders, liking neither Randolph's conduct at the polls nor his breaking a promise, chose Duval and Adams at the new election which was held some time before March 24.[7]

Burgesses of Henrico

William Randolph. Two families monopolized representation from 1750 until 1771: the Randolphs and the Bowler Cocke-Adams. William Randolph, who in 1749 was burgess from Henrico and clerk of the House of Burgesses, was the third son of William Randolph II of Turkey Island, who had laid the foundation of wealth and aristocracy for the Randolph family. Proudly claiming descent from Pocahontas, the Randolphs had become by education, wealth (especially in lands from the crown), and marriage, in

106

the minds of many, the leading family of Virginia. They were related to almost every important family in the colony, rivaling the Byrds, the Carters, and the Harrisons, who were themselves relatives, in that respect. William Randolph was born at Turkey Island about 1719 and, after he reached maturity, moved to Wilton, where he built a fine house. His wife was Anne Harrison, daughter of Benjamin and Anne Carter Harrison of Berkeley, Charles City County; Benjamin Harrison, the "Signer," was therefore Randolph's brother-in-law. William Randolph's brothers held places of prominence in the colony. Beverley died in 1751 while a burgess from the college; Peter was on the council; and their sister, Elizabeth, was the wife of John Chiswell, burgess from Hanover and the father-in-law of Speaker John Robinson.[8] Burgess Randolph from Henrico died in office after the election of 1761, and Philip Mayo,[9] about whom practically nothing is known, filled out his unexpired term. But in 1765 William's nephew, Richard, was elected and stayed in office until the irregular election of 1771. At this late date, it is impossible to find out why Richard did not immediately succeed his uncle. Was he out of the colony, did he hold some office that made him ineligible to a seat in the House, or did he run and was he defeated? We frankly do not know.

Richard Randolph was the son of Richard Randolph of Curles Neck and therefore the grandson of William Randolph II of Turkey Island. He was the nephew of William and of Peter Randolph of the council, first cousin to Jane Randolph Jefferson (Peter Jefferson's wife and mother of Thomas, both of them burgesses) and Dorothy Randolph Woodson (wife of John Woodson of Goochland), Speaker Robinson's wife, and countless others.[10] He had married Anne Meade of Nansemond County about 1750; their second daughter, in turn, married her close kinsman, David Meade, who represented his native county in the assembly from 1769 on.[11] The oldest daughter became the wife of Benjamin Harrison, the "Signer," of Berkeley. Randolph's sister Jane was the wife of Anthony Walke of Fairfield, of Princess Anne County; Archibald Cary, burgess from Chesterfield, was the husband of Mary Randolph, another sister.[12] Like most of his class, Richard Randolph had been vestryman, sheriff, and justice.[13] His wealth seems to have consisted chiefly of large tracts of land in Albemarle and other counties.[14]

The *Bowler Cockes* were father and son; they were in office continuously after 1752 until 1769, first the father and after 1765 the son. In 1769 Richard Adams, whose mother was a sister of the elder Cocke, who had moved into Henrico from New Kent, took office. He remained there through the Revolution. Bowler Cocke, Sr., died in 1771,[15] and his son was still living in 1784.[16] Death did not remove them, so it may be assumed that they and Adams took turns doing their duty for the county. The elder

107

Cocke had married Mrs. Elizabeth Hill Carter, widow of the secretary of the colony, John Carter (Robert "King" Carter's eldest son); and through her he acquired Shirley, where later the Cockes lived. In Henrico, the family lived at Bremo. Both Bowler Cockes were vestrymen, justices, and large property owners, with land and lumber for sale.[17]

Richard Adams was no novice at politics, nor was he the social or economic inferior of the Randolphs. The son of Ebenezer Adams, who had migrated from England some time before 1714, Richard had served New Kent, his native county, from 1752 until 1765. Just when he moved to Richmond is uncertain, but he was burgess from Henrico from 1769 until the end of the colonial period. With land which he had acquired by purchase and patent, he was the largest property owner in Richmond City. There he built a fine residence on what he called Adams Hill (now Church Hill) in the vicinity of historic St. John's Church. How large his holdings were in the pre-Revolutionary period is unknown, but in 1787–1788 he is listed among the one hundred largest property holders in the state. At that time he had 10,865–½ acres of land in six counties, 108 slaves, 36 horses, 134 head of cattle and two lots in Richmond. Half of this land was in the newly created county of Henry on the North Carolina border.[18] From time to time he advertised land for sale.

His economic interests were not confined to land. He had a lumber business in Richmond which he considered a good investment. In 1769 his lumber curing shed was damaged to an estimated two hundred pounds when lightning struck it, setting it on fire. The loss was even greater because a large quantity of hemp, belonging to some people from Augusta, probably customers of his brother, Thomas Adams, was stored there. The hemp blazed up at once, threatening to set fire to four barrels of gunpowder stored there by one J. Stuart. Fear of the inevitable explosion kept everyone from going near enough to put out the blaze. Finally, Adams in desperation persuaded one other person to go with him, and the two of them rolled out two barrels before the heat became too great for them. Less than ten minutes later the remaining powder blew up causing "a most shocking sight." This explosion, however, was the "circumstance of saving the rest of the town, as it blew down the house and in some measure scattered and abated the force of the fire." With all the property damage no lives were lost nor anyone badly injured.[19]

A third interest of Adams was commerce. His brother Thomas, four years his junior, went to England about 1762, where he was in business as a merchant until his return sometime before May 1774. Richard carried on the American end of the partnership, buying tobacco, getting cargo, selling goods sent out, and establishing himself as a leading merchant in Richmond.[20] The voluminous Adams papers in the Virginia Historical Society, most of which are correspondence between the two brothers, are primarily about business.

As the leading businessman of the town that was already making overtures toward becoming the capital of the colony, Adams was active in attempts to open up the Falls of the James to commerce. As an accommodating citizen and neighbor, he was manager of the lotteries of William Dudley and Harry Tompkins, who were using this method of raising money to pay off their debts.[21] As a merchant and patriot, he signed the Virginia Association in 1769 and was a leader in the meeting of merchants in 1774.[22] He was an ardent patriot throughout the Revolution and one of the most enterprising public-spirited men of his day and city.[23]

The Adamses, although they had been in America fewer generations than the Randolphs, could count among their relatives almost as many prominent people. Richard Adams' father, who came from England without a wife, married Tabitha, daughter of Richard Cocke of Bremo, Henrico County.[24] In addition to the two sons, Richard and Thomas, the couple had several daughters who married husbands from prominent families and who became leaders in the colony. The oldest, Tabitha, married Richard Eppes, burgess from Chesterfield; Anne married Colonel Francis Smith of Essex County; and Sarah became the wife of Colonel John Fry, burgess from Albermarle and son of Joshua Fry. Thus Richard Adams was brother-in-law to three burgesses and, through the Cockes, close kin to many more.[25]

Samuel Duval. Adams and the Randolphs, although there seems to have been no blood relationship, were evidently on good terms; if there was any rivalry there is no indication of it. On the other hand Samuel Duval, who defeated Richard Randolph in the 1771 election, was on occasion at cross purposes with the Randolphs,[26] and had a different set of relatives. In fact, if he was related to any prominent family of Virginia's ruling class, the record is lost.

Duval's wife, whom he married in 1772, was a Miss Shepherd of Nansemond County. In the language of the editor of the *Virginia Gazette,* she was "an agreeable young lady"

> Whose charms the coolest breast must fire
> As brightest objects must inspire.
> Like Beauty's queen a thousand Loves,
> Her steps attend wher'e'er she moves.
> Peggy more transports can bestow
> Than crowns confer or monarchs know.

The last lines are hyperbole, but they may also have been an indirect reference to the fortune of the bride, not an uncommon practice in colonial wedding announcements.[27]

Duval was of French Huguenot descent. There is no indication that he was socially inferior to his colleagues or that anyone considered him so. He certainly was as active as Adams in public affairs; he was justice of the peace; and during the war with England he served on many patriotic committees.[28]

His economic interests were as varied as those of Adams. He was already well established as a businessman when he took his Peggy home to Mount Comfort. He had extensive lands both in Henrico and in Lunenburg; five thousand acres above Richmond ideally suited for raising wheat and corn and forested by a large quantity of the best heart pine in the country; and a plantation in Lunenburg on Flat Creek.[29] In 1772, he had lots on Main Street in Richmond for sale and an ordinary at Westham, six miles above Richmond, for rent.[30] His fulling mill in Henrico under the management of Mathew Dick was doing business for the public for prices that ranged from four pence to one shilling six pence per yard.[31] He had either shipping or shipbuilding interests because in the summer of 1768 he offered for sale a part interest in a fifty-ton schooner ready to sail in two weeks.[32]

Whether it was deliberate or not, Duval was the means of breaking the hold of the Randolphs on the county. For more than twenty-five years, that family had monopolized one seat in the House. The Cockes and the the Randolphs were primarily landed aristocrats of the era when Virginia was His Majesty's favorite colony. They represented an era of loyalty and good feeling that by the late 1760's was largely a thing of the past. They were at best lukewarm about the American cause when a showdown came in the 1770's. In contrast, both Adams and Duval were eminent patriots, and this fact may have been a deciding factor in the votes of their constituents.

No county outside the Tidewater is as famous as Albemarle, the home of Thomas Jefferson and James Monroe. It is a beautiful country; its rolling forest-covered hills increasing in size towards the Blue Ridge Mountains, which form a boundary between it and Augusta. In 1750 it had been a county only five years; it was new country, and, the historians tell us, it was led by new men who rose in true democratic fashion where the restraints of class were broken or at least weakened.

Burgesses of Albemarle

We have no information on elections in Albemarle in the quarter century before independence, but we know much about the men who were elected. Three of them have attracted biographers, another left an autobiography, and a third a diary; without exception every man left some kind of records.[33] The burgesses were Dr. William Cabell, William Cabell, Jr., Edward Carter, Henry Fry, John Fry, Joshua Fry, Allan Howard, Peter Jefferson, Thomas

110

Jefferson, John Nicholas, John Walker, and Dr. Thomas Walker.

Allan Howard comes very near fitting the stereotype of the frontiersman. His origins are obscure; but, about 1730, he began acquiring land in the county, at first in small amounts and later in large tracts. It is possible, as one historian of the county points out, that he had an unsavory past. His ears were cropped and slit, a usual eighteenth-century punishment for crime.[34] If this surmise is correct, his career was meteoric. By 1745 he was one of the gentlemen justices of Albemarle along with Peter Jefferson, Joshua Fry, William Cabell, Charles Lynch, and others; in fact, he and William Cabell administered the oaths to Jefferson and Fry at the first meeting of Albemarle County on February 28, 1745. He also became a major in the county militia, being third in command after Fry and Jefferson.[35] His two terms in the assembly were divided, 1752–1755 and 1758–1761. There is no indication of what happened at the election of 1755 except that John Nicholas and Dr. William Cabell were returned. At the 1758 election, William Cabell, Jr., was Howard's colleague.[36] During his last term, Howard brought censure on himself by saying in public what he had previously written one of his constituents, that "the last assembly [of which he was not a member, of course] agreed to give the commissioners for settling the militia accounts and damages done by the Indians forty pounds per day each, that is the way the assembly squanders the country's money."[37]

Joshua Fry was elected with Howard in 1752. Fry had moved to the back settlements "in order to raise a fortune for his family."[38] He was born and educated in England, coming to America sometimes after 1718, when he had matriculated at Wadham College (Oxford), and before 1723, when he was teaching at William and Mary.[39] He was described as a very young man but a good scholar who taught the boys grammar and writing.[40] After some years as head of the Grammar School he was promoted to professor of mathematics and natural philosophy; his salary as a professor was ninety pounds annually plus twenty shillings for every student.[41] In the fifteen or so years that he was associated with the college, he taught many young men who later became leaders in the colony. He kept up his ties with England, so that his recommendation for students going to one of the universities carried weight with the authorities.[42] It is believed that, since his name does not appear in any of the Goochland County records from which Albemarle County was formed, he did not go west until about 1744.[43]

Already a man of solid reputation, he rose rapidly in power and influence in the new county. He was one of the first magistrates and a county militia officer. His chief occupation in Albemarle, however, was surveying. For some years he was engaged in surveying lands in Albemarle, Goochland, and adjoining counties. In 1745 he and Peter Jefferson, who was probably his best friend in the new county, ran the western boundary line for the Fairfax grant.

In 1751 the two completed a map of the "Most Inhabited Parts of Virginia. . . ."[44] For this masterpiece one hundred and fifty pounds was awarded by the colony to each of the surveyors.[45] In 1752 these same men were paid three hundred pounds each for extending the dividing line between Virginia and North Carolina.[46] Fry's familiarity with the frontier was one reason for his being appointed with James Patton of Augusta and Lunsford Lomax, both seasoned Indian diplomats, to negotiate the Treaty of Logstown.[47] During all these surveying activities, Fry was acquiring land for himself—two thousand acres in one tract in 1750, twenty-two hundred acres a year later, and many more.[48] On one tract there were some copper mines, which he sold to John Chiswell, burgess from Hanover, who was developing mining on the frontier.[49]

Fry, like Dr. George Nicholas, Ebenezer Adams, and many others, came to Virginia unmarried. Also like them, he married a wife from a prominent family. His wife was Mrs. Mary Micou Hill, the daughter of an exiled Huguenot physician and widow of Leonard Hill. She had considerable property from Hill's estate which, of course, came into the hands of her new husband. Fry and his wife had several children, two of the sons serving brief terms as burgess from Albemarle. Their daughter, Martha, married John Nicholas, another burgess and clerk of the county; he was the brother of Robert Carter Nicholas, treasurer and one of the most powerful figures in the colony. Henry Fry married Susan Walker, daughter of Dr. Thomas Walker.[50]

At the outbreak of the French and Indian War in 1754, Fry was commissioned colonel of the Virginia forces and went west in the first expedition; youthful George Washington was the second in command. On May 31, 1754, near Wills Creek, Fry was killed, not by the enemy, but in a fall from his horse. Washington, who took charge immediately, was thrust into a position of importance.[51]

Fry's death caused widespread grief. "Our dear acquaintance Joshua is gone from us," wrote Henry Wood from Nelson Hill to Benjamin Waller at Williamsburg. "To me it is almost like losing a limb. My house was his inn when he traveled the road and as he often did, I was as many times happy in his conversation. Such men are but few near me." Wood was sure the House would erect a proper memorial to him because so many of the gentlemen there owed "the foundation of their present knowledge to his great learning and polite instruction." He was moved to pen what he considered a fitting epitaph:

> Here lie the bones of Joshua Fry
> Reader, if thou askest why?
> Because he to his God was dear
> Jehovah said to me be near

His virtues were unknown to thee
Tho plainly understood by me
Modesty, courage, learning great
Could never his firm mind elate
Above what he thought nobly good
Thus writes his old friend Harry Wood.
Let drop one tear, be not ashamed,
For manly sorrow no man blamed.
He died in the service
of his country.[52]

Another contemporary estimate of him, containing fewer flourishes, was that he had a clear head, a mild temper, and a good heart.[53] It was fitting that Peter Jefferson, with whom he had been associated in so many activities, should become his successor in the assembly.

Peter Jefferson. The myth of the cherry tree is no more persistent in American history than the story of the "plain" origin of Thomas Jefferson's father. Everyone knew that Thomas Jefferson's mother was a Randolph and an aristocrat; so, they ask, how else could he have acquired his democratic tendencies unless at his father's knee? This question requires some investigation into the ancestry and career of Peter Jefferson.[54]

The elder Jefferson was born not far down the James River from Richmond in that part of Henrico county which in 1749 became Chesterfield. Osborne, his birthplace, was on the south side of the river; the Byrds, the Harrisons, the Bowler Cockes, the Isham Randolphs, and the William Randolphs all lived on the north side. It has been suggested that there was social stigma attached to living on the banks of the river opposite these wealthy and influential planters. Whether actually true or not, it may be the basis for the story that Peter Jefferson was socially inferior to the family into which he married. Be that as it may, he did not remain on the James River for long after he reached his majority but moved west, first to Goochland and then to Albemarle.[55] In Goochland he became a member of the county court in 1734 along with Dudley Digges, William Randolph, George Carrington, and others—all prominent men.[56] And on September 30, 1737 he was sworn in as sheriff, thus taking over the law enforcement for the county and the responsibility for the prisoners in jail. Of the quitrents he collected as sheriff, he was entitled by law to ten percent; of the debts that were put in his hands to collect, his part was six percent.[57] Sometime in the early 1740's, he moved further west to the area where he built Shadwell, not far from the present city of Charlottesville; there his son Thomas was born in 1743. Peter Jefferson was present at the first county meeting in February 1745 and was second after Fry (who held first place) on the county court. Fry was the surveyor for Albemarle, and

Jefferson had the same office in Goochland, taking the place of William Mayo (in 1744) who had held that post for many years. Jefferson retained that office until 1751 although he lived in the part of Goochland that became Albemarle. Although Fry and Jefferson did a great deal of surveying together, they seem to have maintained separate offices and each paid the other for assistance when the work was being done in his own county. For example, in the John Harvie account book of surveys by Fry in Albemarle, there is a frequent entry of "Peter Jefferson's part."[58] Jefferson, like Fry, was always alert to the possibility of getting unclaimed land he came across in his surveys. Between 1730, when his first patent was granted, until his death in 1757, he had acquired 16,847-2/3 acres. This does not include 2,038 acres which he inherited from his father nor his interest in 800,000 acres of the Loyal Land Company. He had an income from several sources besides his plantation and surveying. He dealt in western lands; he administered estates for several people, including his father-in-law; he had a mill that served the community. Furthermore, for a brief period he was a burgess, which may not have meant a lot of money, but it added to his other resources. At his death, the county still owed him twenty-eight pounds for burgess wages.[59]

His wife was Jane Randolph, daughter of aristocratic and wealthy Isham Randolph of Dungeness. Jane was born in London while her father was agent for the colony. There she spent her childhood and began her education in the things that would fit her for polite society. Writing evidently was not among these, for as long as she lived she signed her name with a mark. Back in Virginia, On October 3, 1739, she and Peter Jefferson were married. The circumstances surrounding the wedding have long since been forgotten, so we can only surmise the reasons for the match. Class lines were not very rigid in colonial Virginia, and it was possible for a bright young man to make his way up in the world, provided he had the drive, the personality—and possibly the vices—that would recommend him to the ruling class. It was possible for such a young man with sufficient lands and adequate expectations to marry into a proud family which had an abundance of eligible girls but little dowry. Marriage in colonial Virginia was not always a matter of sentiment, as the wedding announcements in the *Gazette* (which often gave the size of the bride's fortune) prove. On the other hand, leading families did not take kindly to marriages with social inferiors. In the match between Jane Randolph and Peter Jefferson, the bride's family was not poor, nor even in strained circumstances. Later generations have forgotten what contemporaries knew, that the groom's ancestors were almost, if not fully, as proud as the bride's. His father, Thomas Jefferson, had been a burgess and a captain in the county militia; he had married Mary Field, daughter of a distinguished father and a socially prominent mother. The Randolphs did not openly, if at all, object to the match; and members of the best families assembled at Dungeness to enjoy the wedding festivities—the Woodsons, Dobbs, Mayos, Cockes, Ballews, Cabells, Bollings, Flemings, Eppeses, and numbers of the Randolph clan.[60] It would appear therefore that this was an acceptable match.

The couple had been married about four years when Isham Randolph died, leaving a large and involved property. Peter Jefferson was the administrator for the estate, an office usually entrusted to near relatives and best friends. Two years later (1745) when William Randolph of Tuckahoe, Jane Randolph's cousin and Jefferson's close friend, died, Jefferson was requested in his will to perform like services for him and become guardian of his minor children. In order to look after the estate better, Jefferson moved his family from Shadwell to Tuckahoe; and it was there that Thomas began his schooling under the Rev. William Douglas. The elder Jefferson was no mere overseer, but the executor with complete control over the estate within the terms of the will and the extent of the law.[61]

At Jefferson's death when he was not yet fifty, his possessions compare favorably with those of his neighbors. His biographer, after examining inventories and wills of other residents of Albemarle, is convinced that his estate and the appointments of his house were equalled only by those of Colonel John Harvie and the Reverend Robert Rose, and excelled by none at all. His Albemarle estates were valued at £2,129.10.1–½, the slaves alone on the Rivanna River plantation at £1,509.15.0, and at £283.3.0 at Snowden. Debts due him, most of them from the Joshua Fry and William Randolph estates for which he was an administrator, amounted to £201.18.8–¾, while his own total indebtedness was only £67.7.2–½. If this summary is correct—and there is no reason to believe otherwise—Peter Jefferson was in comfortable circumstances, and his estate was not debt-ridden as many Virginia estates were.[62] His personal estate included a sizeable number of books on history, law, religion, and travel. These, with a bookcase and a cherry-tree desk, he fittingly left to his son Thomas, who was one of the administrators of his estate. The lands and slaves were to be divided between Thomas and the other son, Randolph; and the three daughters were to get marriage portions;[63] his personal effects and estate were to be his wife's for life or widowhood.[64]

This record of Peter Jefferson with his Tidewater origins, his ancestry, estate, numerous public trusts, and evident acceptance by the Randolphs does not make him appear a social inferior. The charge has been made that he was a social climber, always looking for the main chance. This may have an element of truth in it, but the allegation could apply equally to the Randolphs and practically every other family or person who got ahead in Virginia.

115

John Nicholas. The two burgesses who next sat for Albemarle were John Nicholas and Dr. William Cabell. Nicholas was brother of Robert Carter Nicholas, burgess and Treasurer after 1766. John, like his brothers, had been born in Williamsburg where his father, Dr. George Nicholas, had been a leading physician and burgess for the college for at least one term. Dr. Nicholas was a native of England and had been in America a relatively short time before he married the rich young widow of Nathaniel Burwell, the daughter of Robert "King" Carter. Governor William Gooch reported that it was against the "advice of all her friends that she married a man brought up, as he says, at St. Johns College . . . he practices physic here with good success," though Gooch believed he never took any degree. The Governor had misgivings about the man of whom he had heard "strange stories," but admitted that he was an excellent physician. The marriage lasted only a few years. In June 1734, Gooch wrote his brother in England, "The doctor formerly of St. Johns is dead." The dejected man had been "undone" by the death of his wife some four months before and "must have been poor and miserable, if not in gaol. . . ."[65] John Nicholas must have been very young when he was thus suddenly orphaned. His father had no relatives in Virginia, and apparently little estate, so it may be assumed that the boys were reared by some of the numerous Carters. On reaching maturity, John migrated to Albemarle,[66] where he became clerk of the county in 1749, an office which he and his son, who succeeded him, held until 1815. His wife was Martha, daughter of Joshua Fry.[67]

Dr. William Cabell, like Fry, was English born; his native town was Bugley, near Warminster, in Wiltshire. After migrating to Virginia, he married Elizabeth Burks in 1726. He pushed into the interior, became an Indian fighter, surveyor, deputy sheriff, justice of the peace, trader, planter, and surgeon. He set up a private hospital on the fringe of the forest where he dispensed medicines and made wooden legs. By 1741 he had "carried settlements fifty miles westward." The biographer of his son describes him as a "tall, lithe, blackeyed man, audacious in action, liberal in thought, and scientific in method" who by 1753, having acquired twenty-six thousand acres of choice land, "tossed his surveyor's mantle" to his eldest son. Dr. Cabell died in 1774, and was, therefore, not involved in the Revolution; but in spite of his English birth, his free and daring spirit would likely have made him a patriot. His son became a notable one.[68]

The son, *William Cabell, Jr.,* who was elected burgess in 1758, did very well indeed with his father's "surveyor's mantle" and whatever other blessings and privileges may have gone with it. As early as 1751, the Council granted him a tract on "Huffs the Beaver Pond" that alone contained 3,000 acres, and another of 1000 acres in Albemarle. By patent and purchase, mostly the former, he added to his holdings until by 1788 he was one of the richest men in the state with 15,237 acres of land, all but 400 acres of which was in Amherst.[69]

Young Cabell represented Albemarle only one term, 1758–1761. It was in Amherst (cut off from Albemarle in 1761) that he made a name for himself as a leading citizen and patriot. From there he went faithfully to Williamsburg, recording in his diary the number of "daies" the assembly sat, the amounts he received from the treasurer for wages, the debts he collected on the way, and the other business he transacted during the trip.[70] He was a leading lawyer of Amherst, an active land speculator, and an extensive planter. For some of his plantations, which were scattered over a wide area, he hired overseers; but others he let out at a yearly rental.[71] After the Revolution, during which he had served on many patriotic committees, often as chairman, he continued in the state senate and the House of Delegates, retiring from the last body only in 1788.[72] Eckenrode describes him as "six feet high, corpulent, with capacious forehead, he was of superior brain, strikingly liberal in mind and pocket, of ceaseless energy and infinite capacity for work. . . . Fate designed him to be primarily a builder of Virginia."[73]

John Fry. The two sons of Joshua Fry served very briefly in the assembly and seem to have made little impression on that body. John, the elder, was elected in 1761 but resigned in 1764 to become coroner; later he was sheriff. His wife was Sarah Adams, the sister of Richard Adams of New Kent and Henrico; and their son, Joshua, married Peachy, one of the younger daughters of Dr. Thomas Walker of Castle Hill, burgess from Louisa, Hampshire, and Albemarle.[74] Henry Fry succeeded his brother; but, if he ran at the next election, he was defeated. Neither of them again sat in the assembly.

Henry Fry was a friend of Thomas Jefferson in his youth; he had read widely and speculated, if not deeply, at least piously. While he was a student at the college, he lived with his uncle, Thomas Hornsby, and aunt in Williamsburg. The aunt was a very pious woman and his uncle (a leading merchant) something of a skeptic. Together, Fry said, they took care of every phase of life—"the old gentleman careful for the present, and my aunt laying for a future life." The attitudes of his aunt and the death of his father while he was still a student made a deep impression on him. His schooling over, young Fry returned to Albemarle, where he became deputy clerk of the county under John Nicholas, his brother-in-law. In 1764 he married a daughter of Dr. Thomas Walker. Living in an ague-infested area made a near-invalid of him; and, taking the advice of a friend, he began to keep himself "warm with spirits during the season." The remedy, he admitted, was worse than the disease, and he became an alcoholic, incapable of doing business. He tried many remedies, but nothing helped him overcome his besetting sin. Finally in desperation, he turned from the Anglican Church, in which he had been reared, and started attending meetings of the Baptists. He was repelled by some of their practices; and, upon hearing a Methodist circuit rider preach a powerful sermon on the text, "Faith is the substance . . . ," he underwent a religious experience that gave peace and joy to his soul. He turned a room originally designed for music and dancing into a chapel; and, when occasion required, he even could officiate as a lay preacher or class leader. Eventually he became an ordained Methodist Episcopal minister.[75]

Edward Carter. In colonial Virginia, the old feudal laws of primogeniture and entail still held. However, land was abundant and easily acquired. Consequently, younger sons often had estates that equalled or even excelled the ancestral manor. A good case in point is Edward Carter, burgess for one term, 1765–1768. Edward was the son of Secretary John Carter, who before his death in 1743 had acquired by his own efforts and the influence of his father, Robert "King" Carter, land in the Northern Neck and in several western counties outside the Fairfax Grant. The patrimonial estate, Corotoman in Lancaster County, went to his oldest son, Charles, and his vast property in Albemarle to Edward, the second son. Edward, like many of his contemporaries, patented, bought, and sold land throughout his life. By 1787 his total holdings amounted to 20,550 acres (and four lots) in three counties, on which he had 297 slaves.[76] When he made his will in 1792, he was able to give a plantation to each of his eight sons. He freed many of his skilled slaves.[77]

Edward Carter had many business interests. For some years he handled tobacco on consignment and conducted a retail mercantile business in Fredericksburg with Peter Field Trent, brother of Alexander Trent, burgess from Cumberland. Early in 1774 the partnership was dissolved, and Trent took over the store formerly run by Carter. This kind of business required extensive financial connections in England; William Lee, brother of Francis Lightfoot Lee, was one of the merchants Carter dealt with.[78] Carter was likewise one of the investors in the Albemarle Iron Works in which he held five hundred pounds or one-sixth of the capital investment. William Cabell, Alexander Trent, and Thomas Walker held like amounts. John Wilkinson, who owned a third of the stock, had begun the operation some time earlier; the new company was organized for putting into repair the furnace and erecting the necessary outbuildings for making pig and bar iron, common and flash casting. Nine months after he had purchased the stock (September 1771), Carter sold half of his one-sixth to a Pennsylvanian.[79] It may have been a patriotic gesture for Carter to give his permission (May 1775) to lease or sell the iron works; the Continental army always needed rifles such as could be made from Virginia iron.

118

Besides dealing in lands, operating a mercantile business, and investing in mines, Carter engaged in many activities in common with his neighbors. He was on the quorum of the county court, he pitted his cocks against those of Col. Anthony Thornton in a widely advertised match, he raced horses, he married, and he reared a large family—thirteen children in all.[80] He seems to have made no attempt to continue in the House after his one term and was succeeded in 1769 by twenty-six-year-old Thomas Jefferson, whose public career began here.

Thomas Jefferson. Most of the significant events in the public life of Thomas Jefferson came after May 26, 1774; but, in the preceding five years, in which he was a member of the House, he made an impression on its course and had a large hand in shaping the resolutions that caused Dunmore to dissolve it.

It is not surprising that Jefferson should have become a burgess because his birth and training had fitted him admirably for the role. Son and grandson of Jeffersons who had been in the House and related to innumerable Randolphs who had held high office, he was following the traditions of good Virginia families by offering his services to the country. He had better than average training for taking a major part in the affairs of the assembly. His education began at Tuckahoe under the Rev. William Douglas, whose abilities did not rate very high with his young pupil. Back in Albemarle sometime before he was nine, Tom was placed under the tutelage of the Rev. James Maury, who was to become the principal figure in the Parsons' Cause. From Maury, Jefferson received a sound foundation in the classics and, what is more important, developed a real love for learning. It was at his own request that he went to study at the College of William and Mary in March, 1760, when he was one month less than seventeen years of age. After his father died in 1757, he had asked his guardian, John Harvie, to permit him to do this in order to save time and money. "As long as I stay at the mountain," he wrote, "the loss of one fourth of my time is inevitable by companies coming here and detaining me from school. And likewise, my absence will, in a measure, put a stop to so much company, and by that means lessen the expense of the estate in housekeeping. . . . By going to college I shall get a more universal acquaintance which hereafter shall be serviceable to me. . . ."[81] That his three years at college meant more to him than the same length of time meant to most of his fellow students is due to two factors: his habit of diligent study and the influence of three men. His chief intellectual stimulus came from his association with Dr. William Small, who held the first chair of mathematics in the college and, for a period, filled the chair of philosophy. Small, who seems to have given his youthful student much of his time, aroused an interest in scientific questions that was to remain with Jefferson

119

his whole life. Small, furthermore, introduced him to Governor Francis Fauquier, probably the most competent governor that the colony had after 1750. George Wythe, one of the ablest lawyers of the colony, "a man of unexceptionable character, for his knowledge of the law, his candor, integrity and inflexibility,"[82] was an intimate friend of Fauquier's and became the fast friend and eventually the devoted teacher of law for the youthful Jefferson. These four—Fauquier, Small, Wythe, and Jefferson—met often for an evening together and, over a bottle of wine, explored many a field of learning. The association was of inestimable influence on the developing mind of Jefferson.

Jefferson studied law under Wythe and began a practice that was to prove successful. He was recognized as an able lawyer. When the duties of the treasurer's office got so heavy that he could no longer do justice to all his clients, Robert Carter Nicholas, reputed to be one of the best lawyers in the colony, asked Jefferson to take over his practice. Jefferson, pleading too little time, declined; but the fact that a leading barrister would trust him thus is evidence of his standing in the profession.[83]

It is mute testimony of the high regard in which his fellow burgesses held him that, the very first day he ever served in the House, he was appointed to draw up a reply to Governor Botetourt's "affectionate speech" delivered at the opening of the new Assembly. This was Jefferson's first state paper and was purely ceremonial in nature. The phrases were traditional, expressing "a firm attachment to His Majesty's sacred person" and thanking him "that our chief Governor shall in future reside among us," rejoicing that the royal family had another princess, assuring His Excellency that they should "with candor" proceed to the important business for which they were called; and acknowledging the interests of Great Britain and of Virginia to be "inseparably the same." Finally, he prayed that Providence and the royal pleasure might long continue His Lordship "the happy ruler of a free and an happy people." Robert Carter Nicholas rewrote this first effort, but some of his phrases remained.[84] When Botetourt dissolved the assembly on May 26, Jefferson was among those who went up the Duke of Gloucester Street to Mr. Anthony Hay's where the late burgesses took matters in their own hands, unanimously elected Peyton Randolph moderator, and proceeded to form a nonimportation plan by which Virginia could retaliate against England for the Townshend Acts. Jefferson was also in the Association formed in June, 1770. Virginians grew lukewarm about the whole question because, they said, of defection in the northern colonies, but Jefferson remained faithful to the Association, even to the point of hesitating to order some needed building material and his wedding apparel.[85]

The government of Virginia was so organized that there was no continuing body from one assembly to another, or even from one session to another. A committee could be set up to make a report on a particular question, but its activities were confined to that one matter. When the governor chose to dissolve an assembly, there was no body or agency through which the people could speak. Sensing this weakness for revolutionary purposes and reasoning that the old leaders lacked the zeal that the times required, Jefferson, Francis Lightfoot Lee, Richard Henry Lee, Patrick Henry, and Dabney Carr (Jefferson's brother-in-law) formed a group and frequently sat down together behind closed doors at the Raleigh Tavern and talked. What the colonies needed, they concluded, was some plan for united action. These young liberals were alarmed over the way patriotic fervor waned as soon as a crisis was past. Someone in the group—Richard Henry Lee is usually given credit for it—suggested a standing Committee of Correspondence. Such a body would be official and, at the same time, permanent.[86] Furthermore, it would be in the tradition of the colony because such a committee had been used at the time of the Stamp Act. Jefferson was also a leader in drawing up the resolves for a day of fasting and prayer for Boston, which caused the governor to dissolve the Assembly on May 26, 1774.

This brief account of the legislative career of Jefferson points out the role that he played and would continue to play in the assembly. No public speaker, he did his most effective work in a small group, whether on an official committee or in an extralegal body. Here his legal training, his wide reading, and his facile pen could be used to best advantage.

Dr. Thomas Walker. One of the best known Virginians of his day was Dr. Thomas Walker, one of the few men in the assembly for the whole 1750–1774 period. Before 1761 he had sat for Hampshire and Louisa, and in one election both counties returned him.[87] He, like the elder Jefferson, Fry, and Carter, had come from Tidewater country. He was born in King and Queen county in 1715. When he was twenty-six he married the twenty-year-old Mildred Thornton Meriwether, widow of Nicholas Meriwether. Through her, Walker became the master of Castle Hill, where he lived the remainder of his life. He sat for three different counties without once changing his residence. Strong in body, courageous, enterprising, and trustworthy, he took a leading part in nearly every movement that concerned the colony. He was at some time during his busy career (and often at the same time) Indian diplomat, physician, surveyor, explorer, leading spirit in the Loyal Land Company, merchant, industralist, lawyer, planter, and statesman. He was the family physician for the Jeffersons and was at the bedside of Peter when he died.[88] As noted earlier, he was one of the stockholders in the Albemarle Iron Works, which was usually in debt to him for the Negro labor, food, and supplies that he sold to it. As a surveyor and land promoter he was commissioned by the Loyal Land Company to

121

explore the 800,000 acre grant of land beyond the mountains, and it was during this trip in the winter of 1749–1750 that he kept a valuable journal of the western country. On this and other expeditions, he was always on the alert for desirable lands for himself and his friends; the section around Kingsport, Tennessee, was long known as the Pendleton district because Walker surveyed it for Edmund Pendleton.[89] As long as he lived, he kept getting land and more land either through the land company or by individual patent.[90]

Walker was a veteran Indian diplomat. In 1755, he was commissary for the Indians under Braddock's command. There was so much criticism of his handling of public funds that he was forced to defend himself in the assembly against charges of fraud brought by Thomas Johnson, member from Louisa.[91] In 1768, he was commissioned by President Blair to be a representative, along with Andrew Lewis, to meet with the Indians in congress at Fort Stanwix.[92]

Whether he actually practiced law is uncertain, but he had a law office, which he willed to his son, Francis, who from "his professional line of business" would have "the greatest share of trouble" in settling the estate.[93]

During the Revolution, Dr. Walker was a member of many patriotic committees, a delegate to the two conventions, and a member of the council of state in the interim between the flight of Dunmore and the election of Patrick Henry as governor. After the war was over he stayed active, serving in the assembly. An English visitor in his home in 1780 found the chief topic of conversation to be politics, "but always with moderation."[94]

John Walker. The last of the burgesses from Albemarle was John Walker, eldest son of Dr. Walker. There is some confusion about the time of his election to the House. The *Virginia Gazette* reported his election along with Jefferson's in 1771, but the *Journal* gives Thomas Walker. Not until the session of March 1773 does the son's name appear in the official records of the House. There is no request for a special election at which the son could have been elected. One has to conclude that either the *Gazette* or the *Journal* is wrong, but it is not certain which; so the way in which he got his seat remains a mystery.[95] The association and friendship of young Walker and Jefferson began in their childhood. Both had been students of the Rev. James Maury; and, since they were near the same age, they may have been in the same class. They were also in college at Williamsburg together and belonged to the Flat Hat Club, a secret but frivolous society which among other things was dedicated to the idea of making each member "a great ornament and pillar of things general and particular." Not long after he left college in 1764, Walker married Betsy Moore, the daughter of Bernard Moore, of Chelsea, in King William County; Jefferson was one of the wedding attendants. "Jack" Walker and his bride settled down on the old Nicholas Meriwether place, Belvoir, about five or six miles from Shadwell, and his friendship with Jefferson continued until the latter left for Washington in 1801.[96]

In some respects the son's career paralleled his father's, and the two men participated in some of the same activities. For example, when Dr. Walker and Andrew Lewis went to Fort Stanwix to meet the Indians (1768), the son went along as the clerk to the commission.[97] Like his father, he was a patriot; and like his colleague, Jefferson, his greatest public service would come after the colonial period. During the war itself, he was chairman of the Albemarle County Committee, a member of the Committee of Safety, a member of Congress, and an aide to Washington. After the war, he was the first United States Senator for the State.[98]

Among the twelve men who sat in the assembly for Albemarle, there were three Frys, two Jeffersons, two Cabells, two Walkers, and one Nicholas. The Walkers and the Frys were related by marriage. Two of the men were English born; all the rest were of Tidewater origin or their fathers were. With the possible exception of Allan Howard, all of them were from good families that were accustomed to holding places in the House of Burgesses or seats in the council. Occupationally, there were two doctors, two merchants, three lawyers, four surveyors, twelve planters, and twelve land speculators. Several of these men were dead before the Revolution, and we can only guess what would have been their attitude when the final break with England came; but of those who were still living, the Walkers, the younger Cabell, Carter and, of course, Jefferson, became outstanding patriots.

Amelia, third in this trio of counties between the Tidewater and the frontier, lies to the southeast of Albemarle and the southwest of Henrico. It contained in 1750 the territory that was cut off in 1754 to make Prince Edward County and also what is now Nottaway County. It was a large county; and, even after the division of 1754, residents complained of the inaccessibility of the court house.[99] Furthermore, there was no town or other focal center of the county. Petersburg, although outside the county, was the trading center.

Elections in Amelia

Unlike their contemporaries in Albemarle, Henrico, and many other counties, the eight men who represented Amelia County in the Assembly left no personal papers that have been discovered in this study. The student, therefore, is dependent on the public records for any information about them. Fortunately, there are a few election returns for the county: the single poll for Capt. Edmund Booker, for 1758, when he was elected with 465 votes, and the complete poll for December 6, 1768.[100] On the latter date Col. Thomas Tabb and Capt. Robert Munford were chosen, with 435 and 332 votes, respectively. The other two candidates, Capt. John Winn and Mr. John Scott, with 218 and 197 votes, brought the total polls to 1182. Since each freeholder had two votes, that means 591 voters cast their ballots.

The men in office before the election of 1752 were Thomas Tabb and Wood Jones; these two men were returned again; but Richard Booker, an unsuccessful candidate, challenged the election on the ground that unqualified people cast votes for Wood Jones. The election stood, but Booker defeated Jones at the 1755 election.[101] Thomas Tabb was again defeated by another Booker, Edmund, in 1758. Richard was reelected, but died before the 1765 election.[102] In the 1761 election, Tabb was returned and remained in office until is death in November 1769.[103] David Greenhill was his colleague but resigned to become sheriff before the 1765 election.[104] In 1765, Robert Munford was chosen, and he with Tabb remained in office until the same date. At the 1771 election, John Winn (who had filled out the term of Richard Booker in 1760–1761) and John Tabb, son of Thomas, were elected and continued to serve Amelia until after Independence. Of these men, only Thomas Tabb remained in office more than two terms. The frequent turnover is partially explained by the fact that three men died in office and one resigned to become sheriff. Winn in 1761, Wood Jones in 1775, and Munford in 1771 were evidently defeated at the polls.

Burgesses of Amelia

The Tabbs. The changes in personnel may be further explained by the occupation of the men involved. The leading burgesses from Amelia were merchants and land agents; and counties where there was a mercantile leadership seem to have had more frequent changes than the counties where the large planters held the power. The Tabbs, for example, were great merchants, members of the firm of Rumbold, Walker, and Tabb, which handled tobacco on consignment, imported slaves, built and chartered ships, and carried on an extensive trade with England. This company had a number of stores west and southwest of Amelia. Thomas Tabb lived in the western part of the county near the Cumberland County line and may have supervised them. He died on November 27, 1769, when he finally lost the battle he had waged for years against dropsy. "Few (if any)," his death notice ran, "traded so extensively as he did, nor with better credit or character, and by his death the colony has lost one of its most useful citizens."[105] He left a very great estate. In one bequest alone he left his daughter, Anne Bolling, ten thousand pounds; the various stores went to his son, John, who was in England at the time of his father's death.[106] The Tabbs were originally from Elizabeth City County where from 1752 until 1761 a John Tabb represented the county in the Assembly. Whether he was the son of Thomas or some other Tabb, the record does not tell us. The John Tabb of Amelia married a wife from Tidewater, Frances Peyton, daughter of Sir John Peyton of Gloucester.[107]

The Bookers, who seem not to have been father and son but may have been brothers or cousins, were also merchants and land speculators. The inventory of Richard's estate shows that he had estates in Prince Edward, Halifax, and Lunenburg Counties.[108] David Greenhill sold land in Dinwiddie, Lunenburg, and Amelia Counties.[109] Captain Wood Jones in 1752 offered for sale one tract alone of 1540 acres at fifteen pounds per hundred acres.[110] John Winn owned or acted as agent for land in Hanover, Amelia, and Lunenburg.[111]

These men, like most of the other burgesses, were vestrymen, churchwardens, justices, and officers in the county militia. Greenhill (and possibly others) took his turn as sheriff; Munford was for many years clerk of Halifax County.[112] By the outbreak of the Revolution, the two Bookers and Thomas Tabb were dead and Munford died during the war; since his will was made in 1771, he may have been in declining health during his later years. Of the eight men, the two we know were still alive and active after 1776, Winn and John Tabb, became leaders in the patriotic forces in the county to the complete satisfaction of their constituents. A meeting of the freeholders in 1775 expressed gratitude "for their disinterested and unwearied attention to the preservation of the just rights and liberties of the people of this country by assisting at the several conventions" that had been held in the colony and at their own expenses, although they had been offered "the cheerful contributions" of their constituents.[113]

While the three counties considered in this chapter are all in the interior, each is in a different geographical area: Henrico on the border between the Tidewater and Piedmont; Albemarle a hundred or more miles to the west, with its borders extending to the mountains; and Amelia on the "southside," traditionally inhabited by fewer of the elite than was the Peninsula and the Northern Neck. Only in Henrico was political leadership stable, and even there a Randolph was turned out of office in 1771. In the other two counties, there was a frequent turnover in representation and sometimes upsets at the polls. In all, twenty-seven men were sent from the three counties to the General Assembly in the twenty-four-year period. In spite of differences in the counties, all these men had certain common characteristics. Almost without exception they were of Tidewater origin or, as in the case of Thomas Jefferson and the younger Frys, the sons of men of Tidewater origin. They were, furthermore, men of a variety of economic interests who were planters first (even the Tabbs in Amelia) and then merchants, lawyers, land speculators, or surveyors. Most of them were closely related by blood and marriage, forming an office-holding elite. Most of them were active in the cause of independence. As far as our knowledge goes, they appear to have been a stable group of men with ample fortune, good family, and better than average education.

Sir Lewis Namier's study of the structure of politics in eighteenth-century England led him to a number of conclusions which may bear comparison with those suggested by this survey of Virginia's politicians in the same period. Most members of the House of Commons, Sir Lewis concludes, came from among the peers, and they entered the House of Commons as the best way to rise in the political world. "You will be of the House of Commons as soon as you are of age," Lord Chesterfield wrote to his son on December 5, 1749, "and you must make a figure there if you would make a figure in your country."[114] The present study of the House of Burgesses reveals that in some respects the situation in Virginia was very similar, but in other respects quite different. In Virginia, as in England, some young men, barely of voting age, were elected to the House of Burgesses, but the vast majority of members already had had experience in the parish or on the county court. They were recognized as leading citizens before they were elected.

Representatives did not have to be residents of the counties which they served. A case in point is Thomas Walker who, without once moving from his residence at Castle Hill, represented three counties in succession. Gabriel Jones was a candidate in three counties at the same election. George Washington, George William Fairfax, Francis Lightfoot Lee, George Mercer, and Thompson Mason were among the number who represented counties in which they did not live. In every known instance in which a nonresident represented a county, it was a county immediately adjacent or further west. Burgesses on the whole were of Tidewater origin. In Henrico, Amelia, and Albemarle, and in many other Piedmont and southside counties this was almost universally true; and a check on the members from Halifax, Cumberland, and other interior counties shows that it was widespread there, too. In the mountain counties, the preference for Tidewater men was also evident. Walker, Gabriel Jones, John Madison, John Wilson, G. W. Fairfax, George Washington, and very likely the Wests either were born in Tidewater counties or lived there when they reached maturity. In Augusta and Frederick, eastern Tidewater men shared the offices with Scotch-Irish immigrants like James Patton, William Preston, and the Lewises, and with Germans from Pennsylvania.

As to social status, the situation in Virginia was very similar to that in England. North, south, east, or west, burgesses came from upper-class families; almost without exception, they were men of social distinction. Social distinction may have been inherited, acquired by marriage, or made by a man in his lifetime; but, whatever the source, it was a prerequisite for a seat in the House. There is every evidence to show that Virginians expected their representatives to be men of note, and elected none but that kind.

Not only were burgesses of high social rank, but they were also closely interrelated. In the counties studied in the foregoing pages, the Carters and the Randolphs and their immediate families were the most numerous; but the Byrds (especially through the daughters in the family), the Harrisons, the Walkers, the Frys, the Cockes, and others appear repeatedly. The leading families had been intermarrying for so many generations that the House of Burgesses (and Virginia aristocracy from which its members came) was one vast cousinship, although many times the relationship was even closer than that of cousin.

7

PROFESSIONAL AND ECONOMIC
INTERESTS OF THE BURGESSES

Few events, conditions, movements, or men in colonial Virginia were uninfluenced by tobacco. The process of successfully curing the plant had assured the survival of the infant settlement, and thereafter the fortunes of the colony were closely connected with the price of the crop. For the first years, tobacco sold at phenomenally high prices, and planters were tempted to over-plant.[1] As a result, prices fell so low that shipping charges were nearly equal to what the commodity brought on the English market. From a high of three shillings per pound, which was the rate agreed on by the Virginia Company in 1618, the price fell to a low of one and one-half to three pence per pound in 1638–1639. Throughout the remainder of the colonial period prices tended to fluctuate and periodically fell below the cost of production. Producer's prices fluctuated greatly, yet production costs were essentially inelastic. Therefore, the fortunes of Virginia planters rose and fell with the market. Colonists tried various expedients to stabilize the trade: price fixing, destruction of a portion of the crop, standardization of varieties, and uniform methods of curing and packing. All were unsuccessful.

The colonists seem to have been largely unaware that the two things that had the greatest influence on the price of their tobacco—weather and the condition of the market—were beyond their control. Wind, rain, floods, hail, and cold could cause untold damage to the size of the crop and the quality of the tobacco. Even more important in influencing the price of tobacco was the fact that the American tobacco had competition on the European market from the Spanish and Turkish crops. Moreover, the manipulations of the great commission houses in London, and even the whims of a prince on the continent, could raise or lower the price the planter received.[2]

In spite of recurrent depressions, Virginia planters in the seventeenth and eighteenth centuries had been able to make comfortable livings, or even fortunes, primarily in tobacco; by 1750, in spite of the fact that prices had been relatively stable for more than a decade, prosperity based on one crop was largely a thing of the past. Virginians kept their plantations and maintained a lively interest in planting; tobacco was still the common medium of exchange; tobacco remained the chief topic of conversation and a leading cause for legislation. Planters were still planters; but, by the middle of the eighteenth century, virtually all of them had turned to an additional profession or business to supplement their income from tobacco. "I should be glad he would be fond of some business," wrote John Smith, of Middlesex County, about his son in an English school, "for planting alone is poor doings, but with other business it will answer very well."[3]

Professor Louis Morton in his *Robert Carter of Nomini Hall* has destroyed the stereotype of the Virginian as an idle gentleman.[4] Carter, the grandson of Robert "King" Carter, inherited vast tracts of lands and bought and patented even more. Yet his business interests extended far beyond his plantations. He was a producer of flour and bread, of salt and other household articles; he was part owner of the Baltimore Iron Works, a business that proved very profitable; he engaged in banking activities and speculated in stocks and bonds; and he sent his ships up and down the Chesapeake and Tidewater to buy produce of the lesser planters, produce which he held until he could sell it at a profit. Almost to a man, the members of the House of Burgesses after 1750 were planters and, like the master of Nomini, men of many economic interests. Generally speaking, their activities fall into six categories: land speculation, administration of estates, trade and commerce, manufacturing, county and colonial offices, law, and miscellaneous business. For Virginia as a whole, land speculation was the most important.

More than a third of the burgesses after 1750 are known to have been active land speculators, and it seems safe to assume that even more were engaged in land speculation. Men in every part of the colony patented land in the frontier counties which they tried to settle or sell. It was possible for an individual to patent lands—and many did—but the great tracts of land were granted to companies. At least four major organizations dealt with lands in the west: James Patton and Associates, The Greenbrier Company, The Loyal Company, and The Ohio Company.

The first known petition for land in the Mississippi Valley by a British subject was made by James Patton of Augusta County. He had already explored the Ohio region on his own initiative before he petitioned in April 1743 for 200,000 acres on the "three branches" of the Mississippi. Not knowing the attitude of the home government, Governor Gooch and the council refused the request because they said they feared such a grant would precipitate a conflict with the French. Word got around that Patton was interested in obtaining land in the region, and others began making overtures in the same direction. The council recognized him as a petitioner, however, and in April 1743 granted him 100,000 acres. He was promised that as soon as he had settled the required one hundred families on the tract, he would be given the second 100,000 acres. His grant was on Woods and Holston rivers. The Prestons, Christians, and Buchanans were his associates in the company.[5]

Speaker John Robinson was as interested in western lands as any other man in Virginia. As early as 1745, he had been successful in getting the council to grant him 100,000 acres on the Greenbrier River. Shortly thereafter, he had organized the Greenbrier Company to survey and sell the land. When in 1749 he learned that a huge tract had been given the Ohio Company, the members of the Greenbrier Company applied for an even greater tract, 800,000 acres, extending north and west from the end of the boundary line between Virginia and North Carolina. The new associates (of whom many had been in the Greenbrier Company) who applied for and received this large tract became known as The Loyal Land Company. Its initial membership of forty-five included at least eight burgesses: John Robinson (King and Queen County); Thomas Walker, Peter Jefferson, and Joshua Fry (Albemarle); Charles Barret (Louisa); John Baylor (Caroline); Peter Hedgman (Stafford); and John Thornton (Spotsylvania).[6] On the same day that the council made the grant to the Loyal Company (June 12, 1749) it made two other grants of great amounts to associates who seem not to have taken formal names. One of these was for 400,000 acres on New River to a group whose membership included Peyton Randolph (James City), Robert Tucker (Norfolk), Benjamin Waller (James City), Armistead Burwell (Williamsburg), and Edmund Pendleton (Caroline). The second tract, of 100,000 acres, "on the waters of the Mississippi" beginning at New River, went to a group of men among whom were Burgesses Bernard Moore (King William), George Carrington (Cumberland), and James Power (New Kent).

Of the formal organizations, the Ohio Company seems to have been the most important in the history of the colony. It began, however, under difficulties not experienced by the other companies. When the men who formed the organization applied to Governor Gooch late in 1747 for land, he refused to grant it. He sent the petition to the Board of Trade with vague comments to the effect that several men in partnership desired a grant of land west of the Alleghenies. Shortly thereafter, one of the Englishmen interested in the project, John Hanbury, laid before the Board a petition in which he requested land for the company and stated the purposes of the members—to settle the Ohio country and extend English trade among the Indians. Such a company, the petitioner emphasized, would be of great benefit to the empire in that it would strengthen the frontier and tap the rich fur trade then in the hands of the French. The Board wanted to know why the Governor of Virginia had not made the grant himself since he certainly had the power to do so. The inquiry led to an exchange of letters with Gooch, who excused his lack of action by saying that he feared the grant would cause trouble with the French at a time when the colony had hopes of securing a general peace in the region. The real reason seems to have been the fact that Gooch favored the Loyal Company and was reluctant to grant land to a rival company in the same general region. After months of consideration, the Privy Council, to which the matter had been referred by the Board of Trade, made the grant on September 2, 1748. Probably because the matter had been taken to England rather than settled the usual way, the Board of Trade stressed the importance of the grant to Britain in her rivalry for the Ohio country. The company received 200,000 acres in the general vicinity of the forks of the Ohio; it was specifically stated that the land was within the boundaries of Virginia. The company was to erect a fort and settle two hundred families on the tract. When that was done, it would be given an additional 300,000 acres nearby. On July 13, 1749 Governor Gooch made the grant to the company as he was instructed.[7]

Thomas Lee, president of the council, was one of the principals in the early maneuvering of the Ohio Company. His sudden death only a few months after the deal had been completed ended his part in this affair. Three of Lee's sons—Philip Ludwell, Thomas Ludwell, and Richard Henry—took over their father's interests. Robert Dinwiddie was not one of the original petitioners, but became an active member very shortly after he arrived as lieutenant governor. Few, if any, seemed to see any impropriety in the chief executive being an active land speculator. John Mercer of Marlborough and his three sons—George, James, and John Francis—were people of importance in the company. John was the secretary and George was sent to London as its agent in the early 1760's. James and George were burgesses. Three Washington brothers were in the Ohio Company: Lawrence, Augustine, and George. George William Fairfax, Lunsford Lomax, George Mason, and others made up a total membership of thirty-seven. A third of them were residents of England, but of the twenty-five who were Virginians, twenty were burgesses either at the organization of the company or sometime later. Of these twenty, nine were elevated to the council, as were the brothers of two others. As Kenneth Bailey, student of the Ohio Company, said, it would be difficult to assemble a more formidable roster of businessmen and politicians in colonial Virginia. Among all the companies interested in settling the west, there were upwards of fifty burgesses.[8]

131

The journals of the Council are replete with grants made to individuals, many of them burgesses—two hundred acres here, a thousand there, eight or ten thousand somewhere else, most of them in Albemarle, Augusta, Fincastle, and Lunenburg Counties. Many speculators and at least twenty-one burgesses were surveyors. Men like Peter Jefferson, Joshua Fry, and Thomas Walker, who were county surveyors, performed their public duties well but, at the same time, increased their own land holdings. Jefferson, for example, often came across unclaimed land in the course of his duties as surveyor for Goochland and entered patents for it. Joshua Fry did the same in Albemarle, and doubtless others did likewise in other counties. Robert "King" Carter had served his own interests in much the same way while he was agent for the Fairfaxes. Land that he had so acquired was in 1750 in the possession of his sons and his grandsons, many of them burgesses.

Planters undoubtedly patented some land for their future tobacco needs; some got land to provide amply for their children. There is abundant evidence, however, to show that most dealers in land got it to sell. All land companies, except the Loyal, apparently were required to settle a specific number of families as a part of their contract. Settling meant selling land to the newcomers. Patton brought many Scotch-Irish and Germans into the Valley. Hundreds of families reportedly were living on the Loyal Company lands by 1763.[9] Every issue of the *Virginia Gazette* offered land for sale, sometimes with improvements but more often in its natural state. Virgin lands were advertised as being especially suited for a particular crop such as tobacco, grain, hemp, or fruit, or for livestock. Sometimes a description of the natural beauty of the land or its accessibility to navigable streams was added as inducement to the buyer. In most cases agreeable terms of credit could be arranged. Since prices are never mentioned, they may have been determined by bargaining. Although sale prices are not known, the margin of profit must have been satisfactory. The cost of surveying and otherwise proving western lands was small and taxes negligible. Ohio Company land was quitrent free for ten years; and, while the record is not clear on this point, individuals and other land companies may have enjoyed the same exemption. Generally speaking, land seems to have become taxable only when it had a plantation established on it. The westward movement, which had been going on all the time since 1607, increased in momentum in the 1770's. The westward movement created a demand for western land, and Virginians had it for sale.

Well over ten percent of the burgesses were executors or administrators of estates. The terms were not synonymous, because an executor handled an estate for which its deceased owner had left a will; an administrator did the same service for an estate for which there was no will. Being either an executor or administrator was more than a final act of kindness for a departed friend or relative. Estates were often extremely complicated with entailed land, debts, mortgages, and multitudinous heirs—usually some of them minors. The lack of a banking system added to the complexity of estates. Tobacco merchants in London, Liverpool, and other British cities acted as bankers and purchasing agents for their Virginia clients. Since orders were sent to England to be paid out of a crop that was sold later, the sales and purchases did not often balance, and the debts and credits of an estate were not easily determined. The debts of an estate had to be paid first; then the terms of the will could be carried out. Many wills made cash bequests to daughters for marriage portions, to other relatives for various reasons, to charity schools, or even churches. There was always a shortage of cash in the colony, and few estates had the required amount. Consequently, in order to comply with the terms of the will, executors had to turn some of the real property into money. In many cases, land, plantations, or slaves were advertised for sale to settle an estate. Sometimes auctions were held and everything was sold at once; at other times, property was sold as buyers could be found. Under most circumstances, settling an estate became a very difficult and complicated business and often dragged on for years.

An example may be illuminating. Robert Carter Nicholas was the principal administrator of the estate of his brother-in-law, Edward Ambler, burgess from Jamestown at his death in 1768. Ambler was classed as wealthy; his father was a successful merchant and his mother was one of the wealthy Jaquelins, from whom he inherited considerable land. He had land on Jamestown Island, in Yorktown, and in Hanover and Caroline Counties; his slaves were numerous enough to maintain an adequate plantation economy. He had an extensive trade in the West Indies, especially with Barbados. Amber had an English education which, along with the training he received from his practical father, should have made him a good business man. He may have been, but at his death his affairs were hardly in first class order. In the years from 1768 to 1779, Nicholas carried on business for the estate to the value of £10,633.1.2. Much of the sum came from outstanding debts that Nicholas was able to collect. Nevertheless, he found the property difficult to administer, and a lawsuit resulting from alleged failure to account for sums due the estate was still before the courts in 1804. At Nicholas' death in 1780, his son Wilson Cary Nicholas followed in his footsteps as executor.[10]

When Speaker John Robinson died, he owed vast sums to the colony; settling his estate required much of Edmund Pendleton's time from 1766 until after 1800.[11] Pendleton handled other estates, too. On December 3, 1754, he was granted permission to be absent from the House of Burgesses

for the rest of the session in order to represent the estate of Richard Taliaferro at Hanover Court. Taliaferro had surveyed a four-thousand-acre tract
of land but died before he received a patent for it. Pendleton had to complete the transaction because the land was needed to pay the debts of the
estate.[12] Peter Jefferson, as administrator for the estates of his wife's father,
Isham Randolph, and her cousin, William Randolph, found it necessary
to move his family to Tuckahoe in Goochland County in order to look after
the estates properly.[13] When Jefferson died in 1757, John Nicholas and
Thomas Walker (and Peter Randolph of the Council, Thomas Turpin, and
John Harvie) administered his estate. Robert Carter Nicholas and Pendleton
were lawyers, but Jefferson, Walker, John Nicholas, and many others had
only a layman's knowledge of English law and colonial custom, which they
had learned as members of the county courts.

Without examining the accounts of specific estates, it is impossible to
say how much money executors and administrators made. Fees for most
offices and duties in the colony were set by the assembly, usually in terms
of tobacco. The laws regarding settlement of estates say simply that executors and administrators should be allowed "all reasonable charges and
disbursements which they shall lay out and expend for selling any estate
. . . and for collecting and receiving the debts" of the testator or intestate;
he was entitled to no other allowances from the estate. What was "reasonable" is not shown, but it must have been enough to make it worth the
trouble entailed in settling the estate.

A few burgesses had interests in iron mining and manufacturing. In
point of time, iron had engaged the attention of Virginians even before
tobacco. However, early attempts to develop iron mining had all ended in
failure. It was not until Governor Alexander Spotswood settled some forty
German refugees above the falls of the Rappahannock that the industry
became successful. These Germans came from the Sieg Valley, where iron
production was the leading industry, and they fitted beautifully into the
Governor's schemes for the frontier. He settled them at a place he named
Germanna (in honor of the refugees and his Queen), where he built a fort
and within a relatively short time started an iron industry. This was between
1714 and 1716.[14] Almost nothing is known about the project until 1732,
when William Byrd II of Westover made his leisurely horseback journey
into the back country, which he recounts in *A Progress to the Mines*.[15] From
it we get the most reliable information about the conditions of mining in
the colonial period.

Byrd visited four centers where both mining and iron manufacturing
were going on: Germanna, Holt's Forge near the Chickahominy River,
Spotswood's air furnace at Massaponax (some fifteen miles from Germanna), and the iron works of the Principio Company of Maryland on

the Stafford County plantation of Augustine Washington. The agent for the Spotswood company was Charles Chiswell, with whom Byrd had many lengthy conversations and from whom he learned much about the industry. After 1750, all these iron works were still in existence. Spotswood was dead, but his sons and grandsons continued for a time the interest of their ancestor. Chiswell's son John, burgess from Hanover and Williamsburg, inherited his father's shares; Chiswell's Mines became a landmark on the frontier. The son was a man of many affairs, with several plantations and an ordinary besides his iron industry, but he gave considerable time to the mines. Almost the last act of his life was a journey to his mines; he died by his own hand a few days after his return.

The career of Isaac Zane as ironmaster with furnaces in Frederick County and markets in Philadelphia, Hobbes Hole, and England has been discussed in another connection.[17] Edward Carter, Thomas Walker, and Alexander Trent were stockholders in the Albemarle Furnace Company (or Albemarle Iron Works as it was sometimes called), which played a useful part in supplying iron for the patriot cause.[18] William Cabell, Jr., of Albemarle and Amherst was an entrepreneur in the Hardware River Iron Company.[19] All mines, even the successful ones like Zane's in Frederick County, had their vicissitudes resulting from primitive methods, unskilled labor, low water, and unavoidable accidents. Some were in difficulties from the beginning, and investors lost their money. Lunsford Lomax of Caroline County dabbled in many projects, most of them unsuccessful. The most notable failure of the period was on the site of another failure—the one at Falling Creek on the James, where the Southhampton Adventurers had tried to operate mines from 1618 to 1622. Archibald Cary, scion of an energetic and distinguished family, inherited the site at Falling Creek from his father. For ten years he tried to produce pig iron ore there, but seems to have lost money from the start. He abandoned the iron works before the Revolution, but continued to operate successful flour mills, a ropewalk in Richmond, and mines of limonite ore in Buckingham County.[20]

Many others, like Cary, had more than one subsidiary enterprise. John Banister of Dinwiddie was one of several who had flour mills; Samuel Duval of Henrico had a fulling mill; Charles Carter of Lancaster produced ship biscuit in quantity; Charles Lynch of Bedford manufactured gunpowder and saltpetre. Horse breeding was a more genteel pastime than a business, yet numerous gentlemen made money breeding and racing horses. At least eight burgesses imported blooded stock between 1740 and 1775.[21] Several burgesses owned ordinaries and advertised them from time to time. George Fisher, in 1755 a recent arrival from England, found most of them dirty and inhospitable. Persons of influence would obtain a license, Fisher said, and then put the ordinary in the hands of some lazy person at a salary or a per-

135

centage of the sales. It was a common practice by which the proprietor avoided the reproach of being an ordinary keeper and the "scandal of what is there transacted" yet reaped the greater share of the profits.[22] Not all prominent men felt an ordinary was a reproach to self-respect. John Chiswell's Ordinary, sixteen miles from Williamsburg, was a landmark.[23] Yelverton Peyton of Stafford seems to have actually kept his ordinary.[24] Among the burgesses there were at least three physicians—Thomas Walker, William Cabell, and Christopher Wright of Princess Anne. Generally speaking, these miscellaneous enterprises were important only because they were necessary in a simple agricultural economy.

Merchants in Virginia were a well-defined group and certainly a significant one in the late colonial period. After 1750, thirty-two burgesses are known to have had stores that served the public. Some of them were retailers and others importers. Fifteen more had commercial connections with other parts of the colony, the West Indies, or England, doing business for more than themselves. In several instances, for men like the Tabbs and Tuckers, the Nortons, Nelsons, and Newtons, trade was the chief occupational concern; for others like Edward Carter, Israel Christian, and Benjamin Harrison, it was only one of many irons in the fire. The merchants were of different origins: John Norton, John Tabb of Amelia, and Israel Christian of Augusta were English born; Edward Ambler of Jamestown and Thomas Nelson, Jr. were sons of merchants who inherited the family business. The Tuckers of Norfolk were long-time residents of the colony.

There is no questioning the fact that merchants were both numerous and important in colonial Virginia. There are, however, a number of observations which indicate that they were considered of secondary political importance. The fifty or so merchants in the House naturally did their most effective work on the Committee of Trade, yet no merchant of first importance was ever the chairman. Lunsford Lomax of Caroline served in that capacity from 1752 until he was out of the House in 1775. Thereafter until the Revolution, Benjamin Harrison of Charles City was the chairman. Both Lunsford and Harrison had mercantile interests and Harrison had an extensive importing business and a large coastwide trade, but both were primarily planters and men-of-affairs. A second observation is that, except for Richard Adams of New Kent and Henrico, the Tabbs of Elizabeth City and Amelia, and Thomas Newton, Jr. of Norfolk, merchants served short terms in the House of Burgesses. In some measure this can be explained by natural causes that had nothing to do with the political scene. John Norton, for instance, left Norfolk for England in the 1760's, but he had already been out of the assembly some time. Robert Tucker, also of Norfolk, and Edward Ambler of Jamestown died in office. Thomas Nelson, Jr. was young when he was elected in 1761, but he served out the colonial period. It is not surprising that the three representatives of Norfolk Borough —William Aitchison, John and Joseph Hutchings—were merchants or that three of the eleven from Norfolk County and two of the four from York County followed trade. Nine of the merchants who made up the committee in 1770 to consider the state of trade in the colony were burgesses. Generally, the merchants who were burgesses were sympathetic to the colonists in the dispute with England; only Aitchison of Norfolk is known to have been openly hostile. Thomas Nelson, Thomas Newton, Fielding Lewis, and many others were notable patriots.

There was no stigma attached to trade in Virginia, as there was in England. John Smith of Middlesex, whose wife was a Jaquelin, one of the most aristocratic families of the whole colony, without apology hoped that his son would be attracted to commerce. Mrs. Smith's sister was the wife of Richard Ambler, a leading merchant of York. Ambler's son, Edward, married a Cary, one of the proudest families in the Tidewater. William Nelson, councilor and father of Thomas Nelson, Jr., was one of the great merchants; his wife was Lucy Burwell, half-sister to Robert Carter Nicholas and granddaughter to Robert "King" Carter. Richard Adams, leading merchant of Richmond, was an aristocrat with the best of family connections. The Moores of King William, the Carters, the Nortons, the Tuckers, the Randolphs, the Harrisons, the Beverleys, the Pages, the Blairs, and many other leading families were connected in some way with trade.

There is not a single shred of evidence to suggest that any of these families considered trade degrading. This attitude may result from several factors. In the first place, wealth was as basic as family for aristocracy. The Nelsons, the Tabbs, the Nortons, the Newtons, the Adamses, and the Harrisons were all successful merchants, with wealth that eclipsed the estates of many planters engaged primarily in agriculture. In the second place, many of the large planters with their own wharves, tobacco warehouses, ships, and trade with England were *ipso facto* merchants. In the early days direct handling of the crop had been necessary; and long established customs, the English credit system, and the navigation laws had continued it whether Virginians considered it commerce or not. As Governor Fauquier reported to the Lords of Trade in late 1764, "almost every man who has a numerous family becomes his own merchant and imports European goods for his own consumption . . . and are then to be dispersed among the importers who are settled on the various rivers of the colony. . . ."[25] In the third place, most merchants were also planters. The Nelsons lived in a solidly built Georgian brick house in Yorktown, and Richard Adams in one equally good on Adams Hill in south Richmond City, but both men owned plantations in which they maintained an active interest.

In the preceding pages, frequent mention has been made of colonial or county offices which burgesses held at one time or another: county clerk, sheriff, coroner, surveyor, tobacco inspector, customs collector, and naval inspector. That the Virginia gentleman was public minded is proved again and again by the fact that he served his county in many capacities. Most burgesses—perhaps the number ran in excess of three-fourths the total— held two offices: vestryman and justice of the peace. In these capacities they ran the affairs of their parishes and counties. Compensation from such services was purely honorary. There were other positions, however, which carried money (or tobacco) rewards that added materially to the income of the holder. Tobacco inspectors and sheriffs were ineligible to retain their seats in the General Assembly, and clerks, coroners, and others were required to resign when they accepted a "place of profit." But, as a matter of fact, in many instances the resigned burgess was returned to the House by his constituents and held both positions. Governor Dunmore, in the 1770's, thought too many county clerks sat in the assembly. All of them, he said, were considered principal people in their counties and had great influence with their constituents. Since the secretary, not the governor, appointed them, there was no way by which he could control their activities.[26] Other officers, like the sheriffs, returned to the House after their stint in the county had been completed.

Some—at least two—officials had a basic salary which was increased by fees for various duties. The clerks and sheriffs were paid 1200 pounds of tobacco annually by the county court for routine services for which there were no fees. Sheriffs, for example, did not collect a fee for holding elections. The fees of officers were set by law and varied according to the time required in executing the service and the seriousness of the cause. County clerks were allowed to collect 200 pounds of tobacco for attending a court for the examining of criminals, 150 pounds for recording deeds of lease and release, 50 pounds for probating a will, 30 pounds for copying a will, 10 for recording the age of a servant or slave, and only 5 for copying a writ.[27] The sheriff was allowed comparable sums: 250 pounds of tobacco for executing a condemned person, 50 pounds for summoning and impaneling a jury, 50 pounds for each day he attended at jury, 30 pounds for making an arrest, 20 pounds each for ducking, whipping, and imprisoning a criminal, and 15 for serving summons.[28] The coroner's chief duty was holding inquisitions over dead bodies, for which he was paid 133 pounds of tobacco for each case, but he could serve warrants (10 pounds), whip a servant (10 pounds), and perform a few other duties of law enforcement for which he was paid a few pounds of tobacco.[29] The surveyor, in addition to locating land which he might appropriate for himself and running lines for land companies and individuals, performed services for his county. For every survey, the law said, he was entitled to 500 pounds of tobacco plus 30 pounds for each hundred acres above the first thousand. Running a line between counties and parishes was a time-consuming task for which 1000 pounds was paid.[30] Naval officers for the rivers were paid 5 shillings for each time they boarded a ship.[31] How much these officers earned from their various offices is impossible to determine. It was, nevertheless, an amount sufficiently large to attract many office-seekers who frankly admitted the money motive.

By the Revolution, the most significant occupational group in the House of Burgesses was the lawyers. Speaker Peyton Randolph and 43 other known lawyers sat in the House from 1750 to 1774. The number included some of the best minds in the colony and many of the staunchest supporters of the American cause: Robert Carter Nicholas, George Wythe, Edmund Pendleton, Richard Bland, Patrick Henry, John Blair, Jr., Zachary Lewis, Thompson Mason, Thomas Jefferson, Dabney Carr, and many others whose names shine with a lustre nearly as bright. In the 1750–1774 period, lawyers held chairmanships of standing committees thirty times to thirty-seven for all other occupations. They were, furthermore, the leading (and often the majority) members of special committees to take into consideration grievances against England and to register protests against the home government. To cite two examples, of the eleven men on the committee to formulate resolutions against the Townshend Acts, Richard Bland was chairman and four other members—Nicholas, Pendleton, Blair, and John Page, Jr.—were lawyers. The Committee of Correspondence of 1773 had seven out of eleven members of the legal profession.

In the early years of the colony, lawyers had been looked on with disfavor and had been prohibited by law from pleading cases in court, but life had increased in complexity so much by the middle of the eighteenth century that the role of the attorney was recognized as important. Several laws, reenacted many times, set the fees that could be legally collected by lawyers.[32] Barristers (supposedly English trained) and attorneys who practiced before the General Court could collect higher fees than the lawyers who pleaded similar cases in the county courts. Barristers and attorneys could charge £1.1.6 for an opinion while a lawyer could collect only 10s for the same service. The former could get 50s. for a suit at common law and £5 for chancery suits, while lawyers could get only 15s. and 30s. for the same kind of suits. Doubtless much of the income of a lawyer came from collecting small debts for which he was allowed 7s.6d. each, and for witnessing surveys of land. For each day's attendance at a survey he was entitled to £1 and 6d. If threats to put the collection of debts into the hands of a lawyer are any indication of the amount of business the lawyers of the colony had, they were more than busy.

Thomas Jefferson and six of his fellow attorneys could complain that the fees allowed, if regularly paid, would barely compensate them for their incessant labors and reimburse their expenses and losses resulting from the neglect of their private business, but others found the profession a means of making a good living.[33] Arthur Lee, who gave up medicine for law, wrote his brother Richard Henry that the legal profession seemed to be the "most lucrative and honorable" profession open in 1771.[34] The existing fee books show that lawyers were doing very well financially. Paul Carrington, whose practice extended over at least eight counties and included many burgesses and other prominent Virginians, had fees in a ten-month period from January 1 to October 1, 1768, which totalled nearly £600. Patrick Henry's fees for 1765 totaled £425; in 1767 Thomas Jefferson collected £213.6.11 and carried on his books as owed him £307.18.11–1/2.[35]

From a very few physicians to many real estate dealers, the occupations represented in the Assembly ran the gamut of eighteenth century economic opportunities. Law, however, had become the profession in which the greatest gain, both in money and power, was to be had. However important these professions were to the financial welfare of the individuals, generally they were considered of secondary importance. The planter was the ideal in the colony and it seems that every burgess was a planter. Few advanced up the ladder of social, economic, or political success without being one. By the same token, few planters succeeded without an additional profession or income.

8

PATTERN OF POLITICS

The freeholders of Virginia elected 399 different individuals to serve them in the House of Burgesses from 1750 to 1774. These men represented sixty-one counties and four boroughs: the college, Jamestown, Norfolk, and Williamsburg. The boroughs and forty-six of the counties were in existence by the February 1752 meeting of the General Assembly. The remaining fifteen counties were created later by acts of the assembly; three of them, Berkeley, Dunmore, and Fincastle, as late as 1772. The forty-six counties elected three hundred fifty-three men; the other fifteen, sixty-eight; and the four boroughs, seventeen. The counties in existence in 1752 elected on the average 7.67 burgesses; the boroughs, 4.25.[1] There was a wide range, however. Warwick had a total of only three in the whole period under consideration; York and Gloucester had four each; Richmond and Prince George, five; but Norfolk County had twelve and Surry thirteen. These figures raise a number of questions. What made this wide difference? Did the rate of turnover conform to a geographical pattern? How much of this change was due to death, to retirement from office, to positions that prohibited keeping a seat in the assembly at the same time, or how many, on the other hand, were defeated at the polls? Were there political factions that help to account for the changes?

Only five men had the distinction of representing their counties for the whole 1752–1774 period: Richard Bland of Prince George, whose legislative career began in 1742; Dudley Digges of York County; Benjamin Harrison of Charles City; William Harwood of Warwick; Edmund Pendleton of Caroline; and Lemuel Riddick of Nansemond.[2] These counties are all in the Tidewater area where, generally speaking, politics had attained a stability not yet reached in some of the newer sections. Every other burgess had his term in the House shortened in some way.

141

There were a limited number of events that could terminate the service of a burgess in the assembly: he could die; he could accept one of three or four "offices of profit" that made him ineligible for the House; he could be defeated at the polls; he could decline to run; or he could be expelled. Let us first eliminate those cases which do not indicate any partisan activity.

There are three cases of expulsion in our period. William Ball of Lancaster County was expelled and made incapable of sitting in the House for the rest of his life for "uttering forged and counterfeit notes, knowing them to be so."[3] Thomas Prosser of Cumberland was given the same treatment for a variety of shady dealings which included antedating deeds and forging the sheriff's name to a summons for a jury.[4] William Clinch in Surry County was removed from office and forever debarred from the Assembly because of his open threats, and actual assault with a loaded pistol, on the life of Burgess John Ruffin.[5] In all three cases the alleged crimes were committed before the men were elected to the House. Since the crimes of Prosser and Ball could not be considered a breach of privilege, we must conclude that, however lenient the House may have been about other matters, there were certain kinds of dishonorable acts that it could not condone.

A detailed study of more than half the counties in Virginia reveals that, except for expulsion, every other possible reason for changing burgesses occurred in every part of the colony. Death was no respecter of persons or places, and all sections of the colony had to replace deceased members. Probably more changes came because the incumbent, like George Mason of Fairfax County, chose not to run again, but information here is very elusive.

There were a few recorded cases of unanimous election,[6] but the number is very small in comparison to the elections in which there were several candidates. The exact number of burgesses who were replaced at the polls will never be known because of the absence of election information for many counties. Nevertheless, there is abundant material in election returns from fifteen counties and testimony in many contested elections which point to a very lively opposition in every part of the colony. A few instances will illustrate.

Accomac County on the Eastern Shore is good to examine because there are both election returns and the report of a contested election. At the election of 1752, ten people offered themselves as candidates, five of whom can be considered as serious contenders for office. The votes for the five stood: Mr. Edmund Allen, 300; Major George Douglas, 215; Colonel Ralph Justice, 201; Mr. John Wise, 122; and William Andrews, 118. At the 1755 election, six candidates received between 129 and 260 votes each, plus three who polled a scattering few. Three years later (June, 1758) ten candidates had a total of 975 votes. Ten years later (November, 1768) there were three leading candidates. Ralph Justice was defeated at the polls in 1758 by Thomas Parramore who, in turn, was defeated by James Henry in 1771.[7]

Northumberland in the Northern Neck had fewer candidates than Accomac; but, at every one of the eight elections (three of which were by-elections), there were from one to three candidates besides the victors. George Ball and Samuel Eskridge made several attempts at the polls before they were elected, and Ball continued to be a candidate after he was defeated.

In Fairfax County, where George Washington, George Mason, and the Wests lived, the situation was somewhat different. No incumbent was defeated at the polls. Every one of the five burgesses who were replaced can be accounted for. George Mason, Gerald Alexander, and George William Fairfax did not run after a single term in the House, and two men died in office. John West and George Washington represented the county continuously from 1758 and 1765, respectively. All the burgesses were neighbors and friends. One has only to read the diaries of Washington and the correspondence of Mason and others to realize how close they were to one another; they hunted together, managed Pohick Church, shared the same dancing teacher for their children, traveled together, and visited one another regularly. There may have been an unwritten agreement that no one in the inner circle would stand for an office until the incumbent voluntarily gave it up. Or in reverse, the incumbent may have persuaded another of his group to run so he could retire to private life.[8]

This account makes the political scene in Fairfax deceptively simple. No one was turned out at an election, but that was not because other candidates were lacking. At one election, for example, William Ellzey lacked two votes of having the same number that the victor, George William Fairfax, had. At the 1765 election, one John Posey polled 131 votes and there were others who received a few votes.[9]

Spotsylvania County lies on the border between the Tidewater and Piedmont. At the 1752 election, there were five candidates; in 1755, four leading ones and three more trailing with a few votes; in 1769, a least four; in 1771, three leading ones. The story for Prince William, Cumberland, Halifax, Surry, and many, in fact almost all, of the other counties is the same—there was an opposition that tried for office and often won.

At the beginning of the chapter, the question was raised as to whether geography made any difference in the number of representatives. The answer is a qualified yes. There are several exceptions, but generally speaking, the frontier and commercial counties had a greater turnover in burgesses than the planting counties. Augusta on the frontier had eight, Frederick in

143

the same western region eleven, Culpepper ten, Albemarle twelve, Hampshire ten. Counties where there were shipping centers with large total representation were Norfolk with twelve, Surry thirteen, Amelia eight, and Spotsylvania twelve.

Candidates were defeated at the polls, but there is no evidence that parties, in the modern sense, or even strong factions influenced the outcome. The record is simply lacking about this. To be sure, men out of office tried to get in; parents exerted influences in behalf of sons and sons-in-law; friends supported friends, and candidates "joined interests" when they electioneered together, but that is hardly party activity. We may dismiss the influence of factions in elections for lack of evidence, but the question of factions per se in the colony remains to be answered. Did the colony have organized parties, political factions, or even important tensions that influenced the course of events? The answers are not easy. That Virginians differed among themselves does not need to be demonstrated again here. Whether differences were clearly defined or permanent will have to be determined by examining the available record.

There was an incident in the House that suggests more than a rivalry between the two representatives from Louisa County. Thomas Walker, one of the burgesses, had had a contract to provision the Virginia troops on the frontier. On the evening of the November 1758 Louisa County Court, Thomas Johnson, the other member, had several guests at his house. According to witnesses, he criticized Walker's conduct as a contractor and found fault with matters "concerning the proceedings of the House of Burgesses in the session held the September before." During the conversation, Johnson said that Mr. Walker had cheated the county out of eleven hundred pounds. On being asked how it was possible for that gentleman to "impose upon" as many people as the House of Burgesses consisted of "and yet not only continue in office, but be courted so to do," Johnson replied, "you know little of the plots, schemes, and contrivances that are carried on there; in short, one holds the lamb while the other skins. Many of the members are in places of trust and profit, and others want to get in, and they are willing to assist one another in passing their accounts. . . . It would surprise any man to see how the country's money was squandered away." To illustrate the trading of the votes and influence, Johnson cited the case of the clerk's salary. When the matter came to a vote, Thomas Walker strode "through the Burgesses and nodded to his creatures or partisans on each side who followed him out of the House," thus voting with him. Johnson also received a nod but disregarded it. But "being particularly beckoned to" he went out and "was solicited by Mr. John Randolph, the clerk, and many of the members to be for the largest sum . . . proposed for the clerk's salary." Johnson refused, but the measure passed anyway.[10]

144

The words "party" and "faction" were not unknown to colonial Virginians. The governors had several occasions to use them. Dinwiddie, for example, complained that "divisions and parties subsist in the House of Burgesses," yet he was unable to bring them to reason. Some months later when the Pistole Fee question seemed more favorable to him, he reported that he hoped for a successful administration if the legislators did not fall into parties. Fauquier had several occasions to note a party of opposition. For Landon Carter, "the Party" was composed of Robinson followers who supported the French and Indian War.[11] The Reverend John Craig, for another example, recorded in his autobiography that there were two parties in his congregation at Tinkling Spring Church led by James Patton and John Lewis, each of whom wanted to be "highest in commission." This may have been primarily a church squabble with rivalry for church office, but apparently it extended to secular offices as well.[12] Governor Fauquier clearly saw a division in the House of Burgesses over a duty on imported slaves. "The contest on this occasion," he wrote the Board of Trade, "is between the old settlers who have bred large quantities of slaves and would make a monopoly of them by a duty, which they hoped would amount to a prohibition, and the rising generation who want slaves and don't care to pay the monopolists for them at the price they have lately bore which was exceedingly high."[13] At the time the House had to choose a new agent, the James River "interests" were opposed to the Northern Neck men on who should be the man chosen for the place.[14] By the outbreak of the Revolution, Landon Carter could see that it had been an unwise policy to subdivide the western counties, thus multiplying the influence of that "untrustworthy" section in the House.[15] Just prior to the 1771 election, a correspondent of the *Gazette* signing himself "No Party Man" urged fellow citizens to go to the polls to elect gentlemen who would be most likely to "preserve inviolate the sacred deposit" which the freeholders entrusted to them.[16] These are random references to incidents and opinions which seemed to have had little more than temporary and local importance and in which terms like "party" and "division" are used very loosely.

Support for this point of view comes from Francis Fauquier. In spite of his comments about the opposition of factions, the governor was of the opinion that there were no permanent divisions. Writing to the Board of Trade, he said, "Whoever charges them with acting upon a premeditated concerted plan, don't know them, for they mean honestly, but are expedient mongers in the highest degree."[17] It is the studied opinion of two modern Virginia scholars, Thad W. Tate and Jack P. Greene, that Fauquier was correct.[18]

As we have seen earlier, there were a number of issues about which

145

Virginians felt very strongly and measures to which they objected vigorously. There was difference of opinion about each of these major events. In some instances we know who was on which side, but not often. The eighteenth-century practice of not recording votes in the *Journals* and of writing letters to the editor under a classical or patriotic pseudonym keep us from identifying more than a very few.

Take the Parsons' Cause. The burgesses were frankly divided over it. The great majority of them were faithful members of the Established Church and at the same time were representatives of the people. When the Rev. John Camm sued York parish for arrears in his salary, the House appointed a committee of Peyton Randolph, Richard Bland, George Wythe, Robert Carter Nicholas, and Dudley Digges to defend its cause.[19] It can be supposed that these men shared the majority view of the assembly about the Parsons' Cause, or they would not have been selected for the committee. On other questions they would take opposite sides, which suggests an absence of any fixed alliances.

A series of problems, however, came to a head around the period of the Stamp Tax and provided the strongest evidence of the period that anything like a party existed. Probably at no time before the outbreak of the Revolutionary War was Virginia faced with so many major problems as it was in the years 1765 and 1766. First, the Stamp Act brought on a crisis in May 1765, when Patrick Henry, aided and abetted by certain "hot and giddy" members, offered his resolves. No one has been able to determine who besides the Flemings and the Johnsons were among the twenty or more burgesses who voted with Henry. On the other hand, we know that Peyton Randolph, Speaker John Robinson, George Wythe, Edmund Pendleton, and Robert Carter Nicholas opposed the "hot and violent" resolutions. Ill-feeling over the act might have been forgotten in a reasonable length of time had it not been for subsequent events, some of them directly connected with the stamp affair and others not at all. The bitter quarrel between the Mercers and the Lees, the death of Speaker John Robinson, and the bloody murder of Robert Routlidge by John Chiswell came almost simultaneously. The governor recognized this state when he wrote:

The Assembly will meet on the last date of the General Court, which I fear will be a very warm one, the Country differ in many points which are to come before it, some of them not of public concern. But the blood of the people is soured by their private distresses, and party feuds will run high.[20]

A difference of the first order developed between Richard Henry Lee and the Mercers over the sale of stamps. George Mercer, the colony's only stamp distributor, was the son of John Mercer of Marlborough, a leading lawyer, uncle of George Mason and one of the most vocal men of his time.

George Mercer, one of two sons who had served gallantly under Joshua Fry in the French and Indian War, came out of the army still young and badly in debt. Apparently trained to no peacetime profession, he proposed to visit the "Court of Britain," seeking some kind of appointment. He went with the approval and good wishes of the governor, the council, and the burgesses, who were "pleased to recommend him to their sovereign in the most genteel terms" and desired the colony's agent to assist him in every possible way.[21] While he was on a trip to Ireland, the Stamp Act was passed and his friends, who were looking for some opportunity for Mercer, were quick to seize for him the job as collector in his home colony. He had been away from America twenty-two months when the appointment was made and had been out of communication with it for several months before he sailed for Virginia. Bringing the stamps for his own colony and Maryland and apparently anticipating no friction, he landed at Hampton on October 30. Instead of a welcoming committee, a hostile crowd was on hand to meet him, demanding that he resign immediately. Under the protection of Governor Fauquier, who had joined the crowd, he was able to delay the answer until the following day. Impressed by the apparently united hostility against the tax and the reported organized opposition in King William, Loudoun, and Westmoreland Counties, he lost no time in giving up his office.[22]

Mercer's resignation only lulled the furor. It was an open secret that the man responsible for the effigies, the Westmoreland Resolves, and other more or less systematic opposition was Richard Henry Lee, burgess from Westmoreland. To the Mercers, Lee was a johnny-come-lately; they had copies of letters proving that Lee had been a very active and even impatient applicant for the position that young Mercer received. When Lee attacked George in the *Gazette* for his unpatriotic activities, the father, whose emotional boiling point was not high at any time, exploded.[23] In a long series of exchanges in the newspaper, Mercer charged Lee with opposing the Stamp Act only after he learned that his application had been refused, pointing out that at the May session that passed the resolves, Lee had been conspicuously absent. John Mercer believed he was waiting for an "important" communication to arrive from England. Lee could not deny that he had been an applicant, but he excused himself on the grounds that, when he applied, the full import of the bill had not reached America. As soon as he realized the full meaning, he said, he withdrew his application. Lee obviously was on the defensive, and the elder Mercer did not overlook the opportunity to attack his vague references to the time at which he made and withdrew his application.[24] As early as August, 1764, Mercer pointed out, the House had discussed the measure in a Committee of the Whole, and Lee knew good and well what it meant for the colony. This started out as a tilt between Lee and George Mercer, but many others joined in the fracas and their verbal exchanges filled pages and pages of the newspaper for more than three months. Each side drew defenders, but the custom of writing under a pseudonym prevents us from knowing who they were. The Corbins and Francis Lightfoot Lee we know were on Lee's side, John Randolph on the side of the Mercers.[25] This quarrel was essentially between people and not over principles, as is further evidenced by the fact that John Mercer supported the Westmoreland Resolves at the same time he was defending his son.[26]

Meanwhile, other Virginians were having troubles of their own. Speaker John Robinson was without doubt the most powerful man in the whole colony. He had been a member of the House since 1727 and its speaker since 1738. As speaker, he was the most influential member in the House of Burgesses. He had the final word in questions relating to the rules of the House; he appointed the committees and named their chairmen.[27] Robinson filled the office with great dignity and outward efficiency. "When he presided the decorum of the House outshone that of the British House of Commons, even with Onslow at their head," wrote Edmund Randolph. "When he propounded a question, his comprehension and perspicuity brought it equally to the most humble and the most polished understanding. When he pronounced the rules of order, he convinced the most reluctant."[28] He was also treasurer, handling all the money raised by local taxation. He was one of the most popular men in the colony, "the darling of the people," but also a loyal friend of the king and his servant, Governor Fauquier, who found him indispensable in carrying out the affairs of his office. In fact, the governor considered him so essential to his success that during Robinson's life he refused, even in the face of strong pressure from the Board of Trade, to make any move to separate the two offices, being sure that, if he did, Robinson would be alienated and any measures the royal government wished passed doomed.[29] He was probably right. Landon Carter, no friend of the speaker's, recorded in his diary that once the speaker lost a motion in the Committee of the Whole where he was accustomed to have his own way and "he gave such proofs of his resentment that no stone was unturned to please the worthy gentleman."[30] His father, John Robinson, Sr., had been a member of the council for many years and was president when he died suddenly in 1749. As councilor, the elder Robinson was a member of the upper house, the General Court, and the executive body at the same time that his son was burgess, speaker, and treasurer.

Speaker Robinson's position was further strengthened by his family connections. His uncle Christopher Robinson, who had supervised the English education of the father, was a bishop. His mother was the daughter of Robert Beverley, the historian, and his three wives were daughters of prominent families; Bernard Moore of Chelsea and John Chiswell of Hanover and Williamsburg were his last two fathers-in-law.[31] A man of great wealth, refined tastes, and devotion to the king, Robinson was acknowledged as the leader of the Tidewater aristocracy. For the eleven years between 1738 and 1749, it would be difficult to find more concentration of power than was in the hands of the two Robinsons. Judicious use of his power had made it possible for the Speaker to crush or eliminate such opposition as arose, and he was running the colony like a well-oiled machine. Shortly after his death, the public began to see what he had been using for oil. His death on May 11, 1766, although universally lamented, revealed one of the worst financial scandals in all Virginia history. The treasurer was in default of a huge sum, reported at figures varying from £60,000 upwards and finally proving to be in excess of £109,000.[32]

Virginia like every other colony was always in need of money. This need had been made more acute by the exigencies of the French and Indian War; keeping troops in the field had required more cash than the treasury afforded. The assembly had attempted to meet the emergencies by issuing paper money in anticipation of taxes, money that was to be withdrawn at specified times and burned. Whether out of sympathy for the hard-pressed planters, as his friends claimed, or for whatever reason, Robinson had not destroyed the notes; he had loaned the money out again, most of it on account only. There was no record of many transactions in the treasury papers.[33]

The list of debtors to the Robinson estate sounds like a roster of Tidewater elite. William Byrd headed it with a debt of more than ten thousand pounds. Carter Braxton, Lewis Burwell, Charles Carter, Jr., Archibald Cary, Bowler Cocke, Jr., Harry Gaines, Benjamin Grymes, Bernard Moore, and Ralph Wormeley owed the next largest sums, all of them more than five hundred pounds each. Hundreds owed smaller amounts. Many of these men were closely related to Robinson and seem to have formed a closely-knit society. Was it a party? In a sense, yes, for these were the men who for long years had held offices in the assembly. With the death of Robinson, however, the Robinson party, if it can be so designated, lost its leader and declined in prestige.

Calamities seldom came singly even in colonial times; before Robinson had been in his grave five months, his father-in-law, John Chiswell, committed suicide and thereby emphasized the existence of a Robinson party.

John Robinson's third wife was Susan Chiswell; her father had been burgess from Hanover and then later from Williamsburg where the family was living in the summer of 1766. Three weeks after Robinson's funeral, Chiswell killed a Scotch trader by the name of Robert Routlidge in a drunken brawl. On June 3 the two men met at Mosby's Tavern at Cumberland Courthouse and spent the biggest part of the day drinking together. Toward evening when both of them were "much in liquor" and Chiswell was swearing freely, trouble began; just who was responsible is difficult to say. Allegedly, Chiswell called Routlidge "a fugitive rebel, a villain who came to Virginia to cheat and defraud men of their property and a Presbyterian fellow." Annoyed by Chiswell's insults and "important manner," the Scot threw a glass of wine in the Virginian's face; Chiswell returned with a bowl of toddy. With a room full of bystanders looking on, Chiswell ordered his servant to bring his sword, and in spite of attempts to stop him, ran through Routlidge with his sword. Whether Chiswell lunged at the trader or Routlidge flung himself at Chiswell and in that way received his mortal wound, the witnesses were never quite agreed. But the fact remained that the Scot was dead and Chiswell's sword was dripping blood. The sheriff of Cumberland County, Jesse Thomas, was called and clapped Chiswell in jail like any common criminal, refusing him bail. This was a case of murder which could be tried only in General Court. As the sheriff was conducting the prisoner to Williamsburg, three members of the Court met them on the road and, without examining the sheriff's papers in the case, took custody of Chiswell on the spot and freed him on bail. The judges were John Blair, William Byrd, and Presley Thornton. This action caused more public disapproval than any local news that hit the *Gazette* in the whole colonial period. Blair defended the three judges, citing similar cases which had been deemed bailable; but many people felt that had Chiswell been any ordinary citizen and not a leading aristocrat and the father-in-law of the late speaker, he would not have received such lenient treatment. Chiswell went on a tour of his western mines but was back on September 11. No doubt unwilling to face the ignominy of a trial for murder, he died at his own hands just before the meeting of the General Court. The *Gazette* of October 17, in announcing his death, stated simply that "On Wednesday last about two o'clock in the afternoon, died at his house in this city, Colonel John Chiswell, after a short illness. The cause of his death by the judgement of the physician upon oath were nervous fits, owing to a constant uneasiness of the mind.[34]

Even before the treasurer's default, the governor was advocating separation of the speaker's and treasurer's posts.[35] A great many people thought the union of the two offices placed too much power in the hands of one person. Robert Carter Nicholas was a mild man but also a moral man with one of the strongest consciences in public office. The misuse of huge sums of public money riled his usually placid nature, and he criticized Robinson openly and severely.[36] He led the fight to have the offices divided as the only way to prevent recurrence of similar incidents.

The events of 1765–1766 tended to separate the friends from the critics of John Robinson. Nicholas, of course, led the latter group joined by the Lees, Patrick Henry, and others unnamed who expressed their views in letters to the *Gazette*. Bernard Moore, Benjamin Grymes, "Metriotes," "Honest Buckskin," and others joined the fray in support of the late treasurer. Edmund Pendleton became the chief executor of Robinson's estate; it took the best years of his life to settle it and repay the treasury. During his lifetime the debtors to the estate were kept secret, but it may be assumed that William Byrd, Charles Carter, Jr. of King George, the Mercers of Stafford, Lewis Burwell, and the Cockes were his partisans since they were heavily indebted to him.

As far as the record tells us, there was no such thing as a formal party. There was, however, an unmistakable coterie of friends who held the best offices in the colony. They looked to the Speaker as the leader, and he helped them out with currency that the law said was to be burned when it was redeemed by taxes. Robinson's friends (both contemporary and present-day) explain the unauthorized loans he made to his friends as growing out of genuine compassion for the distressed. Anyone, they say, regardless of political sympathies, could have borrowed from him. That may be true, but the fact still remains that the Lees, Patrick Henry, and other known opponents were not indebted to the treasury beyond very small sums (which could have been taxes) and that the greater part of the debts were owed by the Tidewater planters. The planters of King William County alone owed more than one-fourth the total amount. In later years, Thomas Jefferson recognized the existence of a faction led by Robinson and other Tidewater planters, and saw in Robinson's death and subsequent discredit the end of one era and the beginning of a new one led by Henry, the Lees, and himself.

The Robinson affair indicates there was one fairly permanent political group. All other alignments were transitory and shifting. Richard Henry Lee is the classic example; one year he was an applicant for the job as stamp collector, and the next he was one of the leading foes of the Stamp Act itself. Nicholas, Peyton Randolph, and George Wythe opposed Henry's resolves, although they had been on Henry's side in the Parsons' Cause. Nearly all burgesses signed the non-importation associations, yet differed when enforcing the rules of the associations. This led to a real rift with England, dividing the burgesses into "worthy gentlemen" and "bill-of-rights gentry."

One is led to the conclusion that, except for the Robinson faction, differences and alliances within the colony were personal, local, and temporary. It was not until Virginians began debating questions regarding the relationship between the colony and mother country that a real and lasting cleavage appeared.[37]

151

9

CONCLUSION

On May 26, 1774, Governor Dunmore called the General Assembly before him and dissolved it. The incident that caused the governor to fly into a rage and order the assemblymen home was some resolves inspired by the Boston Port Act. Word had reached Williamsburg on the 17th that General Gage was in Boston and that on June 1 the harbor would be closed. Feeling that the time had come for some action, Thomas Jefferson, the two Lees (Richard Henry and Francis Lightfoot), Patrick Henry, and a few others drew up some resolves setting aside that day as a day of prayer and fasting.

Other governors had dissolved other assemblies, but there was an air of finality about this dissolution. People in every part of the colony, both in and out of the assembly, were much concerned over the turn of events.[1] Dunmore, unwilling to give opportunity for the House to enter into other violent resolves, might have dispensed with calling any other assembly had it not been for the urging of the Council. No colonial legislation had been passed at the May session and, since the fee bill and "other useful laws" had expired and the Indians were threatening the frontier settlements, some relief was imperative. Very reluctantly, the Governor issued writs for a new election, which was held in July. The new assembly met, but affairs were far from normal. Assemblies in the past had rebelled; this one did nothing. It merely marked time. For example, it debated at great length and in great detail the message from the Governor; it found repeated reasons for tabling motions, or sending bills back to committees. In short, it used all the delaying and time consuming tactics that a veteran lawmaking body finds useful for its purposes. The House had turned itself into a revolutionary body; and, from 1774 on, its chief purposes seem to have been hampering the governor and furthering its own claim to rights. The House of Burgesses on which Vir-

152

ginians had prided themselves died on May 26, 1774, to be reborn in the legislature of the sovereign state.

In summary, what kind of men held membership in the House of Burgesses that ended thus, and what kind of body was it? With few exceptions, burgesses were to the manner born; a dozen or two had arrived from England without wives but soon married into leading families and thereby stepped into ruling circles. A few men like Allan Howard of Albemarle had risen from obscure backgrounds by their own efforts. In every known instance, men in that class had acquired large amounts of land from the crown and had become men of substance. Having become men of local weight, they were made gentlemen justices, an office that gave them extensive experience in handling the cases before the county court; they also became acquainted with freeholders from all parts of the county. The House of Burgesses was the next step in the political ladder, and few reached the House without first having held a place in the county court.

Burgesses did not give up their places on the county commissions when they were sent to Williamsburg. On the contrary, most of them held county office throughout their lives. Many of them took their turns as sheriff; twenty or more were clerks of the county court; and an undetermined number held offices (such as collector of customs or naval officer on one of the rivers) in the bounty of the king; almost all of them were vestrymen and church wardens in their parishes.

They were men of education. Many of the leaders like the Carters, the Randolphs, the Fairfaxes, the Lees, George Wythe, and Thomas Nelson were educated in England. Others like Robert Carter Nicholas, the Harrisons, some of the Cockes, Dabney Carr, and Thomas Jefferson were trained at the College of William and Mary. Still others like Patrick Henry and George Washington were given the rudiments of an education in private schools run, very likely, by the local minister. Many burgesses had libraries, bought books from the printer in Williamsburg, and ordered others from England. Whether they read them or merely used them to adorn the shelves is another question, but judging from the frequent allusions to the classics and current works, we must judge that articulate men like the Carters and the Lees were well read.[2] A surprising number of books they owned and read were on law and religion.

Nearly all the burgesses were members of the Anglican Church; some of them were militantly orthodox, yet almost to a man they were opposed to the establishment of an American episcopate. The issue came to a head in the summer of 1771 when a few "mistaken" clergymen introduced a bill that would lead to the appointment of an American bishop. The burgesses considered it a measure by which much disturbance, great anxiety, and apprehension would certainly take place among His Majesty's faithful Ameri-

153

can subjects who, like Richard Bland, felt they could "embrace the doctrine of the mother church without approving her hierarchy."[3] Although there is no record of it, nonconformists were undoubtedly more disturbed by the prospects of closer ecclesiastical control than were their Anglican brethren. Such a move, they feared, would end participation of Presbyterians and other non-Anglicans in the government of the colony.

Burgess elections went to men of the gentry, but only to those who had an appeal to the general public. A representative of the people could not expect to be reelected unless he pleased his constituents by service in the House or command their respect as a person. Constituents on the whole may have been of low class and "vulgar" but they held in their hands the power to elect or defeat, and hence they had to be treated with some deference, at least at election time. At the polls (or during the previous campaign) the average freeholder enjoyed an attention he received at no other time, with gentlemen nodding to one and all, treating freely, and shaking hands with those whom they scarcely noticed ordinarily.

There was social stratification in colonial Virginia; gentlemen were gentlemen, and servants were servants, with many gradations between. There is no evidence that the lower classes were restive under the domination of the ruling planter oligarchy. During the Revolution, a traveler in the colony observed that, before the war, the spirit of equality was less prevalent there than in other provinces.[4] From the meager evidence, it appears that "the spirit of independency" of the late colonial and early war years developed into notions of equality only during the war. Bearing arms in the American cause seems to have made the "country peasants" think they were on equal footing with their neighbors. The electoral system had inherent democratic characteristics; but, in the colonial period, no one expected the social order to be upset at the polls.

Such, in brief, were the men who represented their counties and boroughs in the House of Burgesses. The House itself was a relatively small body which never had more than 126 members. The total number was never present at any one time; and, therefore, the House appeared even smaller than it was. It was an intimate group for the additional reason that most of its members were closely related. It was a strong body, rapidly becoming the most active part of the government. Virginians could deplore the imbalance of their government which, in their eyes, gave the executive the most power to the hurt of the popularly elected legislative body; but, as a matter of fact, the hands of the governor were tied by local custom, special concessions to the county courts, and agreements with officers like the secretary of the colony. The governor and the council spent most of their time confirming appointments and consenting to measures that had been decided by someone else. After 1750, the House initiated every piece of legislation that was passed by the Assembly; the only two measures which orginated with the council after that date were settled in the negative without so much as a look into their merits.

For the most part, divisions within the House were transitory. The only exception of any consequence was the faction that centered around Speaker John Robinson. Whatever hold it had on the colony was broken by Robinson's death in the summer of 1766. The scandal that was consequently revealed in the treasury dimmed any glow that remained about the role of the late speaker. It is difficult to explain why political alliances were rare and of little consequence. The burgesses were a closely knit ruling oligarchy, but blood relationship has never been a guarantee of harmony. A more plausible answer is that their economic interests were essentially the same. Occupationally all of them were planters with at least one subsidiary interest; any measure that affected one affected all in much the same way. A third possible solution for the general lack of permanent divisions is the nature of business with which the assembly was concerned. An examination of all the laws (including those which were disallowed by the British government) from 1752 to 1774 shows that about sixty percent of them were of a local nature, providing for warehouses at certan locations, bounties on crows and wolves in counties where they were a nuisance, dissolution of vestries, sale of glebe lands, changes in court days, docking entails from land so that it might be sold, and other matters that concerned no one but the people directly involved. Of the bills pertaining to the colony as a whole, many (probably a fourth) were reenactments of laws which, like the fee bill, had time limits. Many others were to amend faulty parts of the militia and defense laws. Since the vote on very few measures is recorded in the *Journals,* there is no way of checking on how burgesses voted, or by what majorities. With most of the business of a local nature, a form of logrolling was required to pass any of it; with most of the public measures of a nature so general that few could object to them, there was little place for political alignments. In fact, the measures over which Virginians differed most markedly were not measures of their own making, but those imposed by the British Parliament, involving the relationship between colony and mother country.

It need not be emphasized here that Virginia furnished more than her proportionate share of leaders for the cause of independence. The reasons for this lie in the political experience of the colony. Most of the planter-gentry had a strong sense of family and community responsibility; the community, of course, was not only the parish but also the county, the colony, and the nation. Some public figures may have been prompted to exert leadership because of their small faith in the wisdom of the "vulgar" masses; nevertheless, they recognized their obligations to make laws that applied equally

155

to all. Virginia had been accustomed to responsible government for generations; the House of Burgesses was her House of Commons. Any measure
designed to reduce the role of the colonial government met with hearty and
remarkably united opposition. When resolves and petitions no longer served
their purposes, independence was the only logical step left. By training and
practical experience they were ready for it.

APPENDIX I

County Polls for Burgesses
with Candidates and their Votes

Accomac

January 30, 1752 — Deeds, 1746–47, pp. 367–370

Mr. Edmund Allen	300
Maj. George Douglas	215
Col. Ralph Justice	201
Mr. John Wise, Jr.	122
William Andrews, Jr.	118
Daniel Cutler	4
Smith Snead	1
Thomas Wishart	1
Col. Edmund Scarbrough	7
Thomas Teackle	2 (1)
	971

December 6, 1755 — Ibid., pp. 623–629

Edmund Allen	260
Charles West	188
James Rule	129
Ralph Justice	190
Coventon Corbin	140
Southey Simpson	163
Col. Thomas Parramore	4
Col. Thomas Hall	2
John Wise, Jr.	4
	1080

June, 1758 — Deeds, 1757–70, pp. 50–56

Col. Thomas Parramore	215
Ralph Justice	177
Edmund Allen	241
Coventon Corbin	141
James Rule	77
Henry Scarbrough	71
Southey Simpson	39
John Watts	2
Thomas Teakle, Jr.	2
John Wise	10
	975

157

November, 1768   Ibid., pp. 593–598

                Thomas Parramore   375
                Southey Simpson   380
                James Henry   260
                                                            ─────
                                                            1015

Amelia

    July 20, 1758   Photostat, VSL

                Capt. Edmund Booker   465

    December 6, 1768   Photostat, VSL

                Col. James Tabb   435
                Capt. Robert Munford   332
                Capt. John Winn   218
                Mr. John Scott   197
                                                            ─────
                                                            1182

Elizabeth City

    July 11, 1758   Deed Book E, pp. 8ff

                Col. John Tabb   76
                Capt. William Wager   95
                Mr. James Wallace   7
                Mr. William Westwood   11
                Mr. William Armistead   1
                Capt. Cary Selden   9
                Capt. Roscoe Sweny   13
                                                            ─────
                                                             212

Essex

    January 15, 1752   Deeds #25, pp. 301–307

                Col. Thomas Waring   206
                Maj. Francis Smith   210
                Col. John Corbin   119
                Capt. John Livingston   49
                William Daingerfield   31
                Capt. William Round (Bound?)   3
                Thomas Atkins   3
                Capt. Wingo Roy   1
                James Moseley   1
                Capt. Sam Hipkins   1
                                                            ─────
                                                             624

    December 4, 1755   Ibid., pp. 248–252

                Capt. James Garnett   158
                Mr. John Upshaw   137
                Col. William Daingerfield   188
                Col. Francis Smith   173
                Capt. Francis Waring   5
                Major Roane   4
                John Jones   1
                John Covington   1
                Capt. William Garnett   39
                                                            ─────
                                                             706

                         158

July 26, 1758   Deeds #29, p. 95ff

    Col. Francis Smith   170
    Col. Francis Waring   208
    Mr. John Upshaw   209
    Capt. John Lee   111
    Col. William Daingerfield   3
                                       ─────
                                     701

May 6, 1761   Deeds #30, p. 17ff

    Francis Waring   211
    John Upshaw   276
    John Lee   243
    John Mortimer   1
    Col. Francis Smith   6
    James Campbell   1
    William Daingerfield   1
                                     ─────
                                     739

July 9, 1765   Ibid., 235–242

    John Lee   300
    Francis Waring   283
    Robert Beverley, Esq.   138
                                     ─────
                                     721   (4)

November 24, 1768   Ibid., pp. 243–248

    Col. Francis Waring   252
    Capt. Meriwether Smith   157
    Capt. William Roane   239
    Mr. Richard Parker   39
                                     ─────
                                     687   (5)

September 15, 1769   Ibid., p. 318ff

    William Roane   231
    Meriwether Smith   124
    James Edmondson   161
                                     ─────
                                     516

November 22, 1769   Ibid., pp. 497–502

    William Roane   170
    James Edmondson   201
    Meriwether Smith   101
    Robert Beverley   10
                                     ─────
                                   482   (6)

Fairfax

December 11, 1755   Washington Papers, L.C.

    Capt. John West   252
    Col. George William Fairfax   222
    Mr. William Ellzey   224   (7)
                                     ─────
                                     698

July 16, 1765   Washington Papers,
                                                          XI, 15–16, L.C.

       George Washington   201
       John West   148
       John Posey   131
       (single votes for Washington)   4
       (single votes for West)   27
       (single votes for Posey)   1
                                                        ____
                                                         512

Fauquier

September, 1769   JHB, 1766–69,
                                                          pp. 290–291

       Mr. Thomas Marshall   329
       Mr. James Scott   273
       Mr. (Thomas) Harrison   196
                                                        ____
                                                         798

Frederick

December, 1755   Washington Papers,
                                                          X, 59–60

       Mr. Hugh West   271
       Capt. Thomas Swearengen   270
       Col. George Washington   40
                                                        ____
                                                         581

July 24, 1758   6 V162–173

       Col. George Washington   309
       Col. Bryan Martin   239
       Mr. West   200
       Capt. Swearengen   47
                                                        ____
                                                         795

May 18, 1761   Washington Papers,
                                                          X, 96–99

       Col. George Washington   505
       Col. George Mercer   399
       Col. Adam Stephens   294
       Robert Rutherford   1
       Col. John Hite   1
       Henry Brinker   1
                                                        ____
                                                        1201

April 8, 1773   Va. Gaz., April 15, Vol. 73, p. 23

       Isaac Zane   273
       Robert Wood   81
                                                        ____
                                                         354   (8)

King George

January 7, 1752   Deed Book No. 3,
                                                       pp. 467–472

              Charles Carter   149
              Thomas Turner   118
              Anthony Strother   82
              Charles Carter, Jr.   17
                                                      _____
                                                       366

December, 1755   Deed Book No. 4,
                                                       pp. 224–229

              Col. Charles Carter   184
              Thomas Turner   118
              Col. Charles Carter, Jr.   144
              Thomas Jett   38
              Col. John Taylor   1
                                                      _____
                                                       485

Lancaster

July 10, 1750   Lancaster Loose Papers, VSL

              Col. William Ball   162
              Mr. Charles Carter   182
              Col. William Tayloe   78
              John Bailey   2
              Richard Chreswell   1
              James Bell   1
              George Heale   1
                                                      _____
                                                       427

January 15, 1752   Ibid.

              Col. Edwin Conway   103
              Mr. Joseph Chinn   90
              Col. William Tayloe   82
              Col. Joseph Ball   82
              Mr. William Dymers   1
                                                      _____
                                                       358

March 4, 1754 (9)   Ibid.

              Col. William Ball   42
              Col. James Ball   108
              Capt. William Dymers   3
                                                      _____
                                                       153

November 10, 1755 (10)   Ibid.

              William Ball   81
              George Heale   24
              Major Richard Selden   9
                                                      _____
                                                       114

December 12, 1755   Ibid.

              Col. William Ball   123
              Major Richard Selden   95

161

Mr. George Heale	63
Col. William Tayloe	1
Samuel Sparks	1
	283

November 30, 1758 (9)   Ibid.

George Heale	109
Capt. Solomon Euell	36
	145

May 11, 1761   Ibid.

Charles Carter, Esq.	161
Mr. Richard Mitchell	126
Mr. George Heale	108
Capt. Dymers	5
Col. William Tayloe	1
	401

July 17, 1765   Ibid.

Charles Carter, Esq.	149
Mr. Richard Mitchell	168
Mr. Richard Ball	21
Mr. Richard Edwards	2
	340

December 2, 1768   Ibid.

Col. James Ball	186
Mr. Charles Carter	145
Mr. Richard Ball	67
Mr. William Edwards	1
Dale Carter	1
Capt. Dymers	1
	401

September 7, 1769   Ibid.

Richard Mitchell	155
Charles Carter	142
Richard Ball	29
	326

Norfolk

November, 1768   Deed Book No. 24,
                                                  pp. 112–115

John Wilson	330
John Brickell	283
Thomas Newton	303
Col. George Veale	229
Joseph Lockhart	13
Joseph Calvert	1
Matthew Phripps	2
John Taylor	1
	1162

September 6, 1769   Ibid., pp. 212–215

    John Wilson, gent.   481
    Thomas Newton, Jr.   334
    Mr. John Brickell   229
    Joseph Lockhart   20
    Thomas Creech   1
    George Veale   1
    Robert Tucker   1
    Joseph Hutchings   1
                                                    ————
                                                 1068

Northumberland

July 19, 1758   Record Book No. 4,
                                                       pp. 283–287

    Presley Thornton   304
    Col. Spencer Ball   255
    Mr. Robert Clarke   98
                                                    ————
                                                 657

May 17, 1761   Record Book No. 5,
                                                       pp. 401–407

    Col. Presley Thornton   342
    Col. Spencer Ball   200
    Capt. George Ball   172
                                                    ————
                                                 714

December 1, 1761   Ibid., pp. 491–497

    Capt. Richard Hull   173
    Capt. George Ball   140
                                                    ————
                                                 313

July 16, 1765   Record Book No. 6,
                                                       pp. 642–646

    Capt. Spencer Ball   227
    John Cralle   159 (11)
                                                    ————
                                                 386

November 24, 1768   Record Book No. 7, pp. 414–420

    Capt. Spencer Ball   195
    Capt. George Ball   146
    Samuel Eskridge   126
    Newton Keene, gent.   143
    John Cralle   67
                                                    ————
                                                 677

September 4, 1769   Ibid., pp. 427–433

    Capt. Spencer Ball   253
    Mr. Samuel Eskridge   163
    George Ball, gent.   143
    Mr. Rodham Kenner   113
                                                    ————
                                                 672

July 25, 1771 (9)	Record Book No. 8, pp. 271–274
Peter Presley Thornton	149
Thomas Downing	147
	296

December 4, 1771	Ibid., pp. 389–394
Peter Presley Thornton	217
Capt. Spencer M. Ball	208
Thomas Downing	156
	581

Prince Edward

March 22, 1754 (9)	17T244–245
John Nash	161
Mr. George Walker	19
Mr. Joseph Norton	15
	195

December 8, 1755 (11)	17T245–247
Charles Anderson	83
George Walker	48
	131

July 17, 1758 (11)	Grigsby Papers, VHS
Charles Anderson	140
Abner Nash	105
	245

Richmond

February 20, 1752	Order Book No. 12, pp. 353–355
Capt. John Woodbridge	231
Landon Carter	176
Capt. John Smith	102
	509

December 5, 1755	Order Book No. 13, pp. 338–340
Landon Carter, Esq.	189
Capt. John Woodbridge	173
Mr. Robert Mitchell	55
	417

July 20, 1758	Order Book No. 14, pp. 264–268
Mr. Woodbridge	197
Col. Carter	123
Col. Tarpley	114
Mr. William Glasscock	24
	458

May, 1761

	Ibid., pp. 380–384
Col. William Peachy	19
Col. Landon Carter	132
Mr. John Woodbridge	196
Col. John Smith	124
	471

September 22, 1769

	Order Book No. 16, pp. 491–495
Mr. Robert Wormeley Carter	178
Col. Francis Lightfoot Lee	173
Mr. Thomas Glasscock	105
	456

November 21, 1771

	Order Book No. 17, pp. 249–253
Col. Robert W. Carter	194
Col. Francis L. Lee	139
Mr. Hudson Muse	167 (12)
	500

Spotsylvania

January 16, 1752

	Deed Book B, pp. 105–106
Col. William Waller	159
Mr. Richard Curtis	143
Mr. William Lynn	32
Mr. Benjamin Grymes	13
Col. Spotswood	2
	349

December 6, 1753 (9)

	Ibid., p. 195
Mr. Zachary Lewis	39
Mr. John Thornton	70
	109

December 13, 1755

	Will Book B, pp. 279–280
Col. Spotswood	96
Mr. Zachary Lewis	91
Col. William Waller	118
Maj. Richard Curtis	108
Mr. John Carter	3
William Bowler	1
John Lewis	1
	418

October 19, 1756 (9)

	Deed Book B, p. 302
Col. Spotswood	98
Mr. Zachary Lewis	60
	158

November 22, 1771   Will Book D,
                                                       pp. 528–532

             Benjamin Grymes   143
             Mann Page   169
             George Stubblefield   259
                                                        ————
                                                         571

Surry

November 25, 1771   JHB, 1770–72, p. 161

             Mr. Hartwell Cocke   176
             Mr. Allen Cocke   134
             Mr. Charles Judkins   95
             Mr. William Simmonds   59
             Mr. William Allen   16
                                                        ————
                                                         480

Westmoreland

January 30, 1752   Records and Inventories
                                                     No. 2, pp. 184–186

             Col. Richard Lee   157
             Mr. John Bushrod   262
             Robert Vaulx   204
             Col. Henry Lee   157
             Robert Carter   34
                                                        ————
                                                         814

September 12, 1754   Records and Inventories
                                                     No. 3, pp. 48a–49a

             Col. Augustine Washington   194
             Richard Lee, Esq.   130
             Robert Carter, Esq.   7
                                                        ————
                                                         331

December 8, 1755   Ibid., pp. 70–72

             Col. Augustine Washington   187
             Col. Philip Ludwell Lee   183
             Richard Lee, Esq.   168
             Mr. William Bernard   138
                                                        ————
                                                         676

April 25, 1757 (13)   Records No. 4, pp. 25–26

             Col. Richard Lee   179

May 16, 1761   Ibid., pp. 137–139

             Richard Lee, Esq.   233
             Col. Richard Henry Lee   222
             Mr. William Bernard   156
                                                        ————
                                                         611

APPENDIX II

Freeholders and Voting

–A–

Freeholders in Ten Counties
Where the Free White Male Population Above Sixteen
Changed Less than Two Hundred
1755–1790

County	White tithables 1755	White males above 16 1790	Freeholders in 1763	Percentage of tithables
Charles City	537	532	231	45.0
Cumberland	704	885	586	83.2
Elizabeth City	316	390	170	53.8
Essex	889	908	620	69.7
James City	394	395	200	50.8
Middlesex	371	407	280	75.5
King William	702	723	400	57.0
Surry	587	732	370	63.0
Warwick	181	176	125	69.1
York	562	530	200	35.6
Average percentage freeholders among white tithables				60.7

–B–

Freeholders in Six Counties
That Kept the Same Boundaries
1755–1790

County	White tithables 1755	White males above 16 1790	Annual rate of increase	Estimated white tithables 1763	Freeholders 1763	Percentage freeholders
Dinwiddie	784	1790	29	1016	650	64.3
Hanover	1169	1637	13	1273	760	59
Norfolk	1132	2650	43	1476	560	38
Spotsylvania	665	1361	20	725	450	62.07
Prince George	650	965	9	722	430	60
Princess Anne	840	1169	9.5	916	520	56.7
Average percent freeholders among white males over sixteen						56.8

Freeholders Voting in Nine Counties
1755

County	White tithables	Actual voters	Percentage of all tithables voting	Percentage of white tithables twenty-one years and older voting	Percentage of all white people voting
Accomac	1,506	540	35.9	47.8	8.9
Essex	889	350	39.5	52.5	9.9
Fairfax	1,312	349	26.6	39.7	8.9
Frederick	2,173	291	13.6	18.9	3.35
King George	720	243	33.7	45.0	8.4
Lancaster	486	142	29.2	39.1	7.3
Richmond	761	209	27.4	36.6	6.8
Spotsylvania	665	209	31.4	41.8	7.9
Westmoreland	944	338	39.9	47.74	8.9
Average			30.83	41.01	7.82

ABBREVIATIONS

AHR   *American Historical Review*
CO   Colonial Office
DAB   *Dictionary of American Biography*
DNB   *Dictionary of National Biography*
CW   Colonial Williamsburg
H   Hening, *Statutes at Large*
JHB   *Journal of the House of Burgesses*
LC   Library of Congress
N   *Lower Norfolk County Antiquary*
PRO   Public Records Office
R   *Virginia Historical Register*
T   *Tyler's Quarterly Historical and Genealogical Magazine*
U.Va.   University of Virginia
V   *Virginia Magazine of History and Biography*
Va.Gaz.   *Virginia Gazette*
          PD   Purdie and Dixon
          D   Dixon
          R   Rind
          Pi   Pinckney
VHS   Virginia Historical Society
VSL   Virginia State Library
W(1)   *William and Mary Quarterly*, first series
W(2)   *William and Mary Quarterly*, second series
W(3)   *William and Mary Quarterly*, third series

For the *Gazette* I have used the order Lester Cappon and Stella Duff did in making their index: the editor, the day of the month, the month, the year, the page and column. For the magazines indexed by Earl G. Swem, *Virginia Historical Index:* the volume, the initial of the magazine, and then the page.

NOTES

Prologue

1. Herodotus, *History of the Persian Wars,* translated by George Rawlinson (Chicago: Regnery, 1949), vol. 1, p. 1.

2. Charles A. Beard. *An Economic Interpretation of the Constitution* (New York: Macmillan, 1914).

3. Lewis B. Namier, *The Structure of Politics at the Accession of George III* (London: Macmillan, 1950); and J. E. Neale, *The Elizabethan House of Commons* (New Haven, Conn.: Yale University Press, 1950).

Chapter 1

1. The sessions of this Assembly were held on the campus of the College of William and Mary because of repairs being made at the capitol. Full accounts of this meeting are to be found in H. R. McIlwaine and J. P. Kennedy, eds., *Journals of the House of Burgesses,* 13 vols. (Richmond: The Virginia State Library, 1905–1915), 1752–1758, pp. 5 ff. (hereafter cited as JHB). Jack P. Greene, ed., *Diary of Landon Carter* (Charlottesville: University of Virginia Press, 1965). The speeches are in R. A. Brock, ed., *The Official Records of Robert Dinwiddle* (Richmond: The Virginia Historical Society, 1883), vol. 1, pp. 24–31 (hereafter cited as Dinwiddie, *Papers*).

2. For possible variations of the religious requirements, see Chapter V.

3. Diary of Landon Carter, March 3–4, 1752, passim.

4. There were, of course, some chartered towns which had separate governments. Edward M. Riley, "The Town Acts of Colonial Virginia," *Journal of Southern History* (August, 1950), vol. 16, pp. 306–23; Leola O. Walker, "Officials in the City Government of Colonial Virginia," *Virginia Magazine of History and Biography,* vol. 75, pp. 35–51 (hereafter cited as V). The volume precedes the publication and the pages follow; i. e., 75V35–51, as used in Earl Gregg Swem, comp., *Virginia Historical Index,* 2 vols. (Roanoke: privately printed, 1934–1936).

5. "Justices of the Peace of Colonial Virginia," *Bulletin of the Virginia State Library* (Richmond: Virginia State Library, 1921), vol. 14, pp. 59, 65, 73.

6. William W. Hening, ed., *The Statutes at Large: Being a Collection of All the Laws of Virginia,* 13 vols. (Richmond: J. W. Randolph, 1810–1823), vol. 5, p. 489 (hereafter Hening is cited as H and the order employed by Swem is used: volume, publication, and page, i. e., 5H489). When a vacancy occurred in the court or it was decided to enlarge it, three names were sent to the governor by the court itself from which the governor named one.

7. Robert Beverley, *History of Virginia* (Chapel Hill: University of North Carolina Press, 1947), p. 72; 3H245–50; 4H292; 5H516; 7H643–48; 8H316; Colonial Papers (1770), Virginia State Library (hereafter cited as VSL); Albert Ogden Porter, *County Government in Virginia: A Legislative History, 1607–1904* (New York: Columbia

University Press, 1947), pp. 27–28; Oliver Perry Chitwood, *Justice in Colonial Virginia* (Baltimore: Johns Hopkins University Press, 1905), pp. 108, 110.

8. 4H412, 500; Porter, *County Government,* pp. 77–78.

9. Lord Dunmore to Hillsborough, May 2, 1772, Public Record Office, Colonial Office, 5/1350 (hereafter cited as PRO, CO). Francis Fauquier to Lord Jeffrey Amherst, February 25, 1763, War Office, 34/37, f. 170 (hereafter cited as WO).

10. Commission to John Buchanan, Draper Collection, State Historical Society of Wisconsin, 2QQ7, September 30, 1758; Fauquier to Board of Trade, January 30, 1763, CO 5/1330, ff. 270 vo–271 vo; Dinwiddie, *Papers,* vol. 1, p. 388.

11. For vestry question see 6H254; 7H153; 7H162; 7H416; 8H607; 8H432; William Meade, *Old Churches, Ministers and Families of Virginia* (Philadelphia: J. B. Lippincott, 1857), pp. 151–52; JHB 1770–1772, pp. 39, 61, 261, and many others; Jack P. Greene, *Quest for Power: The Lower Houses of Assembly in the Southern Royal Colonies, 1689–1776* (Chapel Hill: University of North Carolina Press, 1963), pp. 350–51.

12. A contemporary outline of the government is to be found in a report of Governor Dinwiddie to the Board of Trade, January, 1755. Dinwiddie, *Papers,* vol. 1, pp. 383–84.

13. For instructions to governors see Leonard Woods Labaree, *Royal Instructions to British Colonial Governors, 1670–1776,* 2 vols. (New York: Appleton-Century, 1935).

14. Fauquier to Lord Jeffrey Amherst, August 8, 1761, WO 34/37, f. 81. See the Fauquier correspondence for other letters. (I wish to thank Mr. George H. Reese of Colonial Williamsburg for allowing me to use his transcripts of the Fauquier correspondence.)

15. William Anne Keppel, Earl of Albemarle, who died in 1754, was replaced by John Campbell, 4th Earl of Loudoun. Dinwiddie, *Papers,* vol. 1, pp. xii, 208, passim. Loudoun came to America as an officer in the army, 1757, but it is believed he never visited Virginia. Dinwiddie, *Papers,* vol. 1, pp. 208, 247, 282, 333, 497; ibid., vol. 2, pp. 455, 473, 491, 497, 524, 532, 554, 568, 583, 586, 594, 604, 605, 607, 616, 618, 628, 664, 666, 667.

16. Fauquier to Amherst, November 25, 1759, WO 34/37, f. 30.

17. Amherst to Fauquier, February 15, 1760, WO 34/37, f. 211; Fauquier to Amherst, WO 34/37, f. 34.

18. Diary of Landon Carter, April 7, 1752; JHB 1752–1758, pp. 96, 99; Fauquier to Amherst, November 25, 1759, WO 34/37, f. 30. For printed letters, including some from Amherst's agent in London, see Beverly McAnear, "The Income of the Royal Governors of Virginia," *Journal of Southern History* (May, 1950), vol. 16, pp. 196–211. See Fauquier's report on the salary. Fauquier to Board of Trade, January 30, 1763, CO 5/1330, ff. 275 vo–276 vo.

19. Fauquier to Board of Trade, October 8, 1766, CO 5/1331, ff. 149 vo–150 vo; Fauquier to Egremont, PRO 30/47/13, ff. 1–3.

20. Louis K. Koontz, *Robert Dinwiddie* (Glendale, Calif.: The Arthur H. Clark Company, 1941), pp. 395–96.

21. Ibid., 353–93; *Dictionary of National Biography,* vol. 3, p. 828.

22. Dinwiddie, *Papers,* vol. 1, p. xiii; vol. 2, p. 724; *William and Mary Quarterly,* 2nd ser., vol. 1, pp. 52–53 (hereafter cited as W, preceded by the volume giving the series in parentheses and followed by the pages, i. e., 1 W(2)52–53).

23. Blair to Board of Trade, June 20, 1758, PRO CO 5/1329, pp. 161–66; William G. and Mary Newton Stanard, *The Colonial Virginia Register* (Albany, N. Y.: Munsell's Sons, 1902), p. 20.

24. Fauquier's Will, 8W(1)171 ff; *Virginia Gazette,* PD3Mr68; R10Mr68. For order used in *Gazette* citations, I am conforming to that used in Lester J. Cappon and Stella F. Duff, eds., *Virginia Gazette Index, 1736–1780* (Williamsburg: Institute of Early American History, 1950), the editor, the day, the month, the year and, following the colon, the page and column. See also Dinwiddie, *Papers,* vol. 2, p. 723; JHB 1766–1769, p. 142; George H. Reese, "Portraits of Governor Francis Fauquier," 76V1–10.

25. Robert Carter to [?], March 9, 1768, Robert Carter Letter Book, MS, Colonial Williamsburg (hereafter cited as CW).

26. Standard, *Colonial Virginia Register,* p. 20, says October 28, but according to H. R. McIlwaine and Wilmer L. Hall, eds., *Executive Journals of the Council of Colonial Virginia, 1760–1771* (Richmond: Virginia State Library, 1925–1945), p. 12a, he first met with the Council on October 26. See also *Georgia Gazette,* 9N68 (courtesy Horace Scheely, formerly of Colonial Williamsburg).

27. George Mercer to brother James, August 16, 1768, MS copy, Mercer Papers, Virginia State Library, hereafter cited as VSL. Printed in Kate Mason Rowland, *Life of George Mason* (New York: G. P. Putman's Sons, 1892), vol. 1, pp. 132–33.

28. Although a leading merchant in Bristol and a large property holder in Gloucester County, he had undergone a series of reverses and was facing financial difficulties in the summer of 1768. Bryan Little, "Norborne Berkeley," 63V379.

29. Ibid., p. 409; Edmund Randolph, "History of Virginia," MS, Virginia Historical Society, Richmond, Virginia (hereafter cited as VHS); William Nelson to Arthur Lee, March 31, 1769, Lee Papers, MS, University of Virginia Library (printed in *Southern Literary Messenger,* September, 1858); Robert Carter Nicholas to Arthur Lee, March 31, 1759, Adams Papers, MS, VHS; Roger Atkinson Letter Book, University of Virginia Library; William Nelson to Fauquier, September 16, 1769, VSL; JHB 1766–1769, pp. 188, 189, 199; Thomas Everard to Norton and Son, August 1, 1770, Norton Papers, MS, CW; John Page, Jr., to John Norton and Son, April 10, 1769, Norton Papers, MS, CW; Lord Botetourt to Secretary of State, State Paper Office (hereafter cited as SPO), Va. vol. 189, Bancroft Transcripts. These transcripts are taken from the Public Record Office but follow their own system of numbering which I am using here.

30. Address of the Quakers . . . , November 24, 1768, enclosure in Botetourt's no. 5, CO 5/1372, f. 32.

31. JHB 1766–1769, pp. 188 ff.

32. Botetourt to Secretary of State, SPO, Va. vol. 189, no. 14, Bancroft Transcripts; JHB 1766–1769, p. 218; William Nelson to Fauquier, September 16, 1769, Nelson Letter Book, VSL.

33. Text of these resolutions is in Julian P. Boyd, ed., *Jefferson Papers* (Princeton, N. J.: Princeton University Press, 1951), vol. 1, pp. 27–30; Henry Piper to Dixon and Littledale, June 8, 1769, Henry Piper Letter Book, MS, University of Virginia Library; R. C. Nicholas to John Norton, May 31, 1769, Norton Papers, CW; JHB 1766–1769, p. xxiv; *Va. Gaz.* PD18Mr69:22.

34. John Page, Jr., to John Norton, May 27, 1769, Francis Norton Mason,*Norton and Sons: Merchants of London and Virginia* (Richmond: The Dietz Press, 1937), p. 94; September 16, 1769, Nelson Letter Book, VSL.

35. Diary of Landon Carter, October 15, 1770; Henry Piper to Dixon and Littledale, November 3, 1770, Henry Piper Letter Book, MS, University of Virginia Library; William Nelson to Hillsborough, October 15, 1770, SPO, Va. vol. 190, no. 1, Bancroft

Transcripts; William Nelson to Samuel Athawes, December 6, 1770, Nelson Letter Book, VSL.

36. Richard Bland to Thomas Adams, August 1, 1770, MS copy, Adams Papers, VHS.

37. December 23, 1771, Sabine Hall Papers, University of Virginia Library.

38. William Reynolds to Mrs. Courtenay Norton, October 19, 1771, Mason, *Norton and Sons*, p. 94; William Nelson to Samuel Athawes, November 19, 1771, Nelson Letter Book, VSL.

39. Bland to Thomas Adams, August 1, 1771, Adams Papers, VHS.

40. Dunmore went to Williamsburg unwillingly. He preferred to stay in New York where he knew he had the good will of the people and the climate was better for his family. Dunmore to Hillsborough, June 4, 1771, CO 5/1547, ff. 11–12; October 3, 1771, CO 5/1349, f. 24.

41. *Dictionary of American Biography,* vol. 5, pp. 519–20; *Dictionary of National Biography,* vol. 13, p. 1285.

42. December 23, 1771, Sabine Hall Papers, University of Virginia Library; Greene, *Quest for Power,* pp. 25–26.

43. There are only two instances after 1750 in which the Council attempted to initiate an act, and both of these were vetoed by the House with lightning speed. See Diary of Landon Carter, April 13, 1752; JHB 1758–1761, p. 151.

44. Dinwiddie, *Papers,* vol. 1, p. 384; Virginia Almanac, 1773, VHS; "A Journal of a French Traveller in the Colonies, 1765," *American Historical Review,* vol. 26 (1921), p. 742.

45. Fauquier to Board of Trade, July 31, 1762, SPO, Va. vol. 27y67, Bancroft Transcripts.

46. Stanard, *Colonial Virginia Register,* p. 47; Virginia Almanac, 1752 (Williamsburg: William Hunter, 1752): W. L. Grant, James Munro, Almeric W. Fitzroy, eds., *Acts of the Privy Council of England, Colonial Series* (Hereford, Eng., 1908–), vol. 4, p. 798; Robert Beverley, *The History of Virginia in Four Parts,* second edition (London, 1722), pp. 205 ff. On at least one occasion appointment to the Council was refused because of the distance from Williamsburg. Hillsborough to Botetourt, October 3, 1770, SPO, Va. vol. 190. Later appointments to the Council include William Byrd, III, Philip Ludwell Lee (son of Thomas), John Tayloe, and Robert Carter of Nomini Hall.

47. This idea is elaborated on by Jackson T. Main, *The Upper House in Revolutionary America, 1763–1788* (Madison: University of Wisconsin Press, 1967), pp. 43–49.

48. I have relied heavily on Stanard, *Colonial Virginia Register,* pp. 6–9, for information about these offices. The Secretary's office was doubtless very important but the records were destroyed by fire and consequently too little is known about it.

49. Richard Corbin Letter Book, MS, CW; Thad W. Tate, Jr., "Richard Corbin's Virginia," *Manuscripts,* vol. 7, pp. 150–54.

50. Stanley M. Pargellis, "Procedure in the Virginia House of Burgesses," 7W(2)156–57; JHB 1740–1749, pp. 429–30.

51. JHB 1752–1758, p. 4.

52. 3H248; 5H517. He could serve writs neither on Sunday nor "upon any person attending his duty at any muster of the militia."

53. William Allason to brother, Falmouth, May 21, 1761, William Allason Letter Book, MS, VSL.

54. This was Richard Lee of Westmoreland, JHB 1742–1749, pp. 290–91; Pargellis, "Procedure in the Virginia House of Burgesses," 7W(2)144.

55. CO 5/1368, ff. 39–68.

56. JHB 1758–1761, pp. 16–17.

57. Ibid., pp. 34–35. Other instances of "scandalous and malicious libel" are to be found in JHB 1752–1758, pp. 143, 372–73; JHB 1758–1761, p. 74.

58. JHB 1752–1758, p. 351. At a later date this Professor Rowe, who taught Philosophy, got into so much trouble that he was dismissed from his post, but only after repeated warnings of the college authorities. They said his conduct had been in several respects "very exceptional." Specifically, he was charged with being publicly drunk on the streets of Williamsburg and York, with uttering "horrid oaths and execrations" in ordinary conversation, with attempting to destroy the authority of President Dawson of the College, with leading the students in an attack on the town apprentices which ended in a riot, and with being excessively absent from his duties at the College, or, as the charge said, "you have been too frequently observed riding about the country at very improper seasons when the duty of your office demanded your attendance at College." Above all, he set a bad example to his students and engaged in such despicable conduct that would "highly aggravate the scorn and contempt of every good and virtuous man. . . ." Fulham Palace Papers, Lambeth Palace; Minutes of the Rector and Visitors, College of William and Mary, March–August, 1760.

59. JHB 1752–1758, pp. 351, 421, 436.

60. JHB 1758–1761, p. 5. Clinch was afterwards reelected from Surry but was of course debarred. By resolution of the House, Clinch and another member, James Power from New Kent, were allowed to waive their privileges so that they might answer indictments against them in the General Court which was then sitting. JHB 1752–1758, p. 366. A case similar to this happened in 1769 when Walter Coles had "uttered certain scandalous words" against Nathaniel Terry, representative from Halifax County. Terry was involved in a notorious irregular election. JHB 1766–1769, p. 209.

61. JHB 1758–1761, pp. 91, 97, 98, 99, 103, 120, 125, 143, 150. Freedom from arrest extended to servants on business for their masters and to witnesses ordered by a burgess to appear before one of the standing committees. JHB 1752–1758, p. 103; JHB 1770–1772, p. 207.

62. JHB 1752–1758, pp. 469, 476. Getting Claiborne to the House, summoning and paying witnesses, etc., cost 3,344 pounds of tobacco. Ibid., p. 480.

63. JHB 1761–1765, pp. 285–86.

Chapter 2

1. Jack P. Greene, *The Quest for Power: The Lower Houses of Assembly in the Southern Royal Colonies, 1689–1776* (Chapel Hill: University of North Carolina Press, 1963), p. 9.

2. Richard Bland, *A Modest and True State of the Case,* ed. W. C. Ford, in *Winnowings in American History, Virginia Tracts* (Brooklyn Historical Printing Club, 1891), p. 31.

3. H. R. McIlwaine and Wilmer L. Hall, eds., *Executive Journals of the Council of Colonial Virginia* (Richmond: The Virginia State Library, 1925–1945), 1744–1752, p. 537 (hereafter cited as *Executive Journals*).

4. *Executive Journals*, 1752–1760, p. 35, April 28, 1753. The letter from the Board of Trade was dated January 17, 1753. A pistole was worth approximately $3.60 in

present-day money. *William and Mary Quarterly,* 1st series, vol. 10, p. 147 (hereafter cited as W and the order employed by Swem is used. The volume precedes the publication, the series appears in parentheses, and the pages follow, i. e., 17W(1)147).

5. H. R. McIlwaine and J. P. Kennedy, eds., *Journals of the House of Burgesses of Virginia,* 13 vols. (Richmond: The Virginia State Library, 1905–1915), 1752–1758, pp. 121, 129, November 14, 21 (hereafter cited as JHB). There is no indication of who the petitioners were, but it seems safe to assume that they were interested in land. Albemarle County was the home of Peter Jefferson, Joshua Fry, Thomas Walker, and many others who had organized the Loyal Land Company in 1749. See *Executive Journals, 1744–1752,* pp. 296–97, July 12, 1749.

6. JHB, 1752–1758, p. 154, December 4, 1753.

7. Ibid., pp. 132–36.

8. Ibid., p. 141.

9. Ibid., p. 154.

10. Robert Dinwiddie to Bishop Serlock, January 29, 1753, Fulham Palace Papers, No. 15, Lambeth Palace; William Stith to Bishop of London, April 21, 1753, Fulham Palace Papers, No. 13. Dinwiddie complained that the burgesses were following a "Republican wav of Thinking," making encroachments on the prerogatives of the Crown. Dinwiddie to Earl of Fairfax, March 12, 1754, R. A. Brock, ed., *The Official Records of Robert Dinwiddie,* 2 vols. (Richmond: The Virginia State Library, 1883), vol. 1, pp. 100–101. Hereafter cited as Dinwiddie, *Papers.*

11. JHB, 1752–1758, p. 154.

12. *Executive Journals, 1752–1760,* p. 80, December 15, 1753. In addition to the records in the *Journal,* official testimony on the pistole fee is contained in W. L. Grant, James Munro, and Sir Almeric W. Fitzroy, eds., *Acts of the Privy Council of England, Colonial Series* (Hereford, Eng., 1908–), vol. 4, pp. 232–35, and the Chalmers Papers, the originals of which are in New York Public Library. The most authoritative secondary accounts are Glenn Curtis Smith, "The Affair of the Pistole Fee, 1752–1755," (who makes no use of the testimony at the hearings before the Privy Council) and Jack P. Greene, "The Case of the Pistole Fee: The Report of a Hearing on the Pistole Fee Dispute Before the Privy Council, June 18, 1754," both found in *The Virginia Magazine of History and Biography,* vol. 48, pp. 209–21, and vol. 66, pp. 399–422, respectively (hereafter cited as V. The volume precedes the publication and the pages follow; i. e., 75V35–51, as used in Earl Gregg Swem, comp., *Virginia Historical Index,* 2 vols. (Roanoke: privately printed, 1934–1936). After an introduction, Mr. Greene edits the testimony at the Cockpit found in the Hargrave papers. The action of the House of Burgesses in appropriating the sum out of public funds was without the consent of the Council and was unprecedented in Virginia history. There was strong belief that Dinwiddie would have Randolph removed from the Attorney General's office but it must be said to his credit that he did so only temporarily. After Randolph had sent the governor a letter "acknowledging his errors" and promising a proper conduct for the future, he was restored. JHB, 1752–1758, pp. 168–69; Edmund Randolph, "History of Virginia," p. 100, unpublished MS in the Virginia Historical Society, hereafter cited as VHS; Dinwiddie, *Papers,* vol. 2, p. 2; JHB, 1758–1761, p. 288.

13. Grant, Munro, and Fitzroy, eds., *Acts of the Privy Council,* vol. 4, p. 232.

14. Chalmers Papers. Copies of the testimony from all parties concerned are in this collection. Colonial Williamsburg, hereafter cited as CW, has this on microfilm. See also *Dictionary of National Biography,* vol. 13, p. 1308.

15. An authoritative reason for it being quitrent free has not been found, but it

seems reasonable to assume that it was so because it had been neither alienated nor surveyed. Lands to the Ohio Company were quitrent free for ten years, and this same principle may have applied to other grants. See Kenneth P. Bailey, *The Ohio Company of Virginia* (Glendale, Calif.: The Arthur H. Clark Company, 1939), pp. 302–308.

16. "Mr. Forrester" remains unidentified. Peyton Randolph did not appear in the testimony, possibly because he was not qualified to appear before the Privy Council.

17. Grant, Munro, and Fitzroy, eds., *Acts of the Privy Council*, vol. 4, p. 235; Board of Trade to Dinwiddie, Public Record Office, Colonia Office 5/1367, London (hereafter cited as PRO, CO), quoted in Louis K. Koontz, Dinwiddie *Correspondence*, pp. 562 ff, microfilm copy, original MS in University of California Library, Berkeley.

18. *Executive Journals, 1752–1760*, p. 56.

19. Jack P. Greene, "Landon Carter and the Pistole Fee Dispute," 14W(3)166–69; Richard Bland, *A Modest and True State of the Case*, p. 31 ff.

20. Diary of Landon Carter, October 17, 1754, University of Virginia Library.

21. "Journal of Colonel James Gordon," 11W(1)98 ff; Rev. Andrew Burnaby, *Travels Through the Middle Settlements in North America in the Years 1759–1760* (London, 1775), pp. 25–30.

22. William W. Hening, ed., *The Statutes at Large: Being a Collection of All the Laws of Virginia*, 13 vols. (Richmond: J. W. Randolph, 1810–1823), vol. 5, p. 489 (hereafter Hening is cited as H and the order employed by Swem is used: volume, publication, and page; i. e., 5H489). In May of this same year, Princess Anne and Norfolk Counties had been allowed to discharge their public dues in money because the two counties normally produced very little tobacco. 6H502.

23. 7H240–41, 277–78, 292.

24. Burnaby, *Travels*, pp. 25–30.

25. 3H141–52.

26. William Meade, *Old Churches, Ministers and Families of Virginia* (Philadelphia: J. B. Lippincott and Company, 1857), vol. 1, p. 218; Rev. James Maury to Rev. William Douglas, Nov. 20, 1759, Maury Papers, University of Virginia Library; *Dictionary of American Biography*, vol. 3, pp. 440–41.

27. "Virginia Committee of Correspondence," 10V340–41; *Executive Journals, 1752–1760*, p. 71; Maury Papers, University of Virginia Library.

28. 10V354–56.

29. "Petition to the King," October, 1760, in Lee Papers, University of Virginia Library, Charlottesville; also printed in *Southern Literary Messenger* (February, 1860), p. 127.

30. In this contest Carter wrote two pamphlets, *A Letter to the Right Reverend Father in God, The Lord Bishop of London, Occasioned by a Letter of his Lordship's To the Lords of Trade on the Subject of the Act of the Assembly passed in the year 1758 entitled an act to enable the Inhabitants of this Colony to discharge their public dues, etc., in money for the ensuing year, from Virginia* (Williamsburg, 1759); and another with an equally lengthy title, *The Rector Detected, being a just Defence of the Two-Penny Act against the Artful Misrepresentations of the Rev. John Camm, Rector of the York-Hampton in his Single and Distinct View containing also a Plain Confutation of his Several Hints, as a Specimen of the Justice and Charity of Colonel Landon Carter* (Williamsburg, 1764). John Camm's contributions included at least two pamphlets: *A Single and Distinct View of the Act Vulgarly entitled Three-Penny Act . . . In which is exhibited a Specimen of Colonel Landon Carter's Justice and Charity,* as well as Colonel Richard Bland's "solus populi," which, because of an unfriendly press in Virginia, he had to have published in Annapolis, 1763; and *A Review of the*

Rector Detected or the Colonel Reconnoitered (1764). For general discussion of the Two-Penny Acts and the Parsons Cause, see JHB 1761–1765, pp. xiii–1; Smith, "The Affair of the Pistole Fee," 48V209–21; "The Parsons Cause, 1755–1765," *Tyler's Quarterly Historical and Genealogical Magazine,* vol. 21, pp. 140 ff (hereafter cited as T and the order employed by Swem is used. The volume precedes the publication and the pages follow; i. e., 21T140 ff). "The Two-Penny Act," 19W(1)10 ff; Greene, *The Quest for Power,* pp. 348–50.

31. *Dictionary of American Biography,* vol. 2, pp. 354–55; Roger Atkinson to Samuel Pleasants, Roger Atkinson Letter Book, May 17, 1774, Virginia State Library (hereafter cited as VSL); James Parker to Charles Stewart, August 14, 1774, Charles Stewart Papers, Microfilm copy at CW, original in National Library of Scotland, Edinburgh.

32. The text of *The Colonel Dismounted* (1763) is in 19W(1)13–41; I have been unable to find the earlier (1760) *A Letter to the Clergy in Virginia in which the Conduct of the General Assembly is Vindicated against the Reflections Contained in a letter to the Lords of Trade and Plantation from the Lord Bishop of London.* The text of the offending bishop's letter is in JHB 1760–1765, pp. viii–1. There was considerable discussion whether the king's disallowance made the act null and void *ab initio.* Bland and Richard Henry Lee believed so. See also "Reasons and Objections to Mr. Camm's appeal," February, 1760, Lee Papers, University of Virginia Library, Charlottesville.

33. 19W(1)36–37.

34. Ibid., p. 37.

35. Ibid., p. 38.

36. Ibid., p. 37.

37. Maury lived in Louisa County, but for some unexplained reason brought suit in Hanover. See James Maury to John Camm, December 12, 1763, Maury Papers, University of Virginia Library, printed in Jacques Fontaine, *A Tale of the Hugenots; or Memoirs of a French Refugee Family* (New York: J. S. Taylor, 1838).

38. William Wirt, *Sketches of the Life and Character of Patrick Henry,* 9th ed. (Philadelphia: Thomas, Cowperthwaite and Co., 1844), pp. 36–46. This is a very spirited account and is, of course, favorable to Henry but contains little that 'the Maury letter does not contain. Henry's father was the presiding magistrate at the Hanover Court and his uncle, the Rev. Patrick Henry, was a leading Anglican minister whom he persuaded to be absent from the trial.

39. See E. S. Morgan, "The Postponement of the Stamp Act," 7W(3)352–92. Like the work of Douglas S. Freeman on Washington, *The Stamp Act Crisis* by Edmund S. and Helen M. Morgan (Chapel Hill: The University of North Carolina Press, 1953) leaves little to be said on the Stamp Act in general.

40. "Proceedings of the Committee of Correspondence," 12V6, 8.

41. The Committee of Correspondence to Edward Montague, July 28, 1764, 12V8–14.

42. Ibid.

43. JHB 1761–1765, p. 256.

44. Ibid.

45. For a summary of the tax burden in the colony see Smith, "The Parson's Cause, 1755–1765," 21T140 ff.

46. JHB 1761–1765, pp. 302–303.

47. CO 5/1331, ff. 1 ro–1 vo.

48. Charles Carter to Stewart and Campbell, London, May 15, 1765, Plummer-Carter Letter Book, University of Virginia Library, Charlottesville.

49. JHB 1761–1765, p. 358.

50. Francis Fauquier to Board of Trade, June 5, 1765, State Papers Office, Virginia, vol. 287, no. 17, Bancroft Transcripts. These transcripts are taken from the Public Record Office, but follow their own system of numbering, which I am using here.

51. This "small altercation" was, according to Thomas Jefferson, an attempt by Peter Randolph of the Council to find a precedent by which he could have the resolves expunged from the record. Cited in Dumas Malone, *Jefferson the Virginian* (Boston: Little, Brown, 1948), p. 93.

52. It seems to be a common belief that the election of Henry was carefully planned. Philip Johnson vacated his seat in the House to become coroner and at a by-election Henry was returned.

53. H. S. Conway to Francis Fauquier, September 14, 1765, Bury St. Edmonds and West Suffolk Records Office, Grafton Papers, 423/788, CO 5/1345, ff. 82–84, London.

54. *American Historical Review,* vol. 26, pp. 745–46.

55. Ibid.

56. JHB 1761–1765, p. 360.

57. These are brought together in Edmund S. Morgan, ed., *Prologue to Revolution: The Stamp Act Crisis, Sources and Documents* (Chapel Hill: University of North Carolina Press, 1959), pp. 82–85.

58. The text of the Act Repealing the Stamp Act, March 18, 1766, is in Edmund S. Morgan, ed., *Prologue to Revolution,* p. 155.

59. October 2, 1765, CO 5/1331, ff. 49 ro–50 vo.

60. Fauquier to Board of Trade, November 3, 1765, CO 5/1331, ff. 54–59.

61. *Virginia Gazette,* 25Oc65s23. For order used in *Gazette* citations, I am conforming to that used in Lester J. Cappon and Stella F. Duff, eds., *Virginia Gazette Index, 1736–1780* (Williamsburg: Institute of Early American History, 1950): the editor, the day, the month, the year and, following the colon, the page and column.

62. Fauquier to Board of Trade, November 3, 1765, CO 5/1331, ff. 54–59. The judges of the General Court were, of course, members of the Council. The stamps which George Mercer brought were deemed unsafe in Virginia and were transferred from the *Leeds* to the *Rainbow* and sent to Annapolis. Fauquier to Gov. Horatio Sharpe, November 8, 1765, *Archives of Maryland,* vol. 31 (Baltimore: Maryland Historical Society, 1883–1919), p. 565; Fauquier to the Board of Trade, November 8, 1765, CO 5/1331, ff. 63 ro–64 vo.

63. *Virginia Gazette,* PD7Mr66:32.

64. November 3, 1765, CO 5/1331, ff. 54–59.

65. H. S. Conway to Governor of Virginia *et al.,* March 1, 1766, CO 5/66, f. 120; Conway to Fauquier, ibid., f. 128; *Virginia Gazette,* PD7Mr66:32; PD12Je66:11. It appears noteworthy that in his letter of March 31, Conway reported on the Declaratory Act, which he calls "for securing the Dependency of the Colonies on the Mother Country," before he mentions the repeal of the Stamp Act.

66. For the public celebrations which were reported in detail see *Virginia Gazette,* PD6Je66:23; PD13Je66:11, 21, 22; and many others.

67. Fauquier to Board of Trade, July 26, 1766, CO 5/1331, ff. 132 ro–132 vo.

68. JHB 1766–1769, pp. 145, 146, 148.

69. Botetourt to Hillsborough, February 17, 1769, no. 9, CO 5/1372, f. 38 ro.

70. JHB 1766–1769, p. 166.

71. Ibid., p. 214.

72. Botetourt to Secretary of State, May 19, 1769, State Papers Office, Va. vol. 189, no. 14, Bancroft Transcripts; *Virginia Gazette,* PD18My69:22. The dissolution of the Assembly and the organization of the Association caused about as much popular comment as the Stamp Act had. See Henry Piper to Dixon and Littledale, June 8, 1769, Piper Letter Book, University of Virginia Library; James Parker to Charles Stewart, June 22, 1769, Charles Stewart Papers, National Library of Scotland (on microfilm, M-68-2, at CW); Roger Atkinson Letter Book, VSL; Martha Jaquelin to John Norton, August 14, 1769, 3T292; *Virginia Gazette,* R25My69:22; James Balfour to John Norton, November 5, 1769, Frances Norton Mason, ed., *John Norton and Sons, Merchants of London and Virginia* (Richmond: The Dietz Press, 1937), p. 110; John Norton to Robert Carter Nicholas, October 14, 1769, Wilson Cary Nicholas Papers, University of Virginia Library; Hillsborough to Botetourt, July 17, 1769, PRO, CO 5/1347; and many, many others.

73. Henry Piper to Dixon and Littledale, June 8, 1769, Henry Piper Letter Book, University of Virginia Library.

74. The text is in Julian P. Boyd, ed., *The Papers of Thomas Jefferson* (Princeton, N.J.: Princeton University Press, 1950), vol. 1, pp. 27–31.

75. May 31, 1769, *Southern Literary Messenger,* vol. 27, p. 184.

76. John Page, Jr., to John Norton, May 27, 1769; Robert Carter Nicholas to John Norton, May 31, 1769, Norton Papers, CW.

77. Diary, 13W(1)50.

78. To his son, John Hatley Norton, January 24, 1770, Norton Papers, CW.

79. Arthur Lee to Richard Henry Lee, May 20, 1770, American Philosophical Society, vol. 1, p. 65. Typescript at University of Virginia Library.

80. JHB 1773–1776, p. 132. The background for this resolution is in Jefferson's Autobiography, quoted in Boyd, ed., *Jefferson Papers,* vol. 1, p. 106.

81. To Arthur Lee, December 20, 1766, James Curtis Ballagh, ed., *The Letters of Richard Henry Lee* (New York: Macmillan, 1912), vol. 1, pp. 19, 21.

Chapter 3

1. *Virginia Gazette,* December 12, 1752, p. 3, column 2. Hereafter the form used by Lester J. Cappon and Stella F. Duff, eds., *Virginia Gazette Index, 1736–1780* (Williamsburg: Institute of Early American History and Culture, 1950) is employed in references to the *Gazette:* the editor, the day, the month, the year and, following the colon, the page and column, i. e., 12D51:32. Also H. R. McIlwaine and J. P. Kennedy, eds., *Journals of the House of Burgesses,* 13 vols. (Richmond: The Virginia State Library, 1905–1915), 1752–1758, p. 3 (hereafter cited as JHB). For the exact date of elections in counties, see Appendix I.

2. JHB 1752–1758, pp. 319–32; R. A. Brock, ed., *The Official Records of Robert Dinwiddie* (Richmond: The Virginia State Library, 1883), vol. 1, p. 300; vol. 2, pp. 269, 273, 274 (hereafter cited as *Papers*).

3. *Virginia Gazette,* 14N55:21; JHB 1752–1758, pp. 335–37.

4. The preface to the *Journal* says the percentage of new personnel was 38, but my count is 39.3. JHB 1752–1758, p. 382, April 24, 1756. Three important items on the agenda were: an appropriation bill for defense of the frontier, "a perusal" of the Treasurer's accounts, and a report on election riots in Augusta.

5. Ibid., pp. 495–506.

6. JHB 1758–1761, pp. 3–45, 183–258.

7. Ibid., p. 258.

8. Ibid.

9. JHB 1761–1765, pp. 315–64.

10. Ibid., pp. 3–4. This number includes at least two (Robert Carter Nicholas and Richard Randolph) who formerly had been in the Assembly but not in 1761–1765. George Mercer, erstwhile stamp agent, from Frederick was not returned.

11. JHB 1766–1769, p. 177; Lord Botetourt to Hillsborough, November 1, 1768, no. 2, Public Record Office, Colonial Office 5/1346 (hereafter cited as PRO, CO). Proclamation was dated October 27, 1768.

12. *Georgia Gazette*, 22F69; JHB 1766–1769, pp. 135, 181, 188–218.

13. JHB 1773–1776, p. 132.

14. William W. Hening, ed., *The Statutes at Large: Being a Collection of All the Laws of Virginia*, 13 vols. (Richmond: J. W. Randolph, 1810–1823), vol. 3, pp. 337 ff. Hereafter Hening is cited as H and in the order employed by Earl Gregg Swem, comp., *Virginia Historical Index*, 2 vols. (Roanoke: Southwest Virginia Historical Society, 1934–1936), i. e., 3H337 ff.

15. For failure to do his duty the Secretary was fined £40 current money, the sheriff 2,000 pounds of tobacco, the minister 1,000 pounds of tobacco, and a non-freeholder voting, 500 pounds of tobacco. 3H237–38.

16. 8H303–17.

17. 4H475–78.

18. 5H153, 205–206.

19. 7H517–30.

20. Francis Fauquier to Board of Trade, March 12, 1763, PRO, CO 5/1330, pp. 396–97. Early in 1764 the news was out that the act was disallowed. Robert Carter to Landon Carter, January 21, 1764, Sabine Hall Papers, University of Virginia Library, Charlottesville. The governor signed the bill December 23, 1762. JHB 1761–1765, p. 164.

21. Matthew Lamb to Board of Trade, PRO, CO 5/1330, p. 403.

22. Richard Henry Lee to Arthur Lee, December 20, 1766, in J. C. Ballagh, ed., *Letters of Richard Henry Lee*, 2 vols. (New York: Macmillan, 1911), vol. 1, p. 18.

23. JHB 1766–1769, p. 272.

24. JHB 1770–1772, pp. 57, 60, 81.

25. Text of the act is in 8H304–17.

26. The dates were June 12, 1771, and March 8, 1773. *Journal of the Commissioners of Trade and Plantations* (London: H. M. Stationery Office, 1937), vol. 13, pp. 257, 345.

27. JHB 1752–1758, pp. 339, 344, 456.

28. JHB 1758–1761, p.82.

29. JHB 1770–1772, pp. 254, 263, 280, 286, 288, 296.

30. JHB 1752–1758, pp. 59, 61.

31. 4H475–78.

32. See charters of Williamsburg and Norfolk in Julius A. C. Chandler, *The History of Suffrage in Virginia* (Baltimore: Johns Hopkins Press, 1901). Burgesses for the College were chosen by the president and professors without any reference to property or residence, yet the men were the same type—and sometimes the same men—who were elected by the freeholders under the laws of the colony. The burgesses from the College after 1751 were: Peyton Randolph, John Blair, John Blair, Jr., George Wythe, and Mann Page.

33. Thomas Jefferson, *Notes on the State of Virginia*, William Peden, ed. (Chapel Hill: University of North Carolina Press, 1955), p. 118.

34. Jackson Turner Main, "The Distribution of Property in Post-Revolutionary Virginia," *Mississippi Valley Historical Review,* vol. 41, pp. 241–58.

35. Dinwiddie, *Papers,* vol. 2, pp. 352–53.

36. Printed in *Virginia Magazine of History and Biography,* vol. 28, pp. 81–82 (hereafter cited as V with volume preceding and pages following).

37. *The First Federal Census* (Philadelphia: Childs and Swaine, 1791).

38. *Notes on the State of Virginia,* p. 86.

39. John Blair, "List of Virginia Counties and Estimated Number of Freeholders, 1763," British Museum, Add. MSS 38337, 321 verso. Blair based his estimates on quitrents. I am indebted to John Hemphill, II, formerly of Colonial Williamsburg, for getting this item in England.

40. The boundaries of these ten counties did not change after 1752. A compilation of colonial population is found in Evarts B. Greene and Virginia D. Harrington, *American Population before the Federal Census of 1790* (New York: Columbia University Press, 1932).

41. J. F. Jameson, "Virginia Voting in the Colonial Period, 1744–1774," *The Nation,* vol. 56, April 27, 1893.

42. Lyon G. Tyler, "Virginians Voting in the Colonial Period," *William and Mary Quarterly,* 1st series, vol. 6, pp. 7–13 (hereafter cited as W, preceded by the volume, the series in parentheses, and followed by the pages, i. e., 6W(1)7–13). The polls from which election information is taken are to be found in Appendix I.

43. Robert E. and B. Katherine Brown, *Virginia, 1705–1780: Democracy or Aristocracy?* (East Lansing: Michigan State College Press, 1964).

44. Lord Dunmore to Hillsborough, November 1, 1771, PRO, CO 5/1349, f. 195.

45. Robert Munford, "The Candidates," 5W(3)227–57. New research on Munford has been done by Rodney M. Baine, *Robert Munford, America's First Comic Dramatist* (Athens: University of Georgia Press, 1967). Dr. Baine is of the opinion that Munford used his neighbors and contemporaries as characters in the play, saving the role of Wou'dbe, the hero, for himself.

46. Robert Stewart to George Washington, February 13, 1761, in S. M. Hamilton, ed., *Letters to Washington, 1755–1775*[*] (Boston: Houghton Mifflin & Co., 1898), vol. 3, p. 201.

47. JHB 1758–1761, pp. 8, 20; Landon C. Bell, *The Old Free State, A Contribution to the History of Lunenburg County and Southside Virginia* (Richmond: privately published, 1927), vol. 3, p. 144.

48. JHB 1752–1758, pp. 30, 73, 74, 75; Diary of Landon Carter, March 31, 1752. Speaker John Robinson was the uncle of Henry Robinson. At the new election Chiswell, later the Speaker's father-in-law, was reelected but Syme was replaced by Robinson. Chiswell later moved to Williamsburg and in 1766 slew a Scotch trader named Robert Routlidge in a drunken brawl. See the 1766 summer issues of the *Virginia Gazette.* Syme, who was a half-brother to Patrick Henry, ran successfully in 1755 and continued to hold his seat until the House of Burgesses was abolished.

49. JHB 1761–1765, pp. 235, 270–71.

50. Fauquier may have considered the arguments trivial but he notified the Board of Trade that he did not intend to oppose the measure should it come up again. May 12, 1761, CO 5/1330, ff. 64 ro–65 ro.

51. "The Candidates," p. 237.

52. Diary of Landon Carter, April 15, May 6, 1755.

53. 5W(3)227–57.

54. Hamilton, ed., *Letters to George Washington,* vol. 2, pp. 241, 245–46.

55. Captain Charles Smith to George Washington, July 26, 1758, Hamilton, ed., *Letters to George Washington,* vol. 2, pp. 397–98; John C. Fitzpatrick, ed., *The Diaries of George Washington, 1748–1799* (Boston: Houghton Mifflin, 1925), vol. 1, p. 301.

56. Charles Campbell, ed., *The Bland Papers* (Petersburg, Va.: E & J Ruffin, 1840–1843), vol. 1, p. 27. "Bumbo" was a slang term for rum.

57. Hamilton, ed., *Letters to George Washington,* vol. 2, pp. 343, 345–46, 372, 374. This campaign is discussed in greater detail in Chapter 5.

Chapter 4

1. Present day Rappahannock was created out of Culpeper in 1833.

2. *Virginia Gazette,* PD8D68:31. For order used in *Gazette* citations, I am conforming to that used in Lester J. Cappon and Stella F. Duff, eds., *Virginia Gazette Index, 1736–1780* (Williamsburg: Institute of Early American History, 1950), the editor, the day, the month, the year, and, following the colon, the page and column.

3. Richmond County Order Book No. 12, 1746–1752, pp. 353 ff, Virginia State Library (hereafter cited as Order Book. Virginia State Library is hereafter cited as VSL). The election was held on February 20.

4. Ibid., No. 13, 1752–1755, pp. 338–40.

5. Ibid., No. 14, 1756–1762, pp. 264–68.

6. Ibid., p. 380.

7. Of this gentleman, Landon Carter recorded in his diary, May 25, 1770, "I met the famous Hudson Muse going there [Capt. Beale's] of whom I took no notice always bearing in mind his opening and exposing private letters that did not in the least affect him." In *William and Mary Quarterly,* 1st series, vol. 13, p. 50 (hereafter cited as W. The volume precedes the publication, the series appears in parentheses, and the pages follow; i. e., 13W(1)50).

8. Order Book No. 16, pp. 491 ff; Order Book No. 17, pp. 249 ff.

9. Woodbridge, listed as "esquire," was the brother-in-law of Col. John Bushrod, burgess from Westmoreland in 1752. *Virginia Magazine of History and Biography,* vol. 7, p. 60 (hereafter cited as V, with the volume preceding the publication and the pages following; i. e., 7V60). H. R. McIlwaine and J. P. Kennedy, eds., *Journals of the House of Burgesses of Virginia, 1727–1740* (Richmond: The Virginia State Library, 1905–1915), p. ix; 8W(1)46; *Virginia Gazette,* PD16Jl67:41.

10. H. R. McIlwaine, ed., *Justices of the Peace of Colonial Virginia, 1757–1775* (Baltimore: Johns Hopkins Press, 1905), p. 82.

11. Sabine Hall Papers, MS, University of Virginia Library, Charlottesville.

12. Paul Carrington to William Wirt, Patrick Henry Misc. MS, Library of Congress, quoted in Robert L. Hilldrup's, *The Life and Times of Edmund Pendleton* (Chapel Hill: University of North Carolina Press, 1939), pp. 59–60. The remaining four were John Robinson, Peyton Randolph, Benjamin Harrison, and Richard Bland, all of them "men of very ordinary talent." Ibid.

13. For text of Robert "King" Carter's will, see 5V408 ff.

14. George William Fairfax to Carter, April 10, 1760, Sabine Hall Papers, University of Virginia Library. Fairfax, another burgess, was kinsman and agent for Lord Fairfax; Robert Wormeley Carter to [?], Carter MSS, folder 19, College of William and Mary, Williamsburg.

15. Thomas Nelson to Carter, May 26, 1763, Sabine Hall Papers, University of Virginia Library; *Virginia Gazette,* R19N72:13; PD24Mr74:32; D25F75:33.

16. Carter MS, 1779, College of William and Mary; abstract of Carter's will is in 29V361–62.

17. Louis Morton, *Robert Carter of Nomini Hall: A Virginia Tobacco Planter of the Eighteenth Century* (Williamsburg: Colonial Williamsburg, 1941), and H. D. Farish, ed., *The Journal and Letters of Philip Vickers Fithian* (Williamsburg: Colonial Williamsburg, 1943) are excellent studies of Carter and his milieu. This Robert Carter was one of the few men who were elevated to the Council without having served in an apprenticeship in the House. He was appointed to the office April 7, 1758, and took the oath October 18. H. R. McIlwaine and Wilmer L. Hall, eds., *Executive Journals of the Council of Colonial Virginia, 1752–1760* (Richmond: The Virginia State Library, 1925–1945), p. 36. Robert II's widow (mother of this Robert Carter) later married John Lewis, also a member of the Council.

18. 21V42. Robert "King" Carter married three times and had ten children. The fifth son was George, immature and irresponsible, who died in England unmarried.

19. R. R. Carter and M. C. Oliver, *The Carter Family Tree* (Richmond, 1897); Morton, *Robert Carter of Nomini Hall*, p. 21n.

20. McIlwaine and Hall, eds., *Executive Journals, 1772–1774*, p. 23; Morton, *Robert Carter*, p. 22.

21. Landon and Charles of Cleve, having common ancestors, named their children the same names. Each had a Maria and a Landon, which is no help in unravelling family events in a voluminous correspondence. The two families seem to have been on the best of terms. Carter MSS, College of William and Mary; Plummer-Carter Letter Book, University of Virginia Library. I have made no attempt to carry relationships beyond first cousins. This is admittedly an arbitrary limitation and one that does not give a true picture of the intermarriage and intricate kinships. Some families had been intermarrying for generations, and the cousinships are beyond anyone except the professional genealogist.

22. W. L. Grant, James Munro, and Sir Almeric W. Fitzroy, eds., *Acts of the Privy Council of England, Colonial Series*, vol. 4 (Hereford, Eng., 1908), p. 798; Colonial Papers, 1754, VSL.

23. 13W(1)41; *Tyler's Quarterly Historical and Genealogical Magazine*, vol. 9, p. 284 (hereafter cited as T, with the volume preceding the publication and the page following). Richmond County Records, VSL, has a marriage contract between Carter and Elizabeth Beale, spinster, April, 1746.

24. *Virginia Gazette*, PDJa67:21; PD11Je67:31; PD13Ag67:22.

25. Ibid., PD11Je67:31; this had a Norfolk dateline.

26. June 22, 1765, James Curtis Ballagh, ed., *The Letters of Richard Henry Lee*, (New York: Macmillan, 1912), vol. 1, p. 8.

27. Monday, April 1776, 16W(1)259–60.

28. There were really two Two-Penny Acts, passed in December, 1755, and October, 1758. William W. Hening, ed., *The Statutes at Large: Being a Collection of All the Laws of Virginia*, 13 vols. (Richmond: J. W. Randolph, 1810–1823), vol. 6, p. 502; vol. 7, pp. 240–41 (hereafter cited as H, with volume preceding the publication and pages following). These acts provided that the ministers' salaries could be paid in money instead of 16,000 pounds of tobacco at the rate of two pence per pound. This was less than the market value.

29. "At a Committee of Correspondence held at the Capitol, November 14, 1759," 10V340–41.

30. The Two-Penny Act was discussed at greater length in an earlier chapter. This was not the first time (nor would it be the last) that Carter opposed the clergy.

As early as 1752, having vowed to clip the wings of the whole clergy in Virginia, he had had his own "parson's cause" with the Rev. William Kay, minister of Carter's parish, Lunenburg. Mr. Kay's version of this is the only one we have. "I had not been long [in the parish]," he wrote, "before I found to my sorrow that I had one wealthy, great, powerful colonel, named Landon Carter . . . whom I could not reasonably please or oblige, very haughty, imperious and fickle. I perceived that he wanted to extort more mean, low, and humble obedience than I thought consistent with the office of a clergyman, all this hauts and insults I little noticed until he publicly declared that I preached against him (which I did not) cursed and attempted to beat me—after this he was my implacable enemy and swore revenge and would not be accountable to the king, bishop, government or any court of judicature." Kay to the Bishop of London, June 14, 1752, in William Stevens Perry, ed., *Papers Relating to the History of the Church in Virginia* (Hartford, Conn.: privately printed, 1870), pp. 389–93; Fulham Palace Papers, Lambeth Palace, London, passim.

31. L. C. to Josias Green, November 4, 1765, contemporary copy, Sabine Hall Papers, University of Virginia Library.

32. November 30, 1765, Sabine Hall Papers. This is in answer to a pamphlet by "Mr. Pym" and, although it has a Boston dateline, sounds very much like Carter's repetitious and, at times, verbose style. He abetted the "Honorable the late worthy House of Representatives of the Province of Massachusetts Bay" for their stand on the Townshend Acts. This piece in the handwriting of Carter is dated 1768.

33. John Tayloe to L. C. (circa 1766), Sabine Hall Papers, University of Virginia Library.

34. Diary of Landon Carter, July 25, 1776. Jack P. Greene has brought together the writings of Carter against the Stamp Act in "Not to be Governed or Taxed, but by . . . Our Representatives," 76V259–300.

35. JHB 1752–1758, pp. 33, 44, 55, 99. The House paid Bryan £250. In lieu of patent laws, this method of compensation was used several times.

36. *Virginia Gazette,* R14Ap74:22. The basic element in his treatment was getting circulation started as soon as possible.

37. *Virginia Gazette,* R31Ja71:21.

38. William Rind to L. C., December 13, 1770; Alexander Purdie to L. C., February 21, 1775; Sabine Hall Papers, Diary of Landon Carter, December 1763.

39. McIlwaine and Hall, eds., *Executive Journals,* vol. 4, p. 331, September 5, 1734; H. R. McIlwaine, *Justices of the Peace of Colonial Virginia* (Baltimore: Johns Hopkins Press, 1905), pp. 82, 100. He is on all the extant lists of justices.

40. Diary of Landon Carter, June 3, 1774.

41. L. C. to Lord Botetourt, November 1, 1768, contemporary copy, Sabine Hall Papers, University of Virginia Library.

42. Diary of Landon Carter, June 3, 1774.

43. "Minutes of the meeting of the County Committee," October 7, 1774, Sabine Hall Papers. Francis Lightfoot Lee, Robert W. Carter, and, of course, others were on this committee.

44. L. C. to George Washington, October 31, 1776, 3T256. He elaborates on this theme in his diary published in 18W(1)43–44.

45. Will proved February 12, 1779, 29V361. Landon Carter was born in 1709, therefore he was nearly seventy years old. His son, born in 1734, lived until 1797. Will proved June 5, 1797, 28V368; R. W. Carter to Thos. Bryan Martin, June 20, 1780, Carter Papers, folder 19, College of William and Mary; "Property of One Hundred," 11W(3)372.

46. Diary of Robert Wormeley Carter, July 14, 15, 30, September 22, MS, Colonial Williamsburg (hereafter cited as CW); *Virginia Gazette,* PD10Ag69:32; R10Ag69:32; Louis Morton, "Robert Wormeley Carter of Sabine Hall: Notes on the Life of a Virginia Planter," *Journal of Southern History,* vol. 12, pp. 345–65.

47. Diary of R. W. Carter, MS, CW.

48. Diary of Landon Carter, April 1, 1776.

49. Even after he became a resident in Richmond County, his brother often called him "Loudoun" or "Brother Loudoun"; see R. H. Lee to Arthur Lee, June 26, 1774, Ballagh, ed., *The Letters of R. H. Lee,* vol. 1, p. 118; and same to same, July 30, 1774, Lee Papers, Harvard Photostats, University of Virginia Library. Arthur Lee is "Brother Templar."

50. *Virginia Gazette,* PD16Mr69:31; R16Mr69:22. The dates for the wedding do not agree. R. W. Carter, who, having received a "slight invitation," was there, says it was on May 25, 1769. Carter would drink no wine at the festivities because of a remark of the bride's mother about debtors' presumption in drinking wine furnished by others. 25V191; 17V374; 30V312.

51. Diary of Landon Carter, April 1, 1776.

52. Edmund Jennings Lee, *Lees of Virginia, 1642–1892, Biographical and Genealogical Sketches of the Descendants of Col. Richard Lee* (Philadelphia: Franklin Printing Company, 1892), p. 215; 9T196.

53. William Lee to Francis Lightfoot Lee, June 5, 1774, Harvard Photostats, University of Virginia Library; Lee, *Lees of Virginia,* p. 217.

54. See Lee Papers, University of Virginia Library, passim.

55. 9T196; *Virginia Gazette,* R16My66:32.

56. 29V163; *Dictionary of American Biography,* vol. 2, p. 105; *Biographical Directory of the American Congress, 1774–1949* (Washington, D. C.: U. S. Government Printing Office, 1950), p. 1448; Julian P. Boyd, ed., *The Papers of Thomas Jefferson* (Princeton, N. J.: Princeton University Press, 1950–), vol. 1, pp. 47, 106n, 109, 432. Rebecca Tayloe Lee died on January 7, 1797, her husband ten days later on the 17th. 6W(1)153.

57. Essex County Deeds, no. 25, pp. 301–307, Virginia State Library (hereafter cited as VSL). Francis Waring was appointed sheriff June 13, 1750. *Executive Journals, 1744–1754,* p. 429.

58. Ibid., no. 27, 1754–1757, pp. 248–52, printed in 7T61.

59. Ibid., pp. 95–99.

60. Ibid., no. 29, 1761–1765, pp. 17–21, printed in 9T284. The others receiving votes were Col. Francis Smith, 6; James Campbell, William Daingerfield, and John Mortimer, one each.

61. Ibid., no. 30, pp. 235–42. The only other time Beverley's name appears as a candidate is in 1771 when he polled a mere 10 votes.

62. Ibid., pp. 318–21.

63. Ibid., pp. 497–502. Meriwether Smith, son of Francis Smith, ran third with 101 votes. There is another poll for burgesses, almost illegible, which looks like June 20, 1773. There is no evidence in the *Journals* that a by-election, which had to be called by the governor on the petition of the House, was held, so this date must be 1778. At that election Meriwether Smith and James Edmondson received 82 votes each. Ibid., no. 31, 1772–1780, pp. 405–406.

64. 11V104, 209–10; JHB 1752–1755, p. 178. Writ for an election to replace Thomas Waring, deceased, was requested on February 14, 1754.

65. JHB 1727–1740, pp. ix, 244, 248, 278, 301, 432; *Executive Journals,* 1737–1763, June 11, 1742; 15V382.

66. 5V191–92. Genealogists do not seem to agree whether it was father or son who married Lucy Cocke. Compare 11V209–10 and 32V63.

67. Thomas Waring, as indicated in his will, had several children. Thomas, the second son, married Betty Payne, "an heiress and owner of Payne's Island," but it is uncertain whether she was the daughter or sister of either of the Payne men who were burgesses. Elizabeth Waring, daughter of Thomas the elder, married Spencer Mottrom Ball of The Cove, Northumberland County, "a near Kinsman of Washington's mother," who was burgess from 1765 until the end of the colonial period. 5V191–92; JHB 1765–1769.

68. *Virginia Historical Register,* vol. 3, p. 17 (hereafter cited as R. The volume precedes the publication and the pages follow; i. e., 3R17); JHB 1758–1761, p. 212.

69. Text of will is in 14T18–20. He, like most other planters, had land in other parts of Virginia which he offered for sale from time to time. *Virginia Gazette,* D17F76:33; P16F76:41.

70. 5W(1)161; William Meade, *Old Churches, Ministers and Families of Virginia,* (Philadelphia: J. B. Lippincott and Company, 1857), vol. 1, pp. 393, 405; William Pitt Palmer, ed., *Calendar of Virginia State Papers,* 6 vols. (Richmond: Virginia State Library, 1875–1893), vol. 1, p. 247.

71. Diary of John Harrower, May 23, 1774. Harrower was the indentured schoolmaster for the Daingerfield children. He admired his master, but had little patience with his mistress. Later Harrower became overseer for Richard Corbin, which explains why the original diary is in the Cobin Papers, CW. The complete journal has now been published. Edward M. Riley, ed., *The Journal of John Harrower* (New York: Holt, Rinehart, and Winston, 1963).

72. *Virginia Gazette,* P12Ap75:32.

73. JHB 1742–1749, pp. viii–ix. For his work in the House see JHB 1752–1758, pp. 216, 238, 371, 411, 432, 442, 454.

74. *Executive Journals* 1752–1760, p. 43; *Virginia Gazette,* PD10Oc71:32; R17Oc-71:33; 2R17; Mead, *Old Churches,* vol. 1, p. 393; 18W(2)80. Upshaw was born July 21, 1715, and died July 23, 1801.

75. He received one vote in the 1765 election, but that hardly qualifies him as a candidate.

76. *Virginia Gazette,* R7F71:32.

77. The guilty were to "be published in the *Gazette* as enemies to America" and the "good people of the colony" were urged to have no dealings with them. P14Je76s11.

78. 5W(1)254; *Virginia Gazette,* PD21Je74p29; R21Je74:23.

79. Lee, *Lees of Virginia,* p. 285; Frederick Warren Alexander, *Stratford Hall and the Lees Connected with Its History* (Oak Grove, Va.: privately printed, 1912), pp. 67–68.

80. Alexander, *Stratford Hall,* p. 67; Lee, *Lees of Virginia,* p. 285; Essex Order Book, VSL.

81. JHB 1770–1772, pp. 6, 51. Roane had an extensive law library. Roane-Harrison-Williams Papers, MSS, Virginia Historical Society (hereafter cited as VHS), Inventory, July 9, 1756.

82. JHB 1770–1772, pp. 51, 170.

83. Ibid., pp. 125, 182.

84. Ibid., pp. 267, 278–79.

85. 7T189.

86. 18W(1)196, 197, 264–65.

87. The Woodbridge family was numerous, judging from Swem's *Historical Index,* but where John fits in is not known.

88. Ten' of these received only one vote each and can hardly be called candidates, but that leaves twenty fairly strong candidates who certainly kept the outcome of elections from being a foregone conclusion.

Chapter 5

1. William W. Hening, ed., *The Statutes at Large: Being a Collection of All the Laws of Virginia,* 13 vols. (Richmond: J. W. Randolph, 1823), vol. 5, pp. 78–80, 257–77 (hereafter cited as H and in the order employed by Earl Gregg Swem, comp., *Virginia Historical Index,* 2 vols. (Roanoke, Va., 1934–1936), i. e., 5H78–80, 257–77. Peter Jefferson and Joshua Fry, Map of Virginia, 1751, University of Virginia Library, Charlottesville.

2. Evarts B. Greene and Virginia D. Harrington, *American Population Before the Federal Census of 1790* (New York: Columbia University Press, 1932); R. A. Brock, ed., *The Official Records of Robert Dinwiddie* (Richmond: The Virginia State Library, 1883), vol. 2, p. 352 (hereafter cited as Dinwiddie, *Papers*); Augusta Vestry Book, Virginia State Library, Richmond; "List of Tithables in Virginia taken 1773," *Virginia Magazine of History and Biography,* vol. 28, pp. 81–82 (hereafter cited as V with volume preceding and pages following). There is no source given for this list. Population figures for Virginia are imaginative, unreliable, and contradictory. Governor William Gooch's estimate of Augusta tithables (1749) is 1423; "A General List of tithables as far as returns were made" (1750), MS, Chalmers Collection, New York Public Library, gives the number as 1670. Dinwiddie's estimate in 1755 is 2,273 plus 40 blacks; the Vestry Book gives 2,227. In 1773 the numbers in the Vestry Book are 3,043, in "List of Tithables," 2,792. It seems logical to assume that the Vestry Book is more reliable than the others, but there is no way of knowing how accurate it is.

3. 6H40–44, 462.

4. An open letter from "Caril" in Botetourt County to brother in Ireland, printed in *Virginia Gazette,* May 18, 1775, p. 1, column 1. Hereafter the form used by Lester J. Cappon and Stella F. Duff, eds., *Virginia Gazette Index, 1736–1780* (Williamsburg: Institute of Early American History, 1950) is employed in references to the *Gazette:* the editor, the day, the month, the year and, following the colon, the page and column, i. e., R18My75:11.

5. JHB 1752–1758, p. 347. This matter came to the attention of the House when no return was made, March 30, 1756.

6. A messenger was paid £12 10s. for bringing down the trio from Augusta. JHB 1752–1758, p. 390.

7. Ibid., p. 381.

8. Ibid., p. 383.

9. Ibid., p. 422.

10. Ibid., p. 446.

11. Ibid., p. 447.

12. The report is from Lunenburg Co., March 30, 1756. *Virginia Historical Register,* vol. 3, p. 76 (hereafter cited as R with volume preceding and page following).

13. JHB 1752–1758, p. 190. Madison, long-time clerk of Augusta, was the father

of the Rev. James Madison, the first Episcopal bishop of Virginia. George McClaren Brydon, *Virginia Mother Church and the Political Conditions Under Which It Grew* (Richmond: Virginia Historical Society, 1952), vol. 2, pp. 474–78; F. B. Kegley, *Kegley's Virginia Frontier: The Beginnings of the Southwest, 1740–1783* (Roanoke: Southwest Virginia Historical Society, 1928), p. 604. His other children married into leading families of the frontier: Thomas married Susannah Henry, sister of Patrick Henry; Rowland married Anne, the daughter of General Andrew Lewis, intrepid Indian fighter and burgess from Botetourt County; Eliza married Colonel Andrew Lewis (1778) whose relationship to the general is disputed; Lucy married William Lewis, son of the general; and William married Elizabeth, daughter of Colonel William Preston.

14. Patton had held either simultaneously or in quick succession the positions of county lieutenant, justice of the peace, sheriff (the county's first), coroner, collector of duties on skins and furs, escheator, and probably others. Draper MSS, 1QQ67, 68, 69, 81 (originals in the Wisconsin Historical Society, Madison); *Virginia Magazine of History and Biography* (hereafter cited as V), vol. 16, p. 20; Louis K. Koontz, *Robert Dinwiddie: His Career in American Colonial Government and Westward Expansion* (Glendale, Calif.: A. H. Clark Co., 1941), p. 138; 13V145n; William P. Palmer, ed., *Calendar of State Papers*, 6 vols. (Richmond: Commonwealth of Virginia, 1875–1893), vol. 1, pp. 244–45; Kegley, *Virginia Frontier*, p. 41. There is in the Draper Manuscripts, an indenture between Peter Burn and James Patton. Burn in return for passage, meat, drink, apparel, and lodging for five years was to serve Patton according to the "Custom of the Country," and, at the end of his term to give him "the usual allowance, according to the custom of the country in like kind." Draper MSS, 1QQ4. Regarding plans for settlement in Virginia, see two letters from William Beverley to Patton, Kercubright, Scotland, August 8, 1738, and August 22, 1738, *William and Mary Quarterly*, 1st series, vol. 3, pp. 226–27 (hereafter cited as W with volume preceding, the series in parentheses, followed by the page numbers). Patton is believed to have settled in Augusta in 1738. Draper MSS, 1QQ introduction.

15. Born in Armagh, Ireland, in 1709 and educated at the University of Edinburgh, Craig migrated to Pennsylvania and settled in Lancaster County in 1736. Sent by Donegal Presbytery as minister to the Presbyterians in the upper valley of Virginia in 1740, he became the first resident minister of that denomination in the whole valley. He organized the Augusta Church eight miles from Staunton in 1740 and the next year the Tinkling Spring congregation near the present day Fishersville, Virginia. He served both churches until 1766 and continued as pastor of the Augusta church until his death in 1774. Charles E. Kemper, "The Settlement of the Valley," 30V176–77; Rev. John Craig's Autobiography, MS, Presbyterian Historical Foundation, Montreat, N. C.

16. John Lewis was also an emigrant from Ireland. He had fled to America after he had split open his lord's head when that gentleman was attempting to evict him from his land. Landing in Philadelphia but soon pushing on to Lancaster where he spent the winter of 1731–1732, he turned southward and finally (1732) settled in what is now Augusta County not far from present-day Staunton, 4R211–17; 5R24-25. His grave at Bellefonte is marked with a simple slab on which is the following inscription:

Here lie the remains of
John Lewis

who slew the Irish Lord, settled Augusta County, located the town of Staunton; and furnished five sons to fight the battles of the American Revolution. He was the son of Andrew Lewis and Mary Calhoun, and was born in Donegal County, Ireland, September, 1678 and died in Virginia, February 1st, 1762. He was a brave man, a true patriot, and a firm friend of Liberty throughout the world. Mortalitate relicta, vivit immortalitate enductus.

17. This statement is subject to question, of course, but this study has revealed little about the public interests of clergymen.

18. November 26, 1772, Draper MSS, 2QQ129. This must be an error in date. There was an election in other counties in late November, 1771. There is a letter from Robert Doack on the same topics dated November 20, 1771. Draper MSS, 2QQ128.

19. JHB 1742–1749, pp. ix, 259; Diary of Landon Carter, March 10, 1752.

20. JHB 1752–1758, pp. 7, 110, 454, 483; JHB 1761–1765, pp. 7, 17, 21 and passim; JHB 1766–1769, passim.

21. JHB 1773–1776, p. 8.

22. William Christian from Camp Point Pleasant, October 15, 1774, Campbell-Preston Papers, Library of Congress, Washington, D. C.; *Virginia Gazette,* PD13Ap74: 22; Pi18My75:11; Pi25My75:41.

23. Ibid., Pi25My75:41.

24. 13W(1)65; 7V214–16; 13V12, 17V323; *Virginia Gazette,* P14Ap75:23; Pi16Mr75:22; D1Ap75:21; *Tyler's Quarterly Historical Register and Literary Companion,* 6 vols. (1848–1853), vol. 4, p. 419 (hereafter cited as T with volume preceding and pages following). James G. Birney, abolitionist and presidental candidate for the Liberty Party, married Agatha McDowell, granddaughter of Samuel McDowell. The McDowells became one of the prominent families in the new state. Betty Fladeland, *James Gillespie Birney: Slaveholder to Abolitionist* (Ithaca, N. Y.: Cornell University Press, 1955), p. 15.

25. Preston material is voluminous. Not only is there the collection of Preston Papers in the Wisconsin Historical Society but there is much more in Dinwiddie, *Papers,* vols. 1 and 2; *Calendar of State Papers,* vols. 1, 2, and 3; 5R62–76; 26V363–79; 27V42–46, 309–18; 28V109–16.

26. Freeman H. Hart, *The Valley of Virginia in the American Revolution* (Chapel Hill: University of North Carolina Press, 1942), p. 55, quoting Augusta Minute Book, May 19, 1761; JHB 1766–1769, p. 29.

27. Kegley, *Virginia Frontier,* p. 325.

28. Virginia Council Journals, December 9, 1762, 16V146. This sum was to be paid by the Receiver-General rather that the Treasurer of the Colony, a member of the House.

29. JHB 1761–1765, pp. 10, 69–70, 207–209, 211, 218. He, Preston, and several others were trustees of the new town. 7H475.

30. Israel Christian to Governor Botetourt, October 23, 1770, Colonial Papers, 1770, Virginia State Library; Kegley, *Virginia Frontier,* pp. 381, 382, 385, 530; *Virginia Gazette,* PD4F73:23; 15V247–51.

31. Clayton Torrance, *Virginia Wills and Administrations, 1632–1800* (Richmond: William Byrd Press, 1931), p. 82.

32. *Dictionary of American Biography,* vol. 10, pp. 169–70; Hugh Blair Grigsby, *The Virginia Convention of 1788* (Richmond: J. W. Randolph, 1890–1891), vol. 2, pp. 16–19.

33. I have relied on Douglas Southall Freeman, *George Washington* (New York: Charles Scribner's Sons, 1948), vol. 1, Appendix 1, pp. 447–513 for the summary of

the Fairfax lands. The definitive study of the northern neck remains to be written and not until that is done can the whole story of Virginia politics be known.

34. William Nelson to E. & S. Athawes, August 12, 1767, William Nelson Letter Book, MS, Virginia State Library. There was complaint that Fairfax lived too far from Williamsburg to be of service on the Council. Nelson would have made his "most dutiful and respectful compliments for the honor" done him but would have begged leave to resign his seat.

35. Poll for Frederick County, Washington Papers, Library of Congress.

36. S. M. Hamilton, *Letters to George Washington* (Boston: Houghton Mifflin & Co., 1898), vol. 1, p. 158; Freeman, *Washington*, vol. 2, p. 147. This is not the first time friends of the young warrior had urged him to try his hand at burgessing. In 1754, when a bill was before the House for dividing Fairfax County, his friend John Carlyle had asked if Washington would consider standing for Fairfax or the new county. He did not give an immediate reply but wrote his brother "Jack" (John Augustine) to "take the pulse" of leading citizens in his neighborhood to see if he stood a chance of winning. The reply was not reassuring so he dropped whatever plans he had for running.

37. Full treatment is given it in Freeman, *Washington*, vol. 2; R. T. Parton, "The First Election of Washington to the House of Burgesses," *Proceedings of the Virginia Historical Society* (Richmond: Virginia Historical Society, 1892), vol. 11, pp. 115–25; Charles S. Sydnor, *Gentlemen Freeholders: Political Practices in Washington's Virginia* (Chapel Hill: University of North Carolina Press, 1952), pp. 68–70.

38. Hamilton, *Letters to Washington*, vol. 2, p. 343.

39. However, Jones was successful in Hampshire which indicates that a man could stand in a number of counties in the same election.

40. July 6, 1758, Hamilton, *Letters to Washington*, vol. 2, pp. 345–46.

41. Ibid., vol. 2, p. 343. Others in the same vein are in ibid., pp. 249, 372.

42. John C. Fitzpatrick, ed., *The Writings of George Washington* (Washington, U. S. Printing Office, 1931–1944), vol. 2, p. 241. Parton calls him a political boss. "The First Election of Washington to the House of Burgesses," p. 122. For low opinion of voters see Hamilton, *Letters to Washington*, vol. 2, pp. 343, 344, 349, 372; vol. 3, p. 201.

43. Ibid., vol. 2, p. 345.

44. Ibid., p. 343.

45. Ibid., pp. 372, 384–85; Sydnor, *Gentlemen Freeholders,* p. 69; "Poll for Burgesses, 1758," Washington Papers, Library of Congress.

46. Hamilton, *Letters to Washington,* vol. 2, pp. 384–85; other congratulatory letters in ibid., pp. 383, 385, 387, 388, 389, 390.

47. The number for Washington varies slightly from 307 to 310.

48. Hamilton, *Letters to Washington,* vol. 2, pp. 389–400.

49. Fitzpatrick, *George Washington,* vol. 2, pp. 249–51.

50. Poll for Burgesses, Washington Papers, Library of Congress. I am unable to find out why Martin did not offer as a candidate.

51. Hamilton, *Letters to Washington,* vol. 3, p. 201. In 1761 Stephens was put in command of the Virginia Regiment engaged in fighting the Cherokees in the absence of Colonel William Byrd. Fauquier implied that he did not trust his judgment. Fauquier to Amherst, October 11, 1761, WO 34/37, ff. 87, 92; Amherst to Fauquier, November 5, 1761, WO 34/37, f. 240.

52. Hamilton, *Letters to Washington,* vol. 3, p. 201.

53. Ibid., p. 204.

54. In 1758 three hundred eighty-four freeholders voted; in the second election, six hundred one.

55. Hamilton, *Letters to Washington*, vol. 3, pp. 15–16.

56. George Washington to Colonel Bassett of Eltham, August 2, 1765, 3R218; *Virginia Gazette*, R15Ap73:23.

George Mercer was not insensitive to the treatment he had received in 1765 and refused to stand in 1768. "As we come to the elections," he wrote his brother James peevishly, "you may from me and by my authority and request decline any offer that may be made of electing me in Frederick. I would not serve a set who had showed so little regard for me in my absence, tho they were more indebted to me than to any man that ever was in this county. Not even were they to elect me without a dissenting voice in the county and of this I beg you will take the trouble to inform them, for I am as fixed as fate and therefore will in time save all expense— and the chance of an opposition." George Mercer to James Mercer, August 16, 1768, copy, Mercer Papers, Virginia Historical Society, Richmond.

57. JHB 1752–1758, p. 197, August 30, 1754.

58. Washington, *Diaries*, vol. 1, p. 110n; 7H489, Fairfax Will Book B, p. 74, Virginia State Library, Richmond.

59. Parton, "First Election of George Washington to the House of Burgesses," p. 118. He became a justice in Berkeley when that county was formed. Freeman points out that the county paid him £20. 16s. 6d. for attending the Assembly in March, 1756. He cites Frederick Order Book No. 7, November 3, 1756.

60. The other two Cary sisters married Robert Carter Nicholas (Anne) and Edward Ambler (Mary), 10V110. Regarding the Fairfax-Cary courtship see Fairfax's letter to his cousin Robert Fairfax, December 12, 1748, 9V108; 36V33.

61. William Nelson to E. and S. Athawes, August 12, 1767, Nelson Letter Book, Virginia State Library; Colonial Papers, 1767, VSL; *Virginia Gazette*, PD11Je67:22.

62. *Virginia Gazette*, R3Je73:23; Lord Dunmore to Secretary of State, December 24, 1774, Colonial Papers, Virginia vol. 195, Bancroft Transcripts. In the summer of 1774 all his household and kitchen furniture, "mostly new and very elegant," was sold at Belvoir. *Virginia Gazette*, PD2Je74:32; R2Je74:22; Pi5Ja75:43.

63. Martin died in 1798, Washington, *Diaries*, vol. 1, 130n; 34V54. He was born in England and came out when he was twenty to be joined shortly by Lord Fairfax. He was county lieutenant, justice, trustee of the towns of Winchester and Bath, and burgress from Frederick and Hampshire. He and Gabriel Jones were executors of Lord Fairfax's estate. He died a bachelor.

64. Parton, "First Election of George Washington to the House of Burgesses," p. 122.

65. Mercer material is voluminous. Besides the newspaper war between the Mercers and Richard Henry Lee about the Stamp Act (*Virginia Gazette*, PD25Je66:21; PD26S66:1-2-3; PD3Oc66:11; PD3Oc66:31), there are the Mercer Papers, VSL, Richmond; the Adams Papers, VHS, Richmond; Lois Mulkearn, ed., *George Mercer Papers Relating to the Ohio Company of Virginia* (Pittsburgh: University of Pittsburgh Press, 1954), and Kate Mason Rowland, *The Life of George Mason* (New York: G. P. Putnam's Sons, 1892) which contain some Mercer correspondence.

66. John C. Fitzpatrick, ed., *The Writings of George Washington*, vol. 1, pp. 130–31.

67. Freeman, *George Washington*, vol. 3, pp. 1–3.

68. Washington to George Mason, April 5, 1769, regarding a nonimportation agreement to nullify the Townshend Acts. Hamilton, *Letters to Washington*, vol. 3, p. 342.

69. For his career as a burgess see Freeman, *George Washington,* vol. 2, pp. 316–21; vol. 3, pp. 1–18; Bernhard Knollenberg, *George Washington, The Virginia Period, 1732–1775* (Durham, N. C.: Duke University Press, 1964), pp. 101–106.

70. *Virginia Gazette,* PD3N74:12; Pi10N74:32.

71. Ibid., R15Ap73:23. The vote stood 273 for Zane, 81 for Robert Wood.

72. Robert Greenhalgh Albion and Leonidas Dodson, eds., *Philip Vickers Fithian: Journal, 1775–1776* (Princeton, N. J.: Princeton University Press, 1934), vol. 2, pp. 14–15.

73. Hart, *Valley of Virginia,* p. 38.

74. Like Washington, Fairfax, Mercer, Martin, and Preston, Zane left a great many papers which are a treasure store for information on frontier industry. The originals of the Zane Papers are in the Library of Congress but are available on microfilm at VSL. See also William Allason Letter Book, VSL. Secondary accounts are to be found in Kathleen Bruce, *Virginia Iron Manufacture in the Slave Era* (New York: Century Company, 1931), p. 21; Carl Bridenbaugh, *The Colonial Craftsman* (New York: New York University Press, 1950), pp. 24–25; Hart, *Valley of Virginia,* p. 25. Roger W. Moss, Jr., "Isaac Zane, Jr., a 'Quaker for the Times'," 77V291–306. Although there are indirect references to a wife in Philadelphia, Mr. Moss is of the opinion he never married.

75. For laborers see *Virginia Gazette,* D13Ja75:43; D30D75:22; P29D75:33. Hall and Gelpin stored the Marlborough iron sent to Alexandria. Isaac Zane to brother, December 10, 1772, Zane Papers. Zane's mother and sister Sarah Jane were occasionally at the iron works and their letters show a lively interest in, and an astute understanding of, the operation of the business. See, for example, Sarah Jane "to her loving brother," September 5, 1772, Zane Papers.

76. Zane paid Byrd's widow £2,000 for it. 9V83.

77. Will, Zane Papers, printed in 6T272. Zane had a great amount of property in buildings in Philadelphia and lands in Virginia.

78. I assume this about Patton, who lived to maturity in the British Isles and whose letters indicate a degree of learning.

79. I find no evidence to the contrary.

80. I have found no concrete evidence that Charles Lewis and Christian were members of a Presbyterian church, but Lewis's father and brother belonged to the Tinkling Spring Church and so did several of Christian's family. See Rev. John Craig, Autobiography, and his Record of Baptisms, 1740–1749, Presbyterian Historical Foundation, Montreat, N. C.; Howard McKnight Wilson, *The Tinkling Spring: Headwater of Freedom* (Fishersville, Va.: Tinkling Spring and Hermitage Presbyterian Churches, 1954). The last contains extracts from session books, including lists of officers and church rolls for several years. See specifically pp. 205, 427, 438.

81. Craig, Record of Baptisms, October 1, 1746.

82. Augusta Vestry Book, VSL.

83. The texts of the usual oaths are found in A. P. Middleton, "The Capitol: A Manual of Interpretation," mimeograph, Colonial Williamsburg; "Toleration Act of 1690," in Andrew Browning, ed., *English Historical Documents, 1660–1714* (New York: Oxford Press, 1953), pp. 400–403; George McClaren Brydon, *Virginia's Mother Church* (Richmond: Virginia Historical Society, 1952), vol. 1, pp. 245, 265; vol. 2, pp. 154–72.

84. Freeman, *George Washington,* vol. 1, pp. 486, 487, 491, 495, 497. See also *The Letters of Robert Carter,* edited by Louis B. Wright (San Marino, Calif.: The Huntington Library, 1940), pp. 61, 65, 114–15.

Chapter 6

1. J. R. V. Daniel, ed., *A Hornbook of Virginia History* (Richmond: The Division of History of the Department of Conservation and Development, 1949), p. 23. Goochland was much sub-divided in the colonial period; Albemarle (1744), Cumberland (1749), Amherst (1761), and Buckingham (1761) were all created from it.

2. H. R. McIlwaine and J. P. Kennedy, eds., *Journals of the House of Burgesses of Virginia* (Richmond: The Virginia State Library, 1905–1915), 1770–1772, p. 195 (hereafter cited as JHB). Sheriffs served two-year terms.

3. In 1770 the justices of Henrico were: Richard Randolph, William Lewis, Samuel Duval, Bowler Cocke, Jr., Ryland Randolph, Joseph Lewis, Richard Adams, Daniel Price, Jr., George Cox (sheriff), and Nathaniel Wilkinson. Colonial Papers, 1770, Virginia State Library. In June of that year the court recommended that William Randolph, Peter Winston Turner, Southall James, Powell Cocke, and John Hailes be added.

4. JHB 1770–1772, p. 195.

5. Ibid.

6. Richard Adams to Thomas Adams, March 24, 1772, Adams Papers, MS, Virginia Historical Society, Richmond (hereafter cited as VHS).

7. Ibid., JHB 1770–1772, pp. 195, 246. Writs for a new election were requested on February 27. There had been five active candidates: Peter Randolph, Richard Randolph, Samuel Duval, Mr. Prosser, and Richard Adams. Richard Adams to Thomas Adams, January 21, 1772, Adams Papers, VHS.

8. For a summary of Randolph relationships, see *Virginia Historical and Biographical Magazine,* vol. 45, p. 69 (hereafter cited as V with volume preceding and page following, i. e., 45V69).

9. It is not infrequent for a little-known person to fill in a breach like this. This raises the question: was he the instrument of the opposition, or, what is more likely, a henchman that could be relied upon until the main candidates were ready?

10. The Randolphs are more difficult to differentiate than even the Carters because there are no Randolph papers of any importance for the eighteenth century. The family was intermarried with the Carters, Bollings, Hills, Lightfoots, Beverleys, and others. It was through the Bollings that Pocahontas became an ancestor. "Authentic Data: Issue of William Randolph II and Elizabeth Beverley his wife," typescript in Virginia Historical Society, is as useful as anything I have found on the family.

11. 45V83.

12. Ibid.

13. H. R. McIlwaine and Wilmer L. Hall, eds., *Executive Journals of the Council of Colonial Virginia, 1744–1753* (Richmond: The Virginia State Library, 1925–1945), p. 481 (hereafter cited as *Executive Journals*).

14. Wilson Cary Nicholas Papers, MS, University of Virginia Library.

15. *Virginia Gazette,* PD22Ag71:22; Richard Adams to Thomas Adams, August 17, 1771, Adams Papers, VHS.

16. *Virginia Historical Register and Literary Companion,* vol. 6, p. 19 (hereafter cited as R, with the volume preceding the publication and the pages following, i. e., 6R19). Extracts from J. F. D. Smyth, *A Tour of the United States of America . . . ,* 2 vols. (Dublin: Price, Moncreiffe *et al.,* 1784).

17. It is almost impossible to sort out the Bowler Cockes because the name persisted for at least six generations, and at times records and correspondence make no distinction between them. Of some help is 4V323; 5V87; 37V232–33. The Cockes,

an old and powerful family, were originally from Surry County where part of the family remained, Benjamin, Hartwell, and Allen Cocke representing that county.

18. Petition for 5000 acres including Rockfish Gap, *Executive Journals,* 1772–1774, p. 22; "Property of the One Hundred, 1787–1788," *William and Mary Quarterly,* 3rd ser., vol. 11, p. 386 (hereafter cited as W, and the order employed by Swem is used. The volume precedes the publication, the series appears in parentheses, and the pages follow; i.e., 11W(3)386; 22V329).

19. Richard Adams to Thomas Adams, July 5, 1769, printed in 5V134.

20. This was not an unusual practice; the Nortons, the Amblers, the Wallers, and the Randolphs all had members of the family in England who took care of the business for them there.

21. *Virginia Gazette,* R19Ag73:22; PD11Ag74:32; R11Ag74:32; PD14Je68:32; PD24S67:21.

22. *Virginia Gazette,* R27Jl69:23; PD30Jl74:27.

23. 5W(1)161, quoting Vestry Book of St. John's Church, pp. 184, 186.

24. 22V379–80. Both the Adamses and the Randolphs used a coat of arms. W. A. Crozier, *Virginia Heraldica* (Baltimore: Southern Book Co., 1953), pp. 7, 15.

25. Ibid. Richard Adams married Elizabeth Griffin of Richmond County, the sister of Judge Cyrus Griffin. Thomas, although never a member of the General Assembly, was a member of the Continental Congress, 1778–1779, and of the Virginia Senate, 1784–1787. His wife was Elizabeth Fountleroy Cocke, widow of his first cousin, Bowler, Jr.

26. In 1770 Richard Randolph registered a complaint against Duval for some misdemeanor in the justice office which the Council dismissed as "trifling." *Executive Journals,* 1760–1771, p. 9.

27. *Virginia Gazette,* PD10S72:22. If this is Duval's first marriage, he must have been a bachelor for some years. His birth date is unknown, but he had been a successful businessman with ads in the papers for years.

28. *Virginia Gazette,* P24N75:13, D11F75s22, and many others.

29. Ibid., 16My55, 23My55, PD27Ag67:31. He had smaller tracts in New Kent.

30. Ibid., PD10D72:31.

31. Ibid., PD4Jl66:32.

32. Ibid., PD16Je68:31.

33. The three who have biographies are Joshua Fry, Peter Jefferson, and, of course, Thomas Jefferson; Henry Fry left an autobiography. Albemarle County was formed in 1744 out of Goochland County. William Anne Keppel, second Earl of Albemarle, for whom it was named, was Governor General at the time.

34. Albemarle Order Book, 1774–1848, p. 386, cited in William Minor Dabney, "Jefferson's Albemarle, History of Albemarle County, 1727–1819," Ph. D. dissertation, University of Virginia, Charlottesville, 1951, pp. 28–29.

35. Ibid.; Edgar Woods, *Albemarle County* (Charlottesville: University of Virginia Press, 1901), p. 375; Edgar C. Hickisch, "Peter Jefferson, Gentlemen," Master's thesis, University of Virginia, Charlottesville, 1940, chapter 3.

36. The two Cabells may be the same, but I assume that since junior is used at the later date, the earlier one was senior.

37. JHB 1758–1761, p. 70.

38. Quoted by Fairfax Harrison, "Virginians on the Ohio and Mississippi Rivers," 30V215. Fry was serving his second term in 1752, having been (with Charles Lynch) the county's first burgess.

39. 5W(1)206; Lois Fell Jackson, "Colonel Joshua Fry, Albemarle's Soldier-

Statesman," Master's thesis, University of Virginia, Charlottesville, 1945; Woods, *Albermarle County,* p. 197.

40. "William and Mary College Recently Discovered Documents," 10W(2)248. The report, which is unsigned and undated, says there were twenty-two or twenty-three boys in attendance and no Indians at all.

41. "Journal of the Meeting of the President and Masters of William and Mary College, March 28, 1732," 1W(1)136.

42. Miss Jackson makes a list of those she knows were students of Fry which includes Archibald Cary, Thomas Dawson, John Fox, Philip Ludwell, Ralph Page, and Charles Pasteur. She offers an additional list of *probable* students which includes the names of thirteen burgesses of later dates. She bases this on *A Provisional List of Alumni, Grammar School Students, Members of the Faculty, and Members of the Board of Visitors of the College of William and Mary in Virginia From 1693 to 1888* (Richmond, 1941), p. 545.

43. The Fry and Jefferson map shows his seat at the north end of the Green Mountains on Hardware River.

44. Plans for this map had been started in 1737 when Fry proposed it to the Assembly. R. A. Brock, ed., *The Official Records of Robert Dinwiddie,* 2 vols. (Richmond: Virginia State Library, 1884), vol. 1, p. 7n (hereafter cited as Dinwiddie, *Papers*).

45. *Executive Journals,* 1744–1753, p. 497.

46. Ibid., pp. 418, 563. Up to this date this line had extended only to Peter's Creek. It was made famous by the account of William Byrd II, *History of the Dividing Line* in *Writings of William Byrd,* edited by John Spencer Bassett (New York: 1901).

47. *Executive Journals,* 1744–1753, pp. 523, 524, 533. This was in December, 1751. Luther F. Addinton, "Virginia's Frontier Blazer and Great Scout" (typescript, University of Virginia Library), p. 86, which is based on the Journal of Christopher Gist. This seems to have been as much an exploring trip to the Ohio as anything else. The Commission is in Brock, ed., Dinwiddie, *Papers,* vol. 1, pp. 7–9.

48. *Executive Journals,* 1744–1753, pp. 416, 425.

49. William W. Hening, ed., *The Statutes at Large: Being a Collection of All the Laws of Virginia,* 13 vols. (Richmond: J. W. Randolph, 1810–1823), vol. 8, p. 270 (hereafter cited as H, with volume preceding the publication and pages following; i. e., 8H270).

50. Woods, *Albemarle County,* p. 197; Elizabeth Hawes Ryland, "The Families of Micou and Hill of Essex Co.," 16W(2)491.

51. 16V136; 29V323; Colonial Papers, 1756, Virginia State Library. This last says that on the tree underneath which he was buried was carved these words: "Here lies the good, just, and noble Frye." Freeman says that he had done no previous fighting, but he "knew men." Washington was 22 years and 3 months old. Douglas Southall Freeman, *George Washington,* 5 vols. (New York: Charles Scribner's Sons, 1948–1952), vol. 1, pp. 339, 381.

52. Waller-Camm typescripts, July 9, 1754, University of Virginia Library. The "Poem" is undated.

53. Quoted, without reference, in Brock, ed., Dinwiddie, *Papers,* vol. 1, p. 7n. For his war services his heirs were entitled to large tracts of land on the Ohio: 7,758 acres at the first distribution and 15,000 acres at a later date. *Virginia Gazette,* R14Ja73:13.

54. For example see: H. S. Randall, *The Life of Thomas Jefferson* (Philadelphia:

J. B. Lippincott & Co. 1865), vol. 1, pp. 5–7; John T. Morse, *Thomas Jefferson* (Boston: Houghton Mifflin, 1889); John Dos Passos, *The Head and Heart of Thomas Jefferson* (New York: Doubleday, 1954).

55. Hickisch is of the opinion that the aristocrats considered the country south of the James River as the eighteenth-century equivalent of the wrong side of the tracks. This may be true, but the Meades lived in Nansemond, some of the Burwells in the Isle of Wight, and several Cockes in Surry.

56. *Executive Journals,* 1736–1743, p. 339.

57. Goochland County Deed Book No. 3, pp. 45, 58, Virginia State Library.

58. John Harvie Account Book, pp. 17, 44, photostat in University of Virginia Library, original at Huntingdon Library.

59. *Ibid.,* p. 1.

60. This is the conclusion of Hickisch, who makes a very good case for his thesis that Peter Jefferson was as well born as any other member of the gentry. He also points out that the first Randolph arrived in America with little more than a determination to get ahead in the New World; he acquired great tracts of land, married into the Isham family which was descended from Scottish barons, and with his property and his wife's breeding and background, he began an American brand of aristocracy. Unfortunately, Hickisch's work is not paged, which lessens its usefulness for the student. He does not give the source of the guest list at the wedding.

61. *Virginia Gazette,* 7Mr51:41; Hickisch, *Peter Jefferson,* chapter 3, passim; Brock, ed., Dinwiddie, *Papers,* vol. 1, p. 95n; *Dictionary of American Biography,* vol. 1, p. 17.

62. Hickisch, *Peter Jefferson,* chapters 4 and 5, summarizes the property at his death; Albemarle County Deed Book 2, pp. 32, 41–48; Will, File 1, Cary Papers, Virginia Historical Society. In 1755 John Smith surveyed at least three pieces of land for Jefferson: one of 300 acres, another of 385, and a third of 400, all in Albemarle County. Surveys made by John Smith, Pocket Plantation Papers, University of Virginia Library.

63. One of the daughters, Mary, married John Bolling on January 29, 1760. Her marriage portion was £200 and a Negro girl valued at £55. John Harvie Account Book, p. 3, photostat in University of Virginia Library, original at Huntingdon Library.

64. The other administrators were John Nicholas, Dr. Thomas Walker, Peter Randolph, Thomas Turpin, and John Harvie.

65. Letters of Gov. William Gooch to his brother in England, July 20, 1733; June 17, 1734, Virginia State Library. He rejoiced that ample estate came to young Mr. Burwell by the death of his mother who, apparently, had held in trust the son's inheritance from his father. There is not a word about the estate of the Nicholas children, who were very young. Robert Carter, the oldest, was born January 28, 1728, and was therefore about six; the other two were younger. *Dictionary of American Biography,* vol. 13, pp. 485–86; 33V43–44.

66. Robert "King" Carter left £200 to the oldest and £100 each to the other Nicholas sons of his dead daughter. The Burwell children, half brothers of the Nicholas boys, were Carter, Robert, and Lewis, whom their grandfather mentions in his will. See text of will, 5V411; 6V21. The Fry-Jefferson Map shows John Nicholas' seat on the south side of the Fluvanna River where Slate River joins it.

67. Dabney, *Jefferson's Albermarle,* p. 30; Woods, *Albemarle County,* p. 289. Like all the other leaders in the area, he was frequently getting western land. *Executive Journals,* 1760–1771, p. 4.

68. *Dictionary of American Biography,* vol. 3, p. 389. I am not absolutely sure that it was Dr. Cabell and not his son who was burgess from 1755 to 1758. But since William Cabell, Jr., was elected in 1758, I am assuming it was the father at the earlier date. Dr. Cabell lived from 1699 until 1774, his son from 1729–1730 to March 3, 1798.

69. *Executive Journals,* 1744–1753, pp. 511, 560; "Property of the One Hundred," 11W(3)371. Buckingham and Amherst were both parts of Albemarle until 1761.

70. The Diaries of William Cabell, 1751–1776, Virginia Historical Society. This diary is best for the period after 1770 and is of no value for Albemarle County. For the May, 1770, session he was paid £23.15. Entry of March 25, 1771.

71. The renting of land and the importance of tenants in colonial Virginia have been pointed out by Louis Morton in *Robert Carter of Nomini Hall: A Virginia Tobacco Planter of the Eighteenth Century* (Williamsburg: Colonial Williamsburg, Inc., 1941). Cabell rented the plantation "above the pounding mill creek" to George Tapscott for £25 per annum if he worked four Negroes and £5 for each additional hand over 16 that he worked. Diary of William Cabell, July 27, 1774. Young Landrum was overseer for two plantations. Others who were overseers were David Reynolds, Ned Tilman, and Theodorick Scruggs. Reynolds was to look after his "Home House" plantation on which there were eleven "shares" and the upper quarter plantation where there were ten "shares." There is no indication of what a "share" was. It may have been an "hand" over sixteen years of age—or was it what in recent years have been called "sharecroppers"? Diary of William Cabell, December 21, 1771.

72. For a summary of his life and patriotic services, see *Dictionary of American Biography,* vol. 1, pp. 389–90. Cabell had a deep interest in education and learning. He hired tutors, bought books, and sent a son to college. Diary of William Cabell, 1773–1774, passim.

73. Joseph Cabell, burgess from Buckingham, was son and brother of the two William Cabells. He, like his brother, was a wealthy man with over 5,000 acres of land in three counties. 11W(3)371.

74. JHB 1761–1765, p. 225; 5W(1)161; *Virginia Gazette,* R25Ja70:11. Like almost everyone else, he and Henry owned and sold land. *Virginia Gazette,* PD23F69:32.

75. 10V40. The Autobiography has the tone of a Methodist "experience meeting" and is filled with platitudes and cliches which the skeptic would call "pious mouthings." Yet, the author sounds very sincere and quite surprised at the marvelous things that had happened to him. See also 22V210; 28V153, 160; 17W(1)168, 169.

76. See "Extracts from Land Patents of Edward Carter, Albemarle," University of Virginia Library; 11W(3)371. Carter married Sarah Champe. Woods, *Albemarle County,* p. 163.

77. Will is dated February 12, 1792, photocopy, University of Virginia Library. Edward's son, Charles, married Fielding Lewis' daughter—another link in the intermarried upper class.

78. William Lee to Francis Lightfoot Lee, July 16, 1774, Harvard Photostats, Lee Papers, University of Virginia; *Virginia Gazette,* PD5My74:31.

79. *Virginia Gazette,* PD18Jl71:21; PD17F74:31; Agreement between Carter and John Old of Birk Co., Penn., September 21, 1771, Walker-Page Papers, University of Virginia Library; Kathleen Bruce, *Virginia Iron Manufacture in the Slave Era* (New York: Century Co., 1931), pp. 65-66. This includes a number of appendices showing the number and extent of iron manufacturing. Carter and Walker had sold out

all their interests by December, 1777, when John Old, Alexander Trent, and John Wilkinson were the sole owners. Ibid., pp. 22, 66n.

80. Sixty-one cocks were entered in the match. *Virginia Gazette*, R14Ap68:33.

81. Thomas Jefferson to John Harvie, January 14, 1760, Julian Boyd, ed., *The Papers of Thomas Jefferson* (Princeton, N. J.: Princeton University Press, 1950), vol. 1, p. 3.

82. Fauquier to Earl of Shelburne, CO 5/1354, ff. 146–47, 151 ro–151 vo.

83. Dumas Malone, *Jefferson the Virginian* (Boston: Little, Brown, 1948), p. 122.

84. Boyd, ed., *Papers of Thomas Jefferson*, vol. 1, pp. 26-27; JHB 1766–1769, pp. 199–200.

85. T. J. to Thomas Adams, February 20, 1771, *Papers of Thomas Jefferson*, vol. 1, pp. 61–62.

86. Autobiography of T. J., quoted in Claude G. Bowers, *The Young Jefferson, 1743–1789* (Boston: Houghton Mifflin, 1945), pp. 77–78.

87. JHB 1758–1761, p. 12. He sat again for Louisa in the 1770's when his son Thomas followed him in Albemarle. JHB 1773–1776, p. 163.

88. Literature on Walker is extensive. Dr. Thomas Walker, *Journal of an Exploration in the Spring of the Year 1750,* Josiah S. Johnston, ed. (Louisville: John P. Morton, 1898); The Page-Walker Papers, University of Virginia Library; *Dictionary of American Biography*, vol. 20, pp. 360–361. Many references appear in historical magazines; i. e., "The Wives of Dr. Thomas Walker," 42V244–46.

89. Samuel Cole William, ed., *Early Travels in the Tennessee Country, 1740–1800* (Johnson City, Tenn.: Watauga Press, 1928), p. 166.

90. Page-Walker Papers, passim, University of Virginia Library; *Executive Journals, 1752–1760*, p. 38.

91. JHB 1758–1761, pp. 88–90; also printed in Kate Mason Rowland, *The Life of George Mason, 1725–1792*, 2 vols. (New York: G. P. Putnam's Sons, 1892), vol. 1, p. 74. At this time Walker himself was a member from Louisa. When asked how he could sustain the charges that Walker had cheated his county even after his constituents had reelected him, Johnson replied, "You know very little of the schemes, plots and contrivances that are carried on in the House of Burgesses; in short, one holds the lamb while another skins, and it would surprise any man to see in what manner the country's money is squandered away."

92. 13V30–36; *Virginia Gazette*, PD1D68:31; PD1D68:23.

93. Will of 1788, Albemarle County Deed Book 3, 1785–1798, Virginia State Library.

94. *Dictionary of American Biography;* Walker, *Journal of an Exploration*, introduction, pp. 26–30; Thomas Anbury, *Travels Through the Interior Parts of America in a Series of Letters* (London: privately printed, 1791), vol. 2, pp. 403-404.

95. *Virginia Gazette*, PD5D71:23; JHB 1770–1772, pp. 113, 123, 143.

96. Malone, *Jefferson the Virginian*, pp. 42, 57, 59, 142, 153–54, 172, and 180. During the years Jefferson was President, a scandalous story was perpetrated (apparently by Henry Lee) of the relations between Jefferson and Mrs. Walker. Jefferson admitted having "offered love" to her in 1768 (before he was married) while her husband was away at Fort Stanwix, but he denied all other allegations. See summary of the affair in ibid., Appendix III, pp. 447–51; Bursar's Book, College of William and Mary, p. 43.

97. Ibid., p. 449; *Virginia Gazette*, PD1D68:31. He was again with his father on a similar journey in 1775. *Virginia Gazette*, D18N75:31.

98. *Dictionary of American Biography,* vol. 19, p. 361; Walker, *Journal of an Exploration,* introduction, p. 30. The youngest son of Dr. Walker was in the national House of Representatives, *Virginia Gazette,* PD4Ag74:23; P8D75:32; D9D75:32; Pi9D75:22; D18D79:21.

99. JHB 1766–1769, p. 90.

100. Photostat of poll, Virginia State Library.

101. JHB 1752–1758, pp. 13, 55, 68.

102. JHB 1758–1761, p. 172, May 20, 1760.

103. *Virginia Gazette,* PD7D69:31; P7D69:33; JHB 1766–1769, p. 313.

104. JHB 1761–1765, p. 315, May 1, 1765.

105. *Virginia Gazette,* 30N59:32; PD1Ag66:31; R8Ag66:41; PD18My69:31; PD28S69:31; PD7D69:31; P7D69:33; PD15Ap73:31; PD24Je73:33; PD18N73:21; text of Thomas Tabb's will, Amelia County Will Book 2x, pp.. 309–10.

106. *Virginia Gazette,* R21S69:23; father's will Amelia County Will Book, 2x, pp. 309–10, April 30, 1769.

107. *Virginia Gazette,* PD22Mr70:22.

108. Amelia County Will Book 1, pp. 181, 196.

109. *Virginia Gazette,* PD7Jl68:31; R3Ag69:31; PD21D69:33.

110. Ibid., 5Mr52:31.

111. Landon Bell, *Sunlight on the Southside* (Richmond: William Byrd Press, 1927), vol. 1, p. 24; *Virginia Gazette,* 5Mr52:32; 15My52:32; 7N55:22.

112. JHB 1761–1765, p. 315; 3T174–76.

113. *Virginia Gazette,* P6Oc75:31.

114. Louis B. Namier, *Structure of Politics at the Accession of George III* (London: Macmillan, 1929), vol. 1, p. 1.

Chapter 7

1. I have relied heavily on Lewis Cecil Gray, *History of Agriculture in the Southern United States to 1860,* 2 vols. (Washington: The Carnegie Institution, 1933), vol. 1, pp. 259–76.

2. The King of Prussia banned tobacco from his kingdom and consequently the merchants had too much of it on their hands. Samuel Athawes to Edward Ambler, 1766, Elizabeth Barbour Ambler Papers, University of Virginia Library, Charlottesville.

3. John Smith to Edward Ambler, June 2, 1751, ibid. Smith was later burgess from his county, and Ambler from Jamestown.

4. Louis Morton, *Robert Carter of Nomini Hall: A Virginia Tobacco Planter of the Eighteenth Century* (Williamsburg: Colonial Williamsburg, Inc., 1941).

5. Kenneth P. Bailey, *The Ohio Company* (Glendale, Calif.: The Arthur H. Clark Co., 1939), pp. 22–23.

6. H. R. McIlwaine and Wilmer L. Hall, eds., *Executive Journals of the Council of Colonial Virginia, 1739–1754* (Richmond: The Virginia State Library, 1925–1945), pp. 269–97; *Tyler's Quarterly Historical and Genealogical Magazine,* vol. 4, p. 86 (hereafter cited as T, with the volume preceding and the page following; i. e., 4T86).

7. Kenneth P. Bailey, *The Ohio Company of Virginia and the Westward Movement, 1748–1792: A Chapter in the History of the Colonial Frontier* (Glendale, Calif.: The Arthur H. Clark Co., 1939), p. 35 and passim. The petitions to the Board of Trade are given in the Appendix, pp. 297–327. In spite of vicissitudes, the company

endured until 1778–1779. Ibid., p. 279; Lois Mulkearn, *George Mercer Papers Relating to the Ohio Company of Virginia* (Pittsburgh: University of Pittsburgh Press, 1954).

8. Bailey, *Ohio Company,* pp. 36–60.

9. 7T226.

10. Ambler and Nicholas papers are abundant. In addition to letters in the Lee Papers, University of Virginia Library; Norton Papers, Colonial Williamsburg, Williamsburg, and William Dabney Papers, University of North Carolina Library, there are three collections available: Elizabeth Barbour Ambler Papers, University of Virginia Library; Wilson Cary Nicholas Papers, University of Virginia Library; and Legal Papers of Nicholas and Wythe, University of Virginia Library.

11. David John Mays, *Edmund Pendleton, 1721–1803,* 2 vols. (Cambridge, Mass.: Harvard University Press, 1952), vol. 1, pp. 174–223, 358–85.

12. Ibid., pp. 87, 320; H. R. McIlwaine and J. P. Kennedy, eds., *Journals of the House of Burgesses of Virginia* (Richmond: The Virginia State Library, 1905–1915), 1752–1757, p. 152 (hereafter cited as JHB). Pendleton also settled the estates of Robert Innes and Lawrence Battaile. Mays, *Edmund Pendleton,* vol. 1, p. 72; vol. 2, p. 165.

13. For more details, see Chapter 6.

14. The early history of iron in the colony is found in Kathleen Bruce, *Virginia Iron Manufacture in the Slave Era* (New York: The Century Co., 1930).

15. William Byrd, *A Progress to the Mines,* in John Spencer Bassett, ed., *The Writings of Colonel William Byrd* (New York: Doubleday, 1901).

16. *Virginia Gazette,* PD12S66:22; PD17Oc66:31; Rev. Andrew Burnaby, *Travels Through the Middle Settlements in North America in the Years 1759–1760 with Observations Upon the State of the Colonies, 1759–1760* (London: T. Payne, 1775), p. 16. Burnaby says Chiswell also had a copper mine on the Roanoke. He used convict servants at his mines. 7T63. He had a thriving mercantile business which handles not only the usual plantation supplies but also such luxury goods as Persian rugs and Irish linen. Colonel John Chiswell's Book, Hanover County (1751–1757), Frederick Hall Plantation Books, Group A, vol. 4. The originals of the Frederick Hall Papers are in the University of North Carolina Library, but have been microfilmed.

17. See Chapter IV.

18. Page-Walker Papers, University of Virginia Library; Bruce, *Virginia Iron Manufacture,* pp. 65–67.

19. *Dictionary of American Biography,* vol. 3, pp. 389–90.

20. Bruce, *Virginia Iron Manufacture,* pp. 18–19; *Dictionary of American Biography,* vol. 3, p. 554; William Meade, *Old Churches, Ministers and Families of Virginia* (Philadelphia: J. B. Lippincott, 1857), p. 455; J. F. D. Smyth, *Tour of the United States of America . . . ,* 2 vols. (Dublin: Price, Moncrieffe, 1784), vol. 1, p. 17.

21. Jackson T. Main, "The One Hundred," *William and Mary Quarterly,* 3rd ser. vol. 11, p. 373 (hereafter cited as W, and the order employed by Swem is used. The volume precedes the publication, the series appears in parentheses, and the pages follow; i.e., 11W(3)373; "Racing in Colonial Virginia," *Virginia Magazine of History and Biography,* vol. 2, pp. 301–303 (hereafter cited as V, with the volume preceding the publication and the pages following; i.e., 2V301–303; "Equine FFV's," 35V329–70.

22. "Narrative of George Fisher," 17W(1)167. The particular ordinary he was

criticizing was owned by "Major R—n" who may have been William Roane of Essex County.

23. Virginia Almanac, 1754. Virginia Historical Society has an extensive collection of almanacs published by the *Virginia Gazette*.

24. *Virginia Historical Register and Literary Companion*, vol. 3, pp. 79–83 (hereafter cited as R, with the volume preceding the publication and the pages following; i.e., 3R79–83).

25. Public Record Office, Colonial Office, 5/1331, ff. 103 ro–104 vo (hereafter cited as PRO, CO).

26. Dunmore to Hillsborough, May 2, 1772, PRO, CO 5/1350. More than twenty clerks are known to have sat in the House, and a close examination of the county court records no doubt would reveal many more.

27. William W. Hening, ed., *The Statutes at Large: Being a Collection of All the Laws of Virginia*, 13 vols. (Richmond: J. W. Randolph, 1810–1823), vol. 5, pp. 42–47 (hereafter cited as H, with the volume preceding the publication and the pages following; i. e., 5H42–47).

28. Ibid.

29. Ibid.

30. Ibid. This act was extended many times but with no major revisions. See 6H200, 6H244, 7H242, 7H278.

31. 6H96–97. Richard Lee of Westmoreland and Edward Hack Moseley of Princess Anne were naval officers.

32. 6H371–72; 7H124–25; 7H397–403; 8H184–85.

33. *Virginia Gazette*, PD20My73:22; R20My73:22.

34. Arthur Lee to Richard Henry Lee, June 11, 1771, Lee Papers, University of Virginia Library.

35. The sum was £594.17.7. Fee Book, 1768, Carrington Papers, Virginia Historical Society. See Clement Eaton, "A Mirror of the Southern Colonial Lawyer: Fee Books of Patrick Henry, Thomas Jefferson, and Waighstill Avery," 8W(3)520–34.

Chapter 8

1. The 4.53 average for the fifteen later counties has little meaning because the dates these counties were created go all the way from 1753 (Hampshire) to 1772. A convenient summary of the counties is found in J. R. V. Daniel, ed., *A Hornbook of Virginia History* (Richmond: Virginia Department of Conservation and Development, 1949), pp. 9–26. See also *Virginia Magazine of History and Biography*, vol. 2, pp. 91ff (hereafter cited as V with the volume preceding and the pages following). These figures total 439 which allows for 40 men serving more than one county.

2. The seven counties examined in Chapters 4, 5, and 6 (Albemarle, Amelia, Augusta, Essex, Frederick, Henrico, and Richmond) will be omitted in this chapter. Dr. Thomas Walker stayed in office most of the period but he served three different counties: Louisa, Hampshire, and Albemarle. See Chapter VI for a discussion of this remarkable man. Information regarding dates of service in the House came from the *Journal of the House of Burgesses* unless otherwise stated.

3. H. R. McIlwaine, ed., *Journal of the House of Burgesses*, 13 vols. (Richmond: Virginia State Library, 1905–1915), 1758–1761, p. 50 (hereafter cited as JHB).

4. JHB 1761–1765, pp. 306, 308, 317–22, 361–62; William W. Hening, ed., *Statutes at Large, Being a Collection of all the Laws of Virginia . . .* 13 vols. (Richmond:

J. W. Randolph, 1823), vol. 8, pp. 173–74 (hereafter cited as H with volume preceding and pages following).

5. JHB 1758–1761, p. 5.

6. See, for example, the election of William Cabell, Jr., in 1769 and 1774 in his Diary, MS, Virginia Historical Society, Richmond.

7. For polls see Appendix I.

8. Ibid.

9. Ibid.

10. JHB 1758–1761, pp. 114, 116, 117.

11. R. A. Brock, ed., *The Official Records of Robert Dinwiddie,* 2 vols. (Richmond: Virginia Historical Society, 1884), vol. 1, pp. 301, 409 (hereafter cited as Dinwiddie, *Papers);* Francis Fauquier to Board of Trade, June 2, 1760, Public Record Office, Colonial Office 5/1345, ff. 182–83 (hereafter cited as PRO, CO); Diary of Landon Carter, August 22, 1754.

12. For more details see Chapter 4.

13. June 2, 1760, PRO, CO 5/1330, f. 37.

14. Arthur Lee to Richard Henry Lee, June 11, 1771, Lee Papers, MSS, University of Virginia.

15. Landon Carter to George Washington, October 31, 1776, printed in *Tyler's Quarterly Historical and Genealogical Magazine,* vol. 13, p. 255 (hereafter cited as T with volume preceding and pages following).

16. *Virginia Gazette* (Purdie and Dixon, editors), April 11, 1771, p. 2, column 3. Hereafter the system used by Lester J. Cappon and Stella F. Duff, eds., *Virginia Gazette Index, 1736–1780* (Williamsburg: Institute of Early American History, 1950) will be followed: the editor, the day, the month, the year and, after the colon, the page and column. The above reference becomes PD11Ap71:23.

17. June 2, 1760, CO 5/1330, ff. 37–39.

18. Thad W. Tate, "The Coming of the Revolution in Virginia: Britain's Challenge to Virginia's Ruling Class, 1763–1776," *William and Mary Quarterly,* 3rd series, vol. 19, pp. 323–43 (hereafter cited as W with series in parentheses, preceded by volume and followed by pages, i. e., 19W(3)323–43). See also Jack P. Greene, "Foundations of Political Power in the Virginia House of Burgesses, 1720–1776," 16W(3)485–506.

19. Fauquier to Board of Trade, May 11, 1766, State Papers Office, Board of Trade, Va. vol. 28Z42, Bancroft Transcripts.

20. Fauquier to Board of Trade, October 18, 1766, CO 5/1331, ff. 149 ro–150 vo.

21. H. R. McIlwaine, ed., *Executive Journals of the Council of Colonial Virginia* (Richmond: Virginia State Library, 1923–1928) 1760–1771, p. 56. *Virginia Gazette,* PD18Jl66:11; R18Jl66:31; Fauquier to Board of Trade, July 8, 1763, SPO, Board of Trade, Va. vol. 27y107, Bancroft Transcripts.

22. *Virginia Gazette,* 25Oc65s32; PD3Oc66:11–2–3; PD3Oc66:33. Even before he arrived, George Mercer was "illtreated in effigie at some places further up the country." Fauquier hoped his arrival would be delayed until after the jurors and witnesses from the back country in town for the General Court had departed. He hoped the colony could "weather the storm which seemed ready to burst over the northern colonies." Fauquier to Board of Trade, October 2, 1765, CO 5/1331, ff. 48 ro–48 vo.

23. *Virginia Gazette,* PD18Jl66:11; R18Jl66:11; PD25Jl66:21; R8Ag66:21–2; PD26S66:11–2–3; PD3Oc66:31–2; PD20Oc66:11.

24. *Virginia Gazette,* R16Ag66:21–2. Lee said it was early in November, 1764, when he first knew about the intention of Parliament to lay a stamp duty. He says that at thát time "perhaps not a single person" in the colony had reflected "on the nature and tendency of the act." It was "just a few days" later that he reflected on the impropriety of an American being concerned in such an affair.

25. Arthur Lee to Richard Henry Lee, n.d., Lee Papers, MSS, University of Virginia; *Virginia Gazette,* PD26S66:12.

26. Kate Mason Rowland, *The Life of George Mason, 1725–1792* (New York: G. P. Putnam's Sons, 1892), vol. 1, p. 125.

27. Robert Carter Nicholas to the editor, *Virginia Gazette,* PD27Jl66:13.

28. Edmond Randolph, "History of Virginia," MS, Virginia Historical Society, Richmond, pp. 110–11; Fauquier to Board of Trade, May 11, 1766, CO 5/1331, ff. 83 ro–83 vo.

29. CO 5/1330, ff. 63 ro–64 ro; CO 5/1329, f. 77.

30. *Diary of Landon Carter,* February 12, 13, 1752.

31. Robinson had three wives, the first was Mary Story who died without children. He married Susan Chiswell in 1760. S. M. Hamilton, *Letters to George Washington* (Boston: Houghton Mifflin & Co., 1898), vol. 3, p. 187; 9V357; 15V448; 17V318.

32. A summary of these debts and the debtors is given in David John Mays, *Edmund Pendleton, 1721–1803* (Cambridge: Harvard University Press, 1952), vol. 1, Appendix II, pp. 358–69. There were rumors before Robinson's death that all was not well with the Treasury and some routine investigation had been undertaken, but nothing had been made public. According to Joseph Albert Ernst, this was not the first incident of embezzlement in which Robinson had been involved. See his "Genesis of the Currency Act of 1764: Virginia Paper Money and the Protection of British Investments," 22W(3)33-74, specifically page 34.

33. This episode has been thoroughly explored by Mays in *Edmund Pendleton,* vol. 1, pp. 174–208. Mays, in spite of his fine work, is inclined to excuse Robinson's actions. Pendleton, protege of the Robinsons, was the leading member of the House-appointed committee to settle the estate of the late Treasurer and to pay off his obligations to the colony. Thanks to inflation, he was able to do this eventually. For a summary of the paper money question see "State of the Treasury Notes and Taxes, 1761–1769," Virginia Miscellany, Virginia State Library; JHB 1766–1769, pp. 155–56; Joseph Albert Ernst, "The Robinson Scandal Redivivus: Money, Debts, and Politics in Revolutionary Virginia," 77V146–73.

34. *Virginia Gazette,* PD20Je66:23; PD4Jl66:22; PD11Jl66:11; PD18Jl66:21–2–3; PD25Jl66:11; PD1Ag66:23; PD17Ag66:22; PD22Ag66:21; PD29Ag66:21–2; PD12-S66:22; PD19S66:22–3; PD10Oc21–2; PD17Oc66:31; Rev. John Camm to Mrs. Mc-Clurg, September 5, 1766, 2W(1)238–39; William Nelson to Samuel Waterman, September 5, 1766, Nelson Letter Book, MS, Virginia State Library, Richmond; John B. Dabney, "Sketches of the Dabney and Morris Family," (1850) MS, Colonial Williamsburg.

35. William Nelson to Samuel Athawes, November 13, 1766, Nelson Letter Book, Virginia State Library; *Virginia Gazette,* PD1Ag66:22; R8Ag66:22; PD4S66:23; PD10Oc66:21; Mays, *Edmund Pendleton,* vol. 1, p. 177.

36. *Virginia Gazette,* PD23My66:31; R30My66:41; PD25Jl66:23; PD5S66:23; R25D66:23; Robert Carter Nicholas to Richard Henry Lee, May 23, 1766, Lee Papers, MSS, University of Virginia. Edmund Randolph, "History of Virginia," Part II, pp. 9–10, MS, Virginia Historical Society.

37. Jack P. Greene in an article published in 1959 examines the leadership of the House of Burgesses from 1720 and concludes that of the 630 who sat in the House after that date only 110 were the leaders. He has some very interesting and useful charts showing the education, profession, and wealth of the leaders. "Foundations of Political Power in the House of Burgesses," 16W(3)485–506.

Chapter 9

1. Julian P. Boyd, ed., *The Jefferson Papers* (Princeton, N. J.: Princeton University Press, 1950), vol. 1, p. 106; Kate Mason Rowland, *The Life of George Mason, 1725–1792* (New York: G. P. Putman's Sons, 1892), vol. 1, 169; James Parker to Charles Stewart, June 7, 1774, Charles Stewart Papers, originals in National Library of Scotland, Edinburgh (microfilm at Colonial Williamsburg); Richard Henry Lee to Samuel Adams, June 23, 1774, J. C. Ballagh, ed., *The Letters of Richard Henry Lee* (New York: Macmillan, 1911–1914), vol. 1, pp. 111–13; R. H. Lee to Arthur Lee, June 26, 1774, ibid., pp. 114–18; *The Journal of John Harrower, 1773–1776*, Edward M. Riley, ed. (New York: Holt, Rinehart and Winston, 1963), June 1, 1774, p. 44; Mr. Hill to Thomas Adams, July 22, 1774, Adams Papers, MSS, Virginia Historical Society; Philip Vickers Fithian, *Journal and Letters of Philip Vickers Fithian, 1773–1774*, Hunter D. Farish, ed. (Williamsburg: Colonial Williamsburg, Inc., 1943), May 29, 1774, p. 47.
2. Louis B. Wright, *The First Gentlemen of Virginia: Intellectual Qualities of the Early Colonial Ruling Class* (San Marino, Calif.: The Huntingdon Library, 1940) exploits this theme.
3. H. R. McIlwaine and J. P. Kennedy, eds., *Journals of the Virginia House of Burgesses,* 13 vols. (Richmond: The Virginia State Library, 1905–1915), 1770–1772, p. 122; Richard Bland to Thomas Adams, August 1, 1771, Adams Papers, Virginia Historical Society; David Meade, *Old Churches, Ministers, and Families of Virginia* (Philadelphia: J. B. Lippincott, 1857), vol. 1, pp. 170–73.
4. Major Thomas Anburey, *Travels Through the Interior Parts of America in a Series of Letters* (London: privately printed, 1791), vol. 2, p. 329.

Appendix I

1. Each freeholder had two votes so the total vote will be twice the number of freeholders participating. When there is an odd number here, someone casts only one vote.
2. A partial return.
3. A different version is printed in *William and Mary Quarterly,* 1st series, vol. 26, pp. 107–108.
4. A printed version in *Tyler's Quarterly Historical and Genealogical Magazine,* vol. 9, p. 284.
5. *Tyler's Magazine* gives figures different from those recorded in the Deed Book.
6. There is another poll for "burgesses" in Deeds No. 31, pp. 405–406, April 20, 1778. By that time, the House of Burgesses had been replaced by the House of Delegates so the heading is a misnomer.
7. Fairfax and not Ellsey was the burgess, so there must have been an error in the count.
8. This was a by-election to elect a burgess in place of Robert Rutherford.
9. A by-election.

10. Another by-election. There is no explanation why it was held so shortly before the general election.

11. This is doubtless only a partial return.

12. Lee, and not Muse, was returned, so there must be an error here. At this election an unusual number of freeholders were objected to—twelve objections for Carter alone. A few refused to "swear." Either they were Quakers or they did not have the required freehold.

13. Colonel Richard Lee's poll only. Appended to the list are eleven names of persons who refused to swear.

BIBLIOGRAPHY

Manuscripts

CHARLOTTESVILLE, VIRGINIA
  University of Virginia Library
    Elizabeth Barbour Ambler Papers
    Berkeley Papers
    Cabell Papers
    Landon Carter Diaries
    Carter-Smith Papers
    Carter Papers, 1729–1758. Typescript.
    Henry Fry, Autobiography
    The Hull Family of Northumberland and Spotsyl-
      vania Counties. Compiled by John W.
      Herndon. Typescript.
    Lee Papers
    Maury Papers
    Legal Papers of Robert Carter Nicholas and
      George Wythe
    Wilson Cary Nicholas Papers
    Page-Walker Papers
    Plummer-Carter Letter Book
    Henry Piper Letter Book
    Pocket Plantation Papers
    Sabine Hall Papers
    Thomas Walker Papers
RICHMOND, VIRGINIA
  Virginia Historical Society
    The Adams Papers
    Diaries of William Cabell, Sr.
    Paul Carrington Papers
    Cary Papers
    Custis Miscellaneous Papers
    Hugh Blair Grigsby Papers
    Preston Papers
    Edmund Randolph, "History of Virginia"
    Roane-Harrison-Williams Papers
  Virginia State Library
    Allason Papers
    John Baylor Letter Book
    Colonial Papers
    Lancaster Loose Papers

William Nelson Letter Book
County Records
    Accomac Deed Books
    Albemarle Deed Book No. 3
    Elizabeth City Deed Book E
    Essex Deed Books Nos. 25, 29, 30
    King George Deed Books Nos. 3, 4
    Norfolk Deed Book No. 24
    Northumberland Record Books Nos. 4, 5, 6, 7, 8
    Richmond Order Books Nos. 12, 13, 14, 16, 17
    Spotsylvania Deed Books B, D
    Westmoreland Records and Inventories
        Nos. 2, 3, 4

WILLIAMSBURG, VIRGINIA
College of William and Mary Library
  Carter Manuscripts
  Robert Pleasant Letter Book, 1771–1775
Colonial Williamsburg Library
  Richard Corbin Letter Book
  Richard Corbin Papers
  Norton Papers
  Rev. Robert Rose Diary and Account Book

Microfilm and Photostats

Bancroft Transcripts. Public Record Office, London.
Robert Wormeley Carter Diaries. William L. Clements Library, University of Michigan, Ann Arbor.
Chalmers Papers. New York Public Library.
Rev. John Craig Diary and Record of Baptisms. Presbyterian Historical Foundation, Montreat, North Carolina.
William Dabney Papers. University of North Carolina, Chapel Hill.
Frederick Hall Papers. University of North Carolina, Chapel Hill.
Wilson Cary Nicholas Papers. Library of Congress.
Preston and Virginia Papers in the Lyman C. Draper Collection. State Historical Society of Wisconsin, Madison.
Charles Stewart Papers. National Library of Scotland, Edinburgh.
George Washington Papers. Library of Congress.
Fulham Palace Papers. London.

Unpublished Theses

Dabney, William Minor. "Jefferson's Albemarle: History of Albemarle County, 1727–1819." Master's thesis, University of Virginia, 1951.
Hemphill, William Edwin. "George Wythe, the Colonial Briton: A Biographical Study of the Pre-Revolutionary Era in Virginia." Master's thesis, University of Virginia, 1937.
Hickish, Edgar C. "Peter Jefferson, Gentleman." Master's thesis, University of Virginia, 1940.
Jackson, Lois Fell. "Colonel Joshua Fry: Albemarle's Soldier-Statesman." Master's thesis, University of Virginia, 1945.

Matthews, John Carter. "Richard Henry Lee and the American Revolution." Master's thesis, University of Virginia, 1939.

Menk, Patricia Holbert. "The Origins and Growth of Party Politics in Virginia, 1660–1705." Ph.D. dissertation, University of Virginia, 1945.

Williams, David Alan. "Political Alignments in Colonial Virginia, 1698–1750." Ph.D. dissertation, Northwestern University, 1959.

Printed Works

Anburey, Thomas. *Travels Through the Interior Parts of America.* 2 vols. London: privately printed, 1791.

Bland, Richard. *A Fragment on the Pistole Fee Claimed by the Governor of Virginia.* Edited by W. C. Ford. *Winnowings in American History, Virginia Tracts,* Brooklyn: Historical Printing Club, 1891.

_____. *A Modest and True State of the Case.* Edited by W. C. Ford. *Winnowings in American History, Virginia Tracts.* Brooklyn: Historical Printing Club, 1891.

Bell, Landon C., ed. *Cumberland Parish* [Lunenburg County] *Vestry Book, 1746–1816.* Richmond: William Byrd Press, 1930.

Burnaby, Rev. Andrew. *Travels Through the Middle Settlements in North America in the Years 1759–1760 with Observations Upon the State of the Colonies.* London: T. Payne, 1775.

Byrd, William, II. *Writings of Colonel William Byrd.* Edited by John Spencer Bassett. New York: Doubleday, Page & Co., 1901.

Campbell, Charles, ed. *The Bland Papers.* 2 vols. Petersburg, Va.: E & J Ruffin, 1840–1843.

Carter, Landon. *The Diary of Colonel Landon Carter of Sabine Hall, 1752–1774.* Edited by Jack P. Greene. Charlottesville: University of Virginia Press, 1965.

Dinwiddie, Robert. *The Official Records of Robert Dinwiddie.* Edited by R. A. Brock. 2 vols. Richmond: Virginia Historical Society, 1884.

_____. *Correspondence.* Edited by Louis K. Koontz. Berkeley: University of California Press, 1951.

Douglas, William. *The Douglas Register: Being a Detailed Record of Births, Marriages, and Deaths Together with other Interesting Notes Kept by Rev. William Douglas from 1750 to 1797.* Edited by W. MacJones. Richmond: J. W. Fergusson and Sons, 1928.

Fithian, Philip Vickers. *Journal and Letters of Philip Vickers Fithian, 1773–1774.* Edited by Hunter D. Farish. Williamsburg: Colonial Williamsburg, Inc., 1943.

Fontaine, Jacques. *A Tale of the Huguenots: or Memoirs of a French Refugee Family.* New York: J. S. Taylor, 1838.

Gist, Christopher. *Journal of Tour Through Ohio and Kentucky in 1751.* Edited by Josiah S. Johnston. Louisville: John P. Morton & Co., 1898.

Grant, W. L.; Munro, James; Fitzroy, Sir Almeric W., eds. *Acts of the Privy Council, Colonial Series.* 6 vols. Hereford, Eng., 1908–1912.

Greene, Evarts B., and Harrington, Virginia D., eds. *American Population Before the Federal Census of 1790.* New York: Columbia University Press, 1932.

Hamilton, S. M., ed. *Letters to George Washington.* 4 vols. Boston: Houghton Mifflin, 1898.

Hansford, Charles. *Poems of Charles Hansford.* Edited by James A. Servies and Carl R. Dolmetsch. Chaptel Hill: University of North Carolina Press, 1961.

207

Harrower, John. *The Journal of John Harrower*. Edited by Edward M. Riley. New York: Holt, Rinehart, and Winston, 1963.

Hening, William W., ed. *Statutes at Large, Being a Collection of All the Laws of Virginia*. 13 vols. Richmond: J. W. Randolph, 1823–1835.

Jarrett, Devereaux. *Life of Rev. Devereaux Jarrett of Bath Parish, Dinwiddie County*. Baltimore: Warner and Hanna, 1806.

Jefferson, Thomas. *Notes on the State of Virginia*. Edited by William Peden. Chapel Hill: University of North Carolina Press, 1954.

_____. *The Jefferson Papers*. Edited by Julian P. Boyd. Princeton, N. J.: Princeton University Press, 1950–.

Jones, Hugh. *The Present State of Virginia*. Edited by Richard L. Morton. Chapel Hill: University of North Carolina Press, 1956.

Lee, Richard Henry. *Letters of Richard Henry Lee*. Edited by James Curtis Ballagh. 2 vols. New York: Macmillan Co., 1912.

McIlwaine, H. R., ed. *Executive Journals of the Council of Colonial Virginia, 1744–1774*. 4 vols. Richmond: Virginia State Library, 1922–1928.

McIlwaine, H. R., and Hall, Wilmer L., eds. *Journals of the House of Burgesses*. 13 vols. Richmond: Virginia State Library, 1905–1915.

Mercer, George. *George Mercer Papers Relating to the Ohio Company of Virginia*. Compiled and edited by Lois Mulkearn. Pittsburgh: University of Pittsburgh Press, 1954.

Morgan, Edmund S. *Stamp Act Crisis: Documents and Sources*. Chapel Hill: University of North Carolina Press, 1952.

Palmer, William Pitt, ed. *Calendar of Virginia State Papers and Other Manuscripts Preserved in the Capitol in Richmond*. 6 vols. Richmond: Commonwealth of Virginia, 1875–1893.

Pendleton, Edmund. *Letters and Papers of Edmund Pendleton, 1734–1803*. Edited by David J. Mays. Charlottesville: University of Virginia Press, 1967.

Smyth, John F. D. *A Tour of the United States of America . . . .* 2 vols. Dublin: Price, Moncrieffe, *et al.*, 1784.

Stanard, William G., and Stanard, Mary Newton. *The Colonial Virginia Register*. Albany, N. Y.: Munsell's Sons, 1902.

Summers, Lewis Preston, ed. *Annals of Southwest Virginia, 1746–1786*. Richmond, 1903.

Virginia State Library. *Justice of the Peace in Colonial Virginia, 1757–1775*. Richmond: Virginia State Library, 1921.

Waddell, Joseph A., ed. *Annals of Augusta County, 1726–1871*. Richmond: William Ellis Jones, 1886.

Walker, Thomas. *Dr. Thomas Walker's Journal of an Exploration of Kentucky in 1750*. Louisville: John P. Morton and Co., 1898.

Washington, George. *Diaries, 1748–1799*. Edited by John C. Fitzpatrick. 4 vols. Boston: Houghton Mifflin, 1925.

_____. *Writings*. Edited by John C. Fitzpatrick. 39 vols. Washington: U. S. Printing Office, 1931–1944.

Secondary Sources

Alexander, Frederick Warren. *Stratford Hall and the Lees Connected with Its History*. Oak Grove, Va.: privately printed, 1912.

Bailey, Kenneth P. *The Ohio Company of Virginia and the Westward Movement,*

1748–1792: A Chapter in the History of the Colonial Frontier. Glendale, Calif.: The Arthur H. Clark Co., 1939.

Bailyn, Bernard. *The Origin of American Politics.* New York: Knopf, 1968.

Baine, Rodney M. *Robert Munford, America's First Comic Dramatist.* Athens: University of Georgia Press, 1967.

Bell, Landon C. *The Old Free State: A Contribution to the History of Lunenburg County and Southside Virginia.* 2 vols. Richmond: William Byrd Press, 1927.

Beveridge, Albert J. *The Life of John Marshall.* 4 vols. Boston: Houghton Mifflin, 1916–1919.

Bodie, John Bennett. *Colonial Surry.* Richmond, 1948.

Bowers, Claude G. *The Young Jefferson, 1743–1789.* Boston: Houghton Mifflin, 1945.

Bridenbaugh, Carl. *Myths and Realities: Societies of the Colonial South.* Baton Rouge: Louisiana State University Press, 1952.

_____. *Seat of Empire: The Political Role of Eighteenth-Century Williamsburg.* Williamsburg: Colonial Williamsburg, Inc., 1950.

Brock, Robert K. *Archibald Cary of Ampthill.* Richmond: Garrett and Massie, 1937.

Bruce, Kathleen. *Virginia Iron Manufacture in the Slave Era.* New York: The Century Co., 1931.

Brydon, George MacLaren. *Virginia's Mother Church and the Political Conditions under which It Grew.* 2 vols. Richmond: Virginia Historical Society, 1952.

Campbell, Thomas E. *Colonial Caroline: A History of Caroline County Virginia.* Richmond: The Dietz Press, 1954.

Cartmell, Thomas Kemp. *Shenandoah Valley Pioneers and Their Descendants: A History of Frederick County.* Winchester, Va.: Eddy Press, 1909.

Chandler, Julian A. C. *The History of Suffrage in Virginia.* Baltimore: Johns Hopkins Press, 1901.

Flippin, Percy Scott. *Royal Government in Virginia, 1624–1775.* New York: Columbia University Press, 1919.

Freeman, Douglas Southall. *George Washington.* 5 vols. New York: Charles Scribner's Sons, 1948–1952.

Gray, Lewis Cecil. *A History of Agriculture in the Southern United States to 1860.* 2 vols. Washington: The Carnegie Institution, 1933.

Grigsby, Hugh Blair. *The Virginia Convention of 1776.* Richmond: J. W. Randolph, 1855.

_____. *The Virginia Convention of 1788.* Richmond: J. W. Randolph, 1890–1891.

Groome, H. C. *Fauquier During the Proprietorship: A Chronicle of the Colonization and Organization of a Northern Neck County.* Richmond, 1927.

Hart, Freeman H. *The Valley of Virginia in the American Revolution, 1763–1789.* Chapel Hill: University of North Carolina Press, 1942.

Hilldrup, Robert L. *The Life and Times of Edmund Pendleton.* Chapel Hill: University of North Carolina Press, 1939.

Kammen, Michael G. *A Rope of Sand: The Colonial Agents, British Politics, and the American Revolution.* Ithaca, N. Y.: Cornell University Press, 1968.

Kegley, F. B. *Kegley's Virginia Frontier: The Beginning of the Southwest: Roanoke of Colonial Days, 1740–1783.* Roanoke: The Southwest Virginia Historical Society, 1938.

Koontz, Louis K. *Robert Dinwiddie: His Career in American Colonial Government and Westward Expansion.* Glendale, Calif.: The Arthur H. Clark Co., 1941.

Labaree, Leonard W. *Royal Government in America.* New Haven, Conn.: Yale University Press, 1930.

Lee, Edmund Jennings. *Lees of Virginia, 1642–1892: Biographical and Genealogical Sketches of the the Descendants of Colonel Richard Lee* . . . . Philadelphia: Franklin Printing Co., 1892.

Lee, Richard Henry. *Life of Arthur Lee* . . . . 2 vols. Boston: Wells and Lilly, 1829.

Lonn, Ella. *The Colonial Agents of the Southern Colonies.* Chapel Hill: University of North Carolina Press, 1945.

Main, Jackson T. *The Upper House in Revolutionary America.* Madison: University of Wisconsin Press, 1967.

Malone, Dumas. *Jefferson The Virginian.* Boston: Little, Brown, 1948.

Mays, David J. *Edmund Pendleton, 1721–1803.* Cambridge, Mass.: Harvard University Press, 1952.

Meade, William. *Old Churches, Ministers, and Families of Virginia.* 2 vols. Philadelphia: J. B. Lippincott and Co., 1857.

Miller, Elmer I. *The Legislature of the Province of Virginia: Its Internal Development.* New York: Columbia University Press, 1907.

Morgan, Edmund S. and Helen M. *The Stamp Act Crisis.* Chapel Hill: University of North Carolina Press, 1953.

Morton, Louis. *Robert Carter of Nomini Hall: A Virginia Tobacco Planter of the Eighteenth Century.* Williamsburg: Colonial Williamsburg, Inc., 1941.

Porter, Albert Ogden. *County Government in Virginia: A Legislative History, 1607–1904.* New York: Columbia University Press, 1947.

Robinson, Morgan P. *Virginia Counties: Those Resulting from Virginia Legislation.* Richmond: Virginia State Library, 1916.

Rowland, Kate Mason. *The Life of George Mason.* 2 vols. New York: G. P. Putnam's Sons, 1892.

Sydnor, Charles S. *Gentlemen Freeholders: Political Practices in Washington's Virginia.* Chapel Hill: University of North Carolina Press, 1952.

Wertenbaker, Thomas J. *The Planters of Colonial Virginia.* Princeton, N. J.: Princeton University Press, 1922.

Wilson, Howard McKnight. *The Tinkling Spring: Headwater of Freedom: A Study of the Church and Her People, 1732–1952.* Fishersville, Va.: Tinkling Springs and Hermitage Presbyterian Churches, 1954.

Wirt, William. *Sketches of the Life and Character of Patrick Henry.* 9th edition. Philadelphia: Thomas, Cowperthwait and Co., 1844.

Woods, Rev. Edgar. *Albemarle County in Virginia.* Charlottesville: The Michie Company, 1844.

Newspapers and Magazines

Journal of Southern History, 1936–.

Lower Norfolk Antiquary, 1895–1906.

Tyler's Quarterly Historical and Genealogical Magazine, 1919–1954.

The Virginia Gazette, 1736–1781. Edited successively by Parks, Hunter, Rind, Purdie, Dixon, and Pinckney. Williamsburg.

Virginia Historical Register and Literary Companion, 1848–1853.

Virginia Magazine of History and Biography, 1893–.

William and Mary Quarterly. First series, 1892–1919; second series, 1921–1930; third series, 1944–.

INDEX

213

214

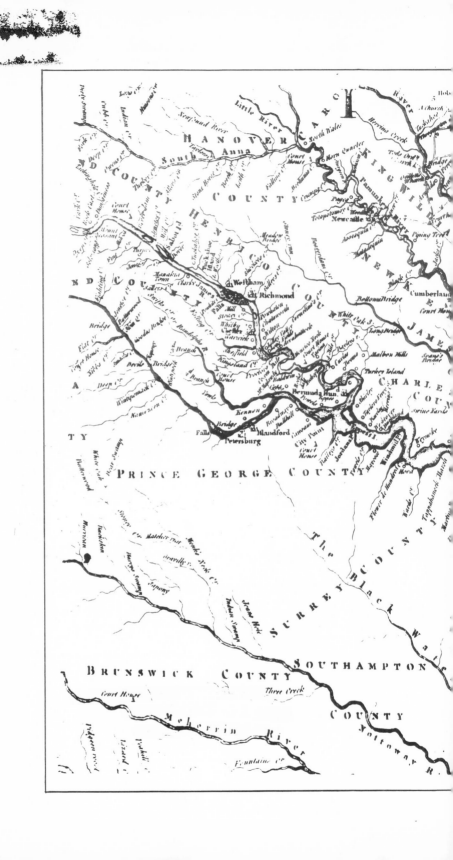